The Holy Spirit

THE KEY TO SUPERNATURAL LIVING

BILL BRIGHT

NewLife PUBLICATIONS
A MINISTRY OF CAMPUS CRUSADE FOR CHRIST

Published by
New*Life* Publications
100 Sunport Lane
Orlando, FL 32809

ISBN 0-86605-158-9

Thomas Nelson Inc., Nashville, TN, is the exclusive distributor of
this book to the trade markets in the United States and the District
of Columbia.

Scripture quotations designated NASB are from the *New American
Standard Bible*, ©1960, 1962, 1963, 1968, 1971, 1972, 1975, 1977 by
the Lockman Foundation, LaHabra, California.

Scripture quotations designated "Living" or TLB are from *The
Living Bible*, ©1971 by Tyndale House Publishers, Wheaton,
Illinois.

Scripture quotations designated KJ are from the *Authorized King
James Version*.

Scripture quotations designated "Phillips" are from the *New
Testament in Modern English*, Revised Edition. ©1958, 1960, 1972
by J.B. Phillips. Reprinted with permission from the MacMillan
Publishing Company, Inc.

For more information, write:
Life Ministries—P.O. Box 40, Flemington Markets, N5W 2129, Australia
Campus Crusade for Christ of Canada—Box 300, Vancouver, B.C., V6C 2X3,
    Canada
Campus Crusade for Christ—Fairgate House, King's Road, Tyseley,
    Birmingham, B112AA, England
Campus Crusade for Christ—P.O. Box 8786, Auckland, New Zealand
Campus Crusade for Christ—Alexandra, P.O. Box 0205, Singapore, 9115,
    Singapore
Great Commission Movement of Nigeria—P.O. Box 500, Jos, Plateau State
    Nigeria,West Africa
Campus Crusade for Christ International—100 Sunport Lane, Orlando FL
    32809, USA

CONTENTS

DEDICATION

To my sons,

Zac

and

Brad

Through whose relationship my Heavenly Father has taught me
— the importance of unbroken fellowship;
— delight in being with them;
— joy and pleasure over their growth and spiritual maturity;
— to earnestly desire more than anything else that they be men of God;
— to delight over every good thing that happens to them;
— the assurance that the disappointments, adversity and heartaches which they experience are actually blessings from God in disguise to draw them closer to Him and to help them to be conformed more into the likeness of Christ;
— the love and gratitude which wells up within me in response to every expression of their love and concern for me.

Through my relationship with Zac and Brad, I have learned so much more about God and my relationship with Him. My heavenly Father loves me and delights in every good thing that happens in my life to make me more like His Son.

To my sons, I am at best a model and encouragement. But my heavenly Father is much more than a model and encouragement to me. He is a teacher, an enabler, constantly with me, helping to maximize my life supernaturally for His glory.

ACKNOWLEDGMENT

In writing this book, I was assisted by a number of people, including those listed below whose contributions and encouragement I especially wish to acknowledge:

Janie Ankenbruck, Nancy Brunner, Helen Mallinson, Marlyse Milburn, Brenda Tate and *Brenda York* for their many long hours of typing, retyping and proofing the manuscript in its various stages of development.

Howard Blandau, Steve Clinton, Steve Douglass, Ron Jenson and *Ted Martin* for their wise counsel and comments on the manuscript.

Erma Griswold and *Dave Enlow* for the final editing of the manuscript

Frank Allnutt for his editorial assistance.

To these dear brothers and sisters in Christ, I give my heartfelt thanks and appreciation for their love and much help.

INTRODUCTION

Some years ago in *Life* magazine, there appeared a full-page picture of the devastation wrought by a mid-western tornado. In the center of the picture was a telephone pole with a straw driven through it. It seemed incredible. How could a flimsy, insubstantial straw be thrust through a rugged, seasoned telephone pole? Here's the answer: the straw, which has no power of its own, was totally empowered by the awesome force of the tornado to penetrate the pole.

The weakest one of God's children, when utterly surrendered to the Spirit of God, is empowered to accomplish the supernatural.

In our morally and spiritually confused world, many are asking — often mutely, "Where is the Lord God of Elijah?" (2 Kings 2:14, King James). He lives! He is still "able to do exceedingly abundantly above all that we ask or think" (Ephesians 3:20, KJ) in and through His children who are fully surrendered to Him.

During the writing of this book, a Christian businessman and friend shared with me the thrilling story of how he and his wife had attended an executive seminar and the miraculous results that followed.

They had heard me speak on, "How to Be Filled with the Holy Spirit," and had responded by appropriating the fullness of the Spirit by faith. Their lives were dramatically changed.

A short time after that, the husband had the opportunity to speak at a church service attended by more than 150 people. He spoke on — you guessed it — "How to Be Filled with the Holy Spirit by Faith," concluding his talk by leading the audience in a prayer for those who wanted to be filled with the Spirit. Then he challenged those who for the first time had appropriated by faith the fullness of the Spirit to stand as an expression of their faith. He reported enthusiastically that nearly everyone present stood.

Several people gathered around him after the meeting. With great excitement they shared how they had understood for the first time the role of the Holy Spirit in their lives. Now they knew how to appropriate that power for holy, righteous living and for being a fruitful witness for Christ. He reported that many went on to witness to others.

This story thrilled my heart, especially because it is an example of how spiritual multiplication takes place in thousands of cases, many of which I am privileged to hear about. Just as a loving father rejoices over the successes of his children and grandchildren, so I rejoice when one whose life God has used me to influence for His glory multiplies himself in the lives of others who in turn influence even more people for our wonderful God.

No truth is more important to the believer than an understanding of the ministry of the Holy Spirit and how to be filled and controlled by Him. As I often say, if I had only one message to share with the Christian world, it would be on this subject.

For that reason, I have written this book, *The Holy Spirit — The Key to Supernatural Living.*

It is my prayer that these truths will help you to experience the reality of the supernatural life that comes from being filled, led and empowered by God the Holy Spirit. May you become a channel of God's Spirit to bring many more people to experience this same fullness of power, even as that young Christian businessman has done and continues to do. Do not keep this good news to yourself. The whole Christian world waits for this life-changing message. Nothing is more important that you could do as a believer, my dear brother or sister, than to communicate these truths concerning the Holy Spirit to everyone who will listen.

Thus you will multiply yourself and the impact of the message of this book in the lives of multitudes throughout the world. God will mightily bless and use you as you do.

Bill Bright
Arrowhead Springs, California

CHAPTER ONE

The Joy of Supernatural Living

A timid young homemaker, who had such low self-esteem that she dreaded even to introduce herself in a small group, learned through our ministry how the Holy Spirit could change her life for the better. Today she happily teaches a Bible study attended weekly by an average of 100 women.

"I've been frustrated in my attempts to serve Jesus Christ," a young advertising executive confessed after hearing me talk at an executive seminar on the supernatural life. "Now I know why: I haven't allowed the Holy Spirit to work in my life."

Since discovering the key to supernatural living, the young man has been in full-time Christian work as a writer. In fact, several of his books have become inspirational top-sellers.

"My life will never be the same after tonight," declared the senior pastor of one of America's leading churches. He had just heard me speak to a group of pastors and laymen on how to experience the joy of supernatural living. "I've been a pastor for more than 20 years," he said, "but I never understood how to live supernaturally until now. I can hardly wait to share this exciting concept with my church members."

A Healed Marriage

An Air Force Colonel, on the verge of divorce and subsequent loss of his children, was led to our international headquarters at Arrowhead Springs in Southern California. While there, he made the wonderful discovery of the supernatural life. Today, with his marriage healed and his family reunited, he is joyfully living and witnessing for the Lord.

"Our lives were changed when we learned how to live supernaturally," a retired businessman and his wife said after traveling halfway across the continent to tell me. "Now we're sharing Jesus Christ with others wherever we go. We've come to ask you to share your unique, life-changing message on nationwide television. Your simple 'how-to' approach reached us, and we want to help you reach millions of others."

First-Century Power

Through the centuries, there have been many followers of Christ who were just ordinary Christians. Nothing spectacular ever happened to them or through them. Then, as happened to Peter and the other disciples, their lives were dramatically changed.

No longer ordinary or average, they became men and women of God — bold in the faith and instruments of God's power. Their defeat turned to victory. Doubts and fear turned to assurance and joy. They were the ones who "turned the world upside down" (Acts 17:6, The Living Bible).

Cowardly Peter, who denied Jesus three times (you and I have denied Him many more times), became the bold Peter of Pentecost who preached fearlessly. On separate occasions, 3,000 and 5,000 believed in Christ and were added to the church as a result of his ministry.

The early disciples possessed a strange new supernatural quality of life, a life of power which transformed the heart of a wicked Roman Empire during the first century. Their supernatural boldness led every one of the original Twelve to a martyr's grave — except John, who died in exile on the Isle of Patmos, and Judas, who committed suicide after betraying the Lord.

The change in the lives of those disciples began on the Day of Pentecost, nearly 2,000 years ago. Just as they were filled with the Holy Spirit and changed by His power, so has this same mighty Spirit changed millions of other ordinary Christians through the centuries into vital, dynamic "world-changers."

Power For Today

Today, that same Holy Spirit — with His life-changing power — is available to you, to enable you to live a supernatural life, holy and fruitful for Jesus Christ.

Yet, tragically, multitudes of Christians do not even know who the Holy Spirit is, much less what it means to be Spirit-filled and to live supernaturally. They go through life without ever experiencing the abundant and fruitful life which Christ promised to all who trust and obey Him.

A Scholar's Search

A young missionary had completed his first term overseas. He came home defeated and frustrated because he saw no results from his diligent, dedicated efforts. He had already earned a degree from seminary, but he returned for advanced study, hoping somehow to discover the key to a fruitful life and ministry.

Several of the seminarians with whom I had shared the ministry of the Holy Spirit sent this missionary to see me, to learn how he too could be filled with the Spirit. I shall never forget the enthusiasm and expectancy with which he came. When I explained to him how he could be filled with the Spirit by faith, he became impatient with me — in fact, a little angry.

"Look," he said. "This is too easy. I can't accept anything so simple, so superficial as what you are suggesting. It really costs something to serve Jesus."

He went on to explain how he had left his family and fortune and had given up everything to live for Christ. "I am prepared to die for Him if necessary," he said. "What you are proposing is a cheap counterfeit of what I believe it costs to serve Jesus."

When he left in impatience and anger, I did not expect to see him again. But I prayed that God would continue to speak to him and help him to realize that what I had shared with him was not only scriptural but also something that he desperately needed for himself.

Several weeks passed. Then one day the telephone rang, and this young man was calling me to say that he had been thinking and praying a great deal about what I had shared with him. Though he said he did not agree with me theologically, he felt I had a certain quality in my life that he wanted in his and asked to see me again.

Once more I explained to him how he could know the fullness of God's Spirit in his life. Reality and power could be his if he were willing to surrender his life totally to Christ and, by faith, appropriate the fullness of the Spirit. Again he refused to accept such a simple solution, but he was sobered and was more receptive to what I had to share.

A few days later, I received a letter from him, filled with praise and thanksgiving to God. He told how he went alone to meditate upon the biblical truths I had shared with him. He had opened his heart and yielded his will to do whatever the Lord wanted — and then the light went on.

He related how he entered into a joyful, meaningful experience with God that had transformed his life. Now, he was writing to thank me because I had taken the time to meet with him and had been patient in spite of his criticism. "Now," he said, "I want to return to the mission field and tell other missionaries, pastors and laymen there what you have shared with me."

"Performing" Christians

Again and again I am reminded of the great contrast between Christ's Church today and His Church in the first century. In J. B. Phillips' introduction to his translation of the New Testament epistles, *Letters to the Young*

Churches, he states:

"The great difference between present-day Christianity and that of which we read in these letters [New Testament epistles], is that to us, it is primarily a performance; to them it was a real experience. We are apt to reduce the Christian religion to a code or, at best, a rule of heart and life.

"To these men it is quite plainly the invasion of their lives by a new quality of life altogether. They do not hesitate to describe this as Christ living in them. Perhaps if we believed what they believed we could achieve what they achieved."

How many of us are "performing" the Christian life? Is being a Christian a *real* experience for you? Has it changed your life-style? Have you made the wonderful discovery of supernatural living? Or have you felt something is missing from your Christian life? Do you know the joy and power of the Holy Spirit? Are you a victorious, fruitful witness for Christ? If not, I have good news. You can be!

CHAPTER TWO

You Can Escape Spiritual Poverty

Some years ago while visiting a brother in Iraan, a West Texas town, I learned of a famous oil field known as the "Yates Pool." During the Great Depression of the 1930s, this field was a sheep ranch owned by a man named Ira Yates.

Because of Yates' inability to make enough money on his ranching operation to pay the principal and interest on the mortgage, he was in danger of losing his ranch. With little money for clothes or food, his family, like many others during the depression years, had to live on government subsidy.

Day after day, as Yates grazed his sheep over those rolling West Texas hills, he no doubt was greatly troubled about how he would be able to pay his bills. Then a seismographic crew from an oil company came into the area and convinced Yates there might be oil on his land. They asked permission to drill a wildcat test well, and Yates signed a lease contract.

Oil!

At 1,115 feet, the drillers struck a huge oil reserve. The first well came in at *80,000 barrels a day.* Translated into today's market value, that would be a gross income of about *$2.5 million a day* from that single well. And that was only the beginning!

Many more wells came in — some more than *twice* as productive as the first. Then, after oil had been pumped for more than 30 years, a government test of just one of the wells showed that it still had a potential flow of 125,000 barrels of oil a day. And the onetime sheep-rancher named Yates owned it all!

The day Yates purchased the ranch, he very likely was more interested in grazing land for his sheep than he was in the oil and mineral rights which were also a part of the purchase. There he was, living on government subsidy, but sitting on a mammoth underground lake of incredibly valuable oil. He was a potential multimillionaire living in poverty!

What was his problem? It was simply that he did not know the oil was there.

Your "Hidden" Resources

How many frustrated, defeated and fruitless Christians are living in spiritual poverty, not knowing the vast resources of God available to them? Like Ira Yates before the oil discovery, they are unaware of the inexhaustible riches of God that are available to them and which are theirs for the taking.

Could it be that you are one of those? Do you find yourself suffering and wasting away in spiritual poverty? Would you like to escape to freedom? To tap God's vast resources and live supernaturally? To know and experience the joy and fulfillment of being a Spirit-filled Christian?

The wonderful truth is that *every* Christian has the potential of entering into the joy of supernatural living. The moment you become a Christian — a child of God through faith in Jesus Christ — you become an heir of God and a joint heir with Christ.

As a result, all of God's possessions are automatically available to you. Everything you need — including wisdom, love, grace and power — to live an abundant, supernatural life as a child of God and to be a fruitful witness for Christ is available to you.

An Exciting Adventure

Every day can be an exciting adventure for the Christian who has discovered the key to supernatural living for such a person knows the reality of being filled with the Holy Spirit and lives constantly, moment by moment, under His gracious guidance and love.

The Holy Spirit has come to give us a supernatural life more wonderful than the human mind can conceive or comprehend. This supernatural life is available to you.

CHAPTER THREE

The Key To Supernatural Life

A minister friend communicated his skepticism to me one day: "I don't like all this talk about the Holy Spirit. I want to talk about Jesus Christ." I reminded my friend that the reason for the Holy Spirit's coming was to exalt and glorify Christ — to "talk about Jesus" (John 16:1-15). A supernatural life is glorifying to Christ, and the key to supernatural living is the person of the Holy Spirit.

Further, I explained that it is impossible even to know Jesus Christ personally as Savior and Lord, apart from the regenerating ministry of the Holy Spirit. It was Jesus of Nazareth, Himself, who said to Nicodemus, "What I am telling you so earnestly is this: Unless one is born of water and the Spirit, he cannot enter the Kingdom of God" (John 3:5, TLB).

It is impossible for us to become Christians, to understand God's Word, to pray, to live holy lives or to witness — apart from the enabling of the Holy Spirit. We can do nothing for the Lord Jesus, and He can do nothing for us, apart from the person and ministry of the Holy Spirit.

Finding the Key

Some years ago, at one of our Lay Institutes for Evangelism in Seattle, Washington, attended by more than 4,000 trainees, I gave a message on how to be filled with the Holy Spirit. Afterward, a missionary who had just retired after 20 years of service in Africa came to see me. He was very excited as he came to share how, during that meeting, he had finally found what he had sought throughout his entire Christian life.

"Today, as you spoke," he said, "I was filled with the Spirit. For 20 years I have tried to serve God on the mission field, but I have served Him in the energy of the flesh and have had very few results. Now, though I have retired and returned to America, I want to go back to Africa.

"This time, I want to concentrate on working just with missionaries, because I know from experience that many of them are still searching for what I have sought all these years. The most important message I can take to them is how they can be filled with the Holy Spirit by faith.

"I want to teach them what you taught me so that they, in turn, will be able to teach the Africans how they too can be filled with the Holy Spirit."

Our Commander-In-Chief

Dr. J. Edwin Orr, a leading authority on spiritual revival, describes the Holy Spirit as "the Commander in Chief of the Army of Christ. He is the Lord of the harvest, supreme in revival, evangelism and missionary endeavor.

"Without His consent, plans are bound to fail. It behooves us as Christians to fit our tactical operations into the plan of His strategy, which is the reviving of the church and the evangelization of the world."

Coming of the Comforter

The first reference to the Holy Spirit appears in Genesis 1:2. His influence is noted throughout the Old Testament, but it becomes more pronounced in the life and ministry of the Lord Jesus Christ. Finally, after the Savior ascended to be at the right hand of the Father, the place of power, He sent the Holy Spirit to be the "comforter" or "helper" to all believers (John 14:26; 15:26).

The Greek word for comforter or helper is *paraclete*, meaning the "one called along beside" the Christian as a companion and friend. It also carries the meaning of one who "energizes," "strengthens" and "empowers" the believer in Christ.

The Holy Spirit came to bear witness to the Lord Jesus Christ and to glorify Him (John 16:13, 14). As Jesus had come to reveal, exalt and glorify the Father, the Holy Spirit was sent to reveal, exalt and glorify the Son, Jesus Christ.

It logically follows, then, that the more we allow the Holy Spirit to control our lives, the more we shall love and serve the Lord Jesus Christ and the more we shall be conscious of His loving and abiding presence.

The Key to Supernatural Living

When we are filled with the Holy Spirit, we are filled with Jesus Christ. Thus, when we are filled with the Holy Spirit, a power much greater than our own is released within us and through us for victorious living and a fruitful witness for the Savior. Without the power and guidance of the Holy Spirit, a Christian cannot experience the joy and wonder of the supernatural life.

But who is the Holy Spirit? And how is He related to every Christian?

The Holy Spirit Is a Person

The Holy Spirit is not some vague, ethereal being or an impersonal force. The Bible tells us He is a person. He has infinite *intellect* (1 Corinthians 2:11), *will* (1 Corinthians 12:11) and *emotion* (Romans 15:30). He possesses all the divine attributes of God. He is equal in every way with God the Father and the Son, Jesus Christ.

The Holy Spirit is referred to in various ways in the Bible: *the Spirit of God* (Genesis 1:2), *the Spirit of the Lord God* (Isaiah 61:1), *the Spirit of your Father* (Matthew 10:20), *the Spirit of grace* (Zechariah 12:10), *the Spirit of truth* (John 14:17), *the Spirit of holiness* (Romans 1:4), *the Spirit of life* (Romans 8:2), *the Spirit of Christ* (Romans 8:9), *the Spirit of adoption* (Romans 8:15), *the Spirit of His Son* (Galatians 4:6), *the Spirit of glory* (1 Peter 4:14), *the Spirit of prophecy* (Revelation 19:10), *the eternal Spirit* (Hebrews 9:14), *My Spirit* (Genesis 6:3), *Thy Holy Spirit* (Psalm 51:11), and *the Helper* (John 14:16, 26).

The Holy Spirit Performs Like a Person

The Bible teaches that the Holy Spirit performs *actions* which cannot be attributed to a mere concept, a thing or an impersonal force. Such actions must be performed by a person, which proves that the Holy Spirit is a person.

He speaks: "He who has an ear, let him hear what the Spirit says to the churches" (Revelation 2:7, NAS). "And while they were ministering to the Lord and fasting, the Holy Spirit said, 'Set apart for Me Barnabas and Saul for the work to which I have called them' " (Acts 13:2, NAS).

He teaches: "But the Helper, the Holy Spirit, whom the Father will send in My name, He will teach you all things, and bring to your remembrance all that I said to you" (John 14:26, NAS).

He witnesses: "When the Helper comes, whom I will send to you from the Father, that is the Spirit of truth, who proceeds from the Father, He will bear witness of Me" (John 15:26, NAS). "The Spirit Himself bears witness with our spirit that we are children of God" (Romans 8:16, NAS).

He guides: "For all who are being led by the Spirit of God, these are sons of God" (Romans 8:14, NAS). "But when He, the Spirit of truth, comes, He will guide you into all truth" (John 16:13, NAS).

He convicts: "But I tell you the truth, it is to your advantage that I go away; for if I do not go away, the Helper shall not come to you; but if I go, I will send Him to you. And He, when He comes, will convict the world concerning sin, and righteousness, and judgment" (John 16:7,8, NAS).

He commands: "And the Spirit said to Philip, 'Go up and join this chariot' " (Acts 8:29, NAS).

He helps: "And in the same way the Spirit also helps our weakness" (Romans 8:26, NAS).

He reaches out to sinners: "My Spirit shall not strive with man forever" (Genesis 6:3, NAS).

He performs miracles: "And when they came up out of the water, the Spirit of the Lord snatched Philip away; and the eunuch saw him no more" (Acts 8:39, NAS).

The Holy Spirit Is Regarded As a Person

The Bible mentions numerous acts which can be performed toward the Holy Spirit. A look at these acts will indicate they must have a personality as their object, which further proves that the Holy Spirit is a person.

He can be obeyed: "And while Peter was reflecting on the vision, the Spirit said to him, 'Behold, three men are looking for you. But arise, go downstairs, and accompany them without misgivings: for I have sent them Myself.' And Peter went down to the men" (Acts 10:19-21a, NAS).

He can be lied to: "But Peter said, 'Ananias, why has Satan filled your heart to lie to the Holy Spirit, and to keep back some of the price of the land?' " (Acts 5:3, NAS).

He can be resisted: "You men who are stiff-necked and uncircumcised in heart and ears are always resisting the Holy Spirit" (Acts 7:51, NAS).

He can be grieved: "And do not grieve the Holy Spirit of God, by whom you were sealed for the day of redemption" (Ephesians 4:30, NAS).

He can be quenched: "Do not quench the Spirit" (1 Thessalonians 5:19, NAS). In other words, do not put out the Holy Spirit's fire and light in your life.

He can be insulted: "How much severer punishment

do you think he will deserve who has trampled under foot the Son of God, and has regarded as unclean the blood of the covenant by which he was sanctified, and has insulted the Spirit of Grace?" (Hebrews 10:29, NAS).

He can be blasphemed (spoken against): "Therefore I say to you, any sin and blasphemy shall be forgiven men, but blasphemy against the Spirit shall not be forgiven" (Matthew 12:31, NAS). The Holy Spirit brings conviction and repentance, and for those with responsive wills He opens the door to forgiveness and eternal life through Jesus Christ.

Therefore, those who hate God and blaspheme Christ can yet be convicted and brought to repentance by the Holy Spirit. But the person whose will totally rejects the overtures of the Holy Spirit closes the door to forgiveness and eternal life.

These acts can be performed only toward a person — not toward some impersonal force. Since these acts are said in the Bible to be performed toward the Holy Spirit, we find in them the scriptural proof that the Holy Spirit is a person.

The Holy Spirit Is Divine God

The Bible describes the attributes — the qualities and inherent characteristics — of the Holy Spirit. These divine, or God-like, attributes further prove that tha person of the Holy Spirit is God Himself. Following is a list of the biblical descriptions of the Holy Spirit's divine attributes:

He is eternal: "How much more will the blood of Christ, who through the eternal Spirit offered Himself without blemish to God, cleanse your conscience from dead works to serve the living God?" (Hebrews 9:14, NAS).

He is omnipresent (everywhere present): "Where can I go from Thy Spirit? Or where can I flee from Thy presence?" (Psalm 139:7, NAS).

He is omniscient (all-knowing): "For to us God revealed them through the Spirit; for the Spirit searches all things, even the depths of God. For who among men knows the thoughts of a man except the spirit of the man, which is in him? Even so the thoughts of God no one knows except the Spirit of God" (1 Corinthians 2:10,11, NAS).

He is omnipotent (all-powerful): "And the angel answered and said to her, 'The Holy Spirit will come upon you, and the power of the Most High will overshadow you; and for that reason the holy offspring shall be called the Son of God' " (Luke 1:35, NAS). "The Spirit of God has made me, and the breath of the Almighty gives me life" (Job 33:4, NAS).

From the above scriptural descriptions of the nature and inherent character of the Holy Spirit, we can see that He possesses God-like attributes, which is possible only because He is divine God.

The Holy Spirit Performs the Work of God

The Bible describes the many works of the Holy Spirit. These works can be performed only by a person with the divine nature of God, which demonstrates further that the Holy Spirit is God.

The first work of the Holy Spirit mentioned in the Bible occurs in the creation account in the book of Genesis: "In the beginning God created the heavens and the earth. And the earth was formless and void, and darkness was over the surface of the waters" (Genesis 1:1,2, NAS).

Now the Holy Spirit was not idle as He moved over the waters: He was participating in the creation. But that was only the literal beginning of the divine work of the Holy Spirit.

The Bible teaches that the Spirit gave inspiration to the writers of Scripture (2 Peter 1:21, 2 Timothy 3:16), caused the miraculous conception and birth of Christ

(Luke 1:35), convicts the world of sin, righteousness and judgment (John 16:8), intercedes (Romans 8:26), gives believers new, holy natures (2 Thessalonians 2:13), produces the fruit of the Spirit (Galatians 5:22,23) and empowers for witnessing (Acts 1:8).

These works could never be performed by a concept or impersonal force — or even by mere man, for that matter. True, man can comfort and intercede and do other similar works, but only God can do them perfectly, absolutely. These works, then, can be performed only be deity, by God, by His divine Holy Spirit.

Who is the Holy Spirit? He is Almighty God!

The Holy Spirit and the Trinity

The Holy Spirit is the third person of the Trinity — co-equal with God, the Father, and God, the Son — Jesus Christ. There is only one God, but He manifests Himself in three persons.

I cannot define the Trinity. No one can. One of my seminary professors once said, "The man who tries to understand the Trinity will lose his mind. The man who denies the Trinity will lose his soul." We who are *finite* do not comprehend God, who is *infinite*.

We try to illustrate the concept of the Trinity, but the attempt is wholly inadequate. For example, I could say that a man has a body, a mind and a spirit — which one is the man?

Or I could describe H_2O as a liquid, a solid or a vapor, depending on whether it was water, ice or steam. Which one is H_2O? Or, I am to my wife a husband; to our sons, a father, and to my parents, a son — yet, I am only one man. No human illustration is adequate. At best it can only suggest what the Trinity is like.

In this chapter, we have examined the Scriptures, which teach that the Holy Spirit is a person, has a divine nature, is God and is the third member of the Trinity. The Holy Spirit is the Spirit of Christ, who has been sent from God to guide and empower us. The Holy Spirit is the risen Christ living within us. He is the key to our supernatural adventure with God as a way of life.

CHAPTER FOUR

A New Spiritual You

Every Christian, at the moment of his spiritual rebirth, enters into an eternal relationship with God (1 John 5:11-13). It is accomplished by the work of the Holy Spirit who regenerates (Titus 3:5, John 3:3), indwells (1 Corinthians 3:16), seals (Ephesians 1:13, 4:30), guarantees (2 Corinthians 5:5), baptizes (Galatians 3:27) and fills (Ephesians 5:17-20) the believer.

These acts on the part of the Holy Spirit place the believer into the Body of Christ — a positional relationship which may or may not be accompanied by an emotional experience.

This is the essence of what Christ meant when He explained, "You in Me, and I in you" (John 14:20, NAS). When we enter into this union with Christ, we exchange our weakness for His power, our sinfulness and defeat for His holiness and victory. When we receive Christ, we immediately possess all the potential necessary to live the supernatural life — a life of power and victory over sin.

This amazing supernatural power of the Holy Spirit — the life of Christ in every believer   is released in our lives by faith as we surrender the control of our lives to the Holy Spirit. Since it is the ministry of the Holy Spirit to glorify Christ, Jesus Christ now has unhindered opportunity to work in and through us to perform His perfect will.

Let us look more closely at the work of the Holy Spirit in the life of the Christian at the time he receives Jesus Christ as Lord and Savior.

The Spirit Regenerates Us

"Regeneration" refers to a believer's spiritual rebirth. "He saved us, not on the basis of deeds which we have done in righteousness, but according to His mercy, by the washing of regeneration and renewing by the Holy Spirit" (Titus 3:5, NAS).

When a person receives Christ as Lord and Savior, the Holy Spirit translates him from his spiritually dead natural state into a new, spiritually alive child of God. "Unless you are born again," Jesus told the Pharisee, Nicodemus, who was a ruler of the Jews and a good and moral religious person, "you can never get into the Kingdom of God" (John 3:3, TLB).

The Spirit Indwells Us

In Old Testament days, the Holy Spirit came *upon* certain men and women of God for the purpose of special service during a time determined by God (Judges 14:19). During Christ's ministry, the Holy Spirit was said to have dwelled *with* the disciples in the person of Christ (John 14:16).

After the coming of the Holy Spirit at Pentecost, the Holy Spirit is described as dwelling *within* believers (1 Corinthians 6:19). "Don't you realize that all of you together are the house of God, and that the Spirit of God lives among you in His house?" (1 Corinthians 3:16, TLB).

The Spirit Seals Us in Christ

At the time we receive Christ, the Holy Spirit places His *seal* on us. Figuratively, the seal indicates that we are children of God and belong to Him and that His Holy Spirit will keep us eternally in God's protective custody, secure from Satan, sin and judgment. "Having also believed, you were sealed in Him with the Holy Spirit of promise . . . sealed for the day of redemption" (Ephesians 1:13; 4:30, NAS).

The Spirit Guarantees Our Inheritance

By the very presence of the indwelling Holy Spirit in our lives, we are given a preview of the inheritance which awaits us in heaven. God, by indwelling us with His Holy Spirit, is giving His promise in the form of a "down payment" that our inheritance is real and waiting. "This is what God has prepared for us and, as a guarantee, He has given us His Holy Spirit" (2 Corinthians 5:5, TLB).

The Spirit Baptizes Us

Most Christians will agree that the Holy Spirit baptizes the believer into the Body of Christ: "For by one Spirit we were all baptized into one body, whether Jews or Greeks, whether slaves or free" (1 Corinthians 12:13, NAS). But the unity of the Body of Christ is divided on earth by many differences over a "second baptism," speaking in tongues and "Spirit-filling."

All believers agree, however, that we are commanded to live holy lives and the Holy Spirit supernaturally makes this human impossibility a reality. He does this when we totally submit ourselves to His indwelling love and power. Or, to use a metaphor of the apostle Paul, "For all of you who were baptized into Christ have clothed yourselves in Christ" (Galatians 3:27, NAS).

The Spirit Fills Us

We are admonished by Paul: "Don't act thoughtlessly, but try to find out and do whatever the Lord wants you to. Don't drink too much wine, for many evils lie along that path; be filled instead with the Holy Spirit, and controlled by Him. Talk with each other much about the Lord, quoting psalms and hymns and singing sacred songs, making music in your hearts to the Lord. Always give thanks for everything to our God and Father in the name of our Lord Jesus Christ" (Ephesians 5:17-20, TLB).

Paul was suggesting that a Spirit-filled Christian will know God's will, and he may give the impression of being "Spirit-intoxicated" because of the joy, radiance, boldness and courage that he frequently demonstrates. Also, as the Ephesians passage suggests, a Spirit-filled Christian talks much about the Lord, is continually praising God, making melody in his heart to the Lord and giving thanks for all things.

He realizes, in a way that he could not realize while in his carnal state, that all that he is and has is by the grace of God. Only the Spirit-filled Christian possesses the key to supernatural living.

To summarize, at the time a person becomes a Christian the Holy Spirit indwells, regenerates, seals, guarantees, baptizes and fills the believer. This work by The Holy Spirit results in the believer becoming a member of the Body of Christ and a child of God forever.

Have You Heard?

Sadly, there are many people who have not entered into the supernatural life. Either they are not Christians or they are not sure that they are Christians, or they are Christians who want to live supernaturally, but do not know how. Certainly, until a person becomes a child of God — a Christian in the true, biblical sense — he cannot become a Spirit-filled person and cannot know and experience the wonderful joy of living supernaturally.

This may come as a surprise to you, as it does to many others, but our personal surveys taken by the millions all over the world indicate that from 50% to 90% of all church members are not sure of their salvation. Like Martin Luther, John Wesley and many others who became mighty ambassadors for Christ, some spend many years "serving God" before they experience the assurance and reality of their salvation.

The pastor of a large fashionable church of 1,500 members once reacted negatively when I shared these statistics, doubting that such large percentages of church members lacked assurance of their salvation. He decided personally to survey his own congregation at the church where he had served as senior pastor for 15 years. To his amazement and shock, more than 75% of the membership indicated they were not sure of their salvation.

The following Sunday, the pastor arranged for the Four Spiritual Laws booklet — which contains the distilled essence of the gospel — to be distributed to each member of the congregation. For his sermon he read the contents of the booklet aloud. Then he invited all who wished to receive Christ as their Savior and Lord to read aloud with him the prayer contained in the booklet. Almost the entire congregation joined in the prayer audibly. As a result the church was changed.

Could it be that you would include yourself in that large number of religious church members who are not sure of their salvation? If so, you will want to read the next chapter without further delay.

For about three decades, the staff of Campus Crusade for Christ has been sharing with millions of people around the world the gospel of Jesus Christ and explaining how a person can become a Christian. This is quite often communicated in one form or another from a little booklet entitled, "Have You Heard of the Four Spiritual Laws?"

To date, more than 700 million copies of this simple guide, telling how to become a Christian, have appeared in literature, books, newspapers and magazines in every major language of the world. In addition, it has been used on film, records, cassette tapes, television and radio.

The complete version of "The Four Spiritual Laws" is reprinted at the back of this book.

CHAPTER FIVE

You Can Be Sure

A dynamic young businessman sat across from me in my office. By almost every standard of human measure he was an outstanding success in both his business and his religion. He was one of the leading men in his field of specialty in the world.

A highly moral, religious person, he was very active in his church. And yet, he was not sure that he was a Christian. He wanted desperately — more than anything in the world — to have real assurance, but he did not know how to go about obtaining it. Step by step, I explained to him from the Bible how he could receive Christ into his life and be sure of his salvation. Soon we were on our knees in prayer, after which he went on his way rejoicing in the assurance of his salvation.

Doubt of Salvation

Many pastors and other Christian leaders, I have discovered, have this same gnawing doubt about their salvation. One pastor who had preached the Bible-centered gospel for 40 years told me that he was still unsure of his salvation.

The wife of an evangelist confided, "During the past 30 years, my husband and I have introduced thousands of people to Christ, but I have never been sure of my own salvation. Never before have I had the courage to share this concern with anyone, but now I am so desperate that I have come to seek your help."

A student who had received Christ after hearing my message on "The Uniqueness of Jesus" stood to his feet after we had prayed together and, with a puzzled, troubled look on his face, said, "I don't feel any different. I guess God didn't hear my prayer. How can I be sure that Christ has come into my life?"

My experience in counseling thousands of students and laymen through the years has convinced me there are literally millions of good, faithful churchgoers who have "received" Christ into their lives through prayer but are not sure of their salvation. Regardless of how hard they try and how disciplined their efforts to please God, they are still uncertain of their relationship with Him.

During the writing of this chapter, I had the privilege of participating in the 1980 World Evangelization-Here's Life Crusade in Seoul, Korea. Police officials estimated that almost 10.5 million people were present for the five evening meetings, about one million attending the first night and 9.5 million more on the following four nights.

I was asked to go before these vast audiences and invite those who had not previously done so to receive Jesus Christ as their Savior and Lord. For three nights I did this, then, on the fourth night, following my message on "How to Be Filled with the Holy Spirit," I invited the audience to pray, and by faith to appropriate the fullness of the Holy Spirit.

Officials estimated that more than one million people responded to the salvation invitation. Almost two million indicated they had, by faith, for the first time, appropriated the fullness of the Holy Spirit.

How could this be? How could the Korean people, who are already so dedicated to Christ and His Church, not be sure of their salvation and not know the reality of being filled with the Spirit? Many Korean pastors and missionaries have explained to me that many Korean Christians were dedicated, disciplined and even devoted to Jesus, but do not know the reality of a personal relationship with Him and the personal assurance of their salvation.

As explained in the previous chapter, this same lack of assurance of salvation is true among church members throughout the world, including America.

Why does this heartbreaking uncertainty exist among so many Christians who genuinely want to know God better and have sought Him for years? I am persuaded that the lack of assurance is due to either misinformation or to a lack of information regarding who God is — the true meaning of the crucifixion and the resurrection and the role of faith in receiving Jesus Christ as Savior.

Threefold Commitment

If you are among that vast multitude who are still looking for God, the next few moments could well be the most important ones of your entire life.

Becoming a Christian involves *receiving* the Lord Jesus Christ. You must receive Him because He is God's gift to you of His love and forgiveness (John 3:16). A gift does not become yours until you receive it.

The Bible tells us that we can receive Christ — God's gift — only by faith: "For by grace you have been saved *through faith*; and that not of yourselves, it is the gift of God; not as a result of works, that no one should boast" (Ephesians 2:8, 9, NAS, italics added). If we tried to pay for our salvation, it would no longer be a gift.

Receiving Christ results in a threefold commitment to a person — the person of the Lord Jesus Christ It is a commitment to Him of one's *intellect, emotions* and *will,* as illustrated below:

SELF-DIRECTED LIFE
S—Self on the throne
†—Christ is outside the life
•—Interests are directed by self, often resulting in discord and frustration

CHRIST-DIRECTED LIFE
†—Christ is in the life
S—Self is yielding to Christ
•—Interests are directed by Christ, resulting in harmony with God's plan

These two circles represent two kinds of lives: the *self-controlled life* and the *Christ-controlled life*. In the *self-controlled life*, (S) finite self rules from the throne of a person's life. In such a life, Christ (+) is outside the life, and interests (o) that are controlled by self often result in discord and frustration.

In the *Christ-controlled life*, Christ is on the throne of the life, self is dethroned and interests are under His gracious, wise and loving control, resulting in harmony with God's plan.

Our relationship with Christ can well be illustrated by the requirements for a marriage relationship. Such a relationship in marriage, ideally, must contain these same three ingredients: the intellect, the emotions and the will.

My own marriage serves as a good example. I was absolutely convinced *intellectually* that my beloved Vonette, the woman who was my intended bride, was the "right one" for me. Furthermore, I was *emotionally* convinced that she was the "right one" for me — I loved her with all my heart. But marriage requires more than intellect and emotions. It also involves the *will*. It was not until Vonette and I, as an act of the *will*, committed ourselves to each other before a minister of authority that we became husband and wife. The two words, "I do," made the difference.

So it is in our relationship with Jesus Christ. It is not enough to be *intellectually* convinced that Jesus Christ is the Son of God, that He died on the cross for our sins, that He rose from the dead. It is not enough to be baptized and active in the church; not even enough to have an *emotional* experience.

Though both the intellect and the emotions are valid and important, a person does not become a Christian until, *as an act of the will, by faith,* he receives Christ into his life as Savior and Lord. At that point he experiences a new birth and becomes a child of God.

Waiting for an Experience

An active church member brought one of his business associates to see me for the purpose of introducing him to Christ. After a brief explanation of who Christ is, why He came to earth, the meaning of His death and resurrection and how to receive Him as Savior and Lord by faith, the man readily responded.

In the course of our conversation, it became apparent that the church member who brought his friend to see me was not a Christian himself. When I asked if he was sure of his own relationship with Christ, he surprised me with this story:

"No," he said, "I am not a Christian, though I want to be. I believe that Jesus Christ is the Son of God and I know that He died for my sins. I am active in the church and keep hoping that someday something will happen and I will become a Christian."

I was puzzled. "What is keeping you from receiving Christ?" I asked.

"I am waiting for an emotional experience like my mother had when she received Christ as a young woman," he answered. "But no matter how hard I try, nothing happens."

As I explained the fallacy of seeking an emotional experience and the scriptural basis for receiving Christ, by faith, he too readily responded. As we prayed together, he had the scriptural assurance that Christ had come into his life.

You will be interested to know that when he received Christ as God's gift by faith, he was filled with great joy. He had sought an emotional experience for years without success. Yet, when he was willing to obey and trust God's Word to him, he experienced the reality of the promise of Jesus recorded in John 14:21, "I will manifest myself to those who obey me."

Threefold Confirmation

How, then, can a person be sure that he is a Christian? Is there not some kind of confirmation that God gives to the man who sincerely receives Christ? Yes, there is. Every person who sincerely invites Christ into his life can be certain that He has come in. This certainty can be based on a threefold confirmation:

Trustworthiness of God

First, we have the external witness, or evidence, of the Word of God. Assurance is based on the authority of God's Word. When you meet God's conditions, as revealed in His Word, you can be assured that you are a child of God.

```
   TRUSTWORTHY WORD  )
CONFIRMING HOLY SPIRIT  } = ASSURANCE
        CHANGED LIFE  )
```

"We believe men who witness in our courts, and so surely we can believe whatever God declares. And God declares that Jesus is His Son. *All who believe this know in their hearts that it is true.* If anyone doesn't believe this, he is actually calling God a liar because he doesn't believe what God has said about His Son.

"And what is it that God has said? That He has given us eternal life and that this life is in His Son. So whoever has God's Son has life; whoever does not have God's Son does not have life. I have written this to *you who believe in the Son of God so that you may know you have eternal life"* (1 John 5:9-13, TLB, italics added).

The Holy Spirit Tells Us

The second confirmation that we have become a child of God is the internal witness, or evidence, of the Holy Spirit. The apostle Paul writes, "For His Holy Spirit speaks to us deep in our hearts and tells us that we really are God's children" (Romans 8:16, TLB).

Paul also emphasizes the validity of the evidence of the presence of the Holy Spirit in the believer: "For when we brought you the good news, it was not just meaningless chatter to you; no, you listened with great interest. What we told you produced a powerful effect on you, for *the Holy Spirit gave you great and full assurance that what we said was true"* (1 Thessalonians 1:5, TLB, italics added).

Changed Lives

Our changed lives are a third witness to the fact that we are Christians. Jesus explained to Nicodemus, a devout religious leader of the Jews, "You must be born again or you cannot see the kingdom of God" (John 3:3, NAS).

This born-again experience was explained by the apostle Paul to the Colossian Christians: "The same good news that came to you is going out all over the world and changing lives everywhere just as it changed yours that very first day you heard it and understood about God's great kindness to sinners" (Colossians 1:6, TLB).

The proof that we have experienced a new birth and have become children of God will be demonstrated by our changed lives, as John recorded:

"And how can we be sure that we belong to Him [Christ]? By looking within ourselves: are we really trying to do what He wants us to? Someone may say, 'I am a

Christian; I am on my way to heaven; I belong to Christ.'
But if he doesn't do what Christ tells him to, he is a liar.

"But those who do what Christ tells them to will learn
to love God more and more. That is the way to know
whether or not you are a Christian. Anyone who says
he is a Christian should live as Christ did" (1 John 2:3-6
TLB).

Unless one has a genuine desire to obey and please
the Lord Jesus, he has a right to question that he is a
child of God.

Jesus said, "He who has My commandments, and
keepeth them, he it is who loves Me; and he who loves
Me shall be loved by My Father, and I will love him, and
will disclose Myself to him" (John 14:21, NAS). As
explained earlier, Jesus is saying here that He will make
Himself known to all who obey Him in such a way that
they *experience* the reality of His presence in their lives.
Such a manifestation will differ, however, according to
the individual and the circumstances.

There *is* a place for emotions in the Christian life, and
we are not to ignore the value of legitimate emotions,
though we should not seek an emotional experience nor
attempt to recapture one from the past.

It is more important to remember that we are to live
by *faith* — in God and in His promises — and not by
seeking an emotional experience.

I reiterate: a valid, emotional, scriptural experience is
the by-product of faith and obedience. But to seek an
emotional experience contradicts the command of faith
and grieves the Holy Spirit. Remember, "The righteous
man shall live by faith" (Galatians 3:11, NAS) and "Without faith, it is impossible to please Him" (Hebrews 11:6,
NAS).

Source of Assurance

We have discussed how you can be sure you are a
Christian in terms of the intellect, the emotions and the

will. We have compared becoming a Christian to a marriage. However, in these two experiences there may be a difference in sequence.

Generally, in the marriage relationship, the sequence of commitment is: first, intellect; then, emotions; and, finally, will. But in commitment to Christ the sequence is: first, the intellect; then the will; and, finally, as a by-product or result, the emotions or feelings. (In some countries and cultures where marriages are arranged, the sequence is generally intellect, then will, then emotions.)

Basic Truths

To be sure that you are a Christian you must be aware intellectually of certain basic truths:

First, that God, who created the universe and every living creature, loves you and offers a wonderful plan for your life.

Second, man is sinful and separated from God; thus, he cannot know and experience God's love and plan.

Third, Jesus Christ is God's only provision for man's sin. Through Him you can know and experience God's love and plan.

Fourth, we must individually receive Jesus Christ as our personal Savior and Lord; then we can know and experience God's love and plan.

Christ said, "Behold, I stand at the door and knock; if anyone hears my voice and opens the door, I will come in to him, and will sup with him, and he with Me" (Revelation 3:20, NAS).

In the Gospel of John we are told, "But as many as received Him, to them He gave the right to become children of God, even to those who believe in His name" (John 1:12, NAS).

Saved Through Faith

It is not enough merely to ask the Lord Jesus Christ into your life. You must have faith to believe that He will do what He said He would. Jesus promised to come into your life if you ask Him in. By faith, I can know that Jesus will come into my life when I ask Him in because He said He would.

God's Word promises, "For by grace you have been saved through *faith*; and that not of yourselves, it is the gift of God; not as a result of works, that no one should boast" (Ephesians 2:8, 9, NAS, italics added).

How would you answer the question, "On what basis do you know you will go to heaven when you die?" If you are depending on your good works, your church membership or your Christian spouse or parents, you will never make it. But if you are depending completely on the grace of God, expressed through the gift of His Son, the Lord Jesus Christ, whom you have received into your life by faith, you can be assured of God's warm welcome to a heavenly home.

Many Christians ask Jesus to come into their lives again and again in times of emotional crises or in response to a moving presentation of the gospel. Yet nothing seems to happen in their lives. Why? There are three possible explanations.

Not Just a Man

First, some ask Jesus to come into their lives without realizing that He is not just a mere man, a historical figure. Jesus of Nazareth is much more than a man of history; He is the God-man — both perfect God and sinless man, the Savior, the promised Messiah of the Old Testament, who died for our sins, was buried and on the third day was raised from the dead.

Jesus is the living Lord of life and history, and He has the power to change the lives of any and all who will receive Him. When a person only superficially "receives" Christ — perhaps just because others are receiving Him, without understanding who He is, nothing is likely to happen.

For example, an alcoholic asked Jesus into his heart for years, but nothing happened. Then one day he was asked, "Are you asking Jesus, the man, into your life? Or Jesus, the omnipotent Son of God and Savior?"

The alcoholic replied, "Jesus, the man."

At that, my friend gave the alcoholic a careful explanation of who the Lord Jesus is and why He came into the world. This time the alcoholic received the living Christ into his life with understanding, and he was immediately changed. Incidentally, he has not had a drink since.

Ask Him Once

The second reason some people invite Christ into their lives over and over again but seem to experience no change in their way of living is that they do not ask Him to come into their lives as an expression of *faith*. They insult Him by asking Him in again and again.

Ask Him to be your Savior once, and thereafter thank Him daily as an expression of faith that He is in your life, for He has promised never to leave or forsake you (Hebrews 13:5).

The third reason why some people do not change after inviting Christ into their lives is that they do not understand who Christ is, what He has done for them and what it means to become a child of God. Our Four Spiritual Laws, which are reprinted in the back of this book, will answer such questions in a simple, understandable way.

Does all that I have shared with you in this chapter make sense? Have you ever personally received the Lord Jesus Christ as your Savior? If you have received Him, do you have the assurance of your salvation? Are you sure that if you died right now, you would spend eternity with God in heaven?

If you cannot answer "Yes" to these questions, may I suggest that you find a quiet place where you can be alone and pray. Receive Jesus Christ into your life today.

If you have never received Him by a definite, deliberate act of your will, by faith, you can do so *right now*, in prayer. And if you are not *sure* that you are a Christian, even though you have asked Christ into your life many times in the past, you can make sure now. In either case, may I suggest that you pray this or a similar prayer of faith, making it your very own:

"Lord Jesus, I need You. Thank you for dying on the cross for my sins. I open the door of my life and receive You as my Savior and Lord. Thank You for forgiving my sins and giving me eternal life. Take control of the throne of my life. Make me the kind of person You want me to be. Amen."

As I was editing this page of the manuscript, a woman seated near me on the plane saw me open the Four Spiritual Laws booklet. Her face lit up as she interrupted my editing to share this story:

"A few days ago," she began, as we flew over Indiana, "I was driving in Colorado when my engine died and refused to start. A woman stopped to help me, and as we talked she gave me a copy of that booklet."

"Did you read it?" I asked.

"Yes," she said.

"Did you receive Christ into your life?" I asked.

Her response was so vague that I asked her another question: "If you were to die today, are you sure you would go to Heaven?"

"No," she replied, "I am not sure, but I would like to be."

I asked her if she believed that Jesus is the Son of God, and if she believed that He died for her sins."

"Yes," she said, "I do."

I referred again to the prayer in the booklet and suggested that when she returned home she should read the first three chapters of the Gospel of John, review the Four Spiritual Laws booklet, then get on her knees and pray the prayer contained in the booklet as an act of faith. This she promised to do, with the kind of conviction that convinced me she was eager to do so. She gave me her address for further follow-up.

You Can Be Sure

Now, if you have prayed the prayer from the booklet and invited Christ into your life for the first time, or if you have previously invited Christ into your life but never really knew for sure whether or not He had come in, *you can now and forever be sure that you are a Christian.*

According to His promise in Revelation 3:20, where is Christ right now in relation to you? Christ said that He would come into your life. Would He mislead you? On what authority do you know that God has answered your prayer? You can know on the basis of the trustworthiness of God Himself and His Word.

You Have Eternal Life

Because assurance is so important, let me repeat: the Bible promises eternal life to all who receive Jesus Christ as their Lord and Savior. "And the witness is this, that God has given us eternal life, and this life is in His Son. He who has the Son has the life; he who does not have the Son of God does not have the life.

"These things I have written to you who believe in the name of the Son of God, in order that you may *know* that you have eternal life" (1 John 5:11-13, NAS, italics added).

Thank God daily, even many times each day, that Christ is in your life and that He will never leave you

(Hebrews 13:5). You can know on the basis of His promise that Christ lives in you and that you have eternal life, from the very moment you invite Him in. He will not deceive you.

Let me reiterate: Never insult Jesus by asking Him into your life again. Thank Him every morning when you awaken — and several times each day — that He is in your life. Ask Him to guide your steps each day and enable you to share His love, which you are experiencing, with others.

What Happened?

The moment that you received Christ by faith, as an act of the will, many things happened. Christ came into your life (Revelation 3:20 and Colossians 1:27). Your sins were forgiven (Colossians 1:14). You became a child of God (John 1:12). You received eternal life (John 5:24). You began the great adventure for which God created you (John 10:10; 2 Corinthians 5:17 and 1 Thessalonians 5:18).

Can you think of anything more wonderful that could happen to you than receiving Christ? Would you like to thank God in prayer right now for what He has done for you? By thanking God, you further demonstrate your faith.

All over the world there are millions of men and women of all ages, in every state of society, who are making this same, wonderful discovery of God's love and forgiveness through Jesus Christ.

A Divine Appointment

For example, I was talking recently with a very prominent businessman in America. The appointment was made by a mutual friend. As we talked together, this outstanding executive, whom I had not met previously, expressed a great hunger for God.

Sensing that God had prepared his heart for our meeting and this was truly a divine appointment, I shared the gospel with him, as presented in the Four Spiritual Laws booklet. He indicated that, as a young person, he had been religious but had never really known Christ personally. But now, he expressed a desire to receive Christ.

So he read aloud the prayer in the booklet, making it his own prayer. Then I prayed for him. Together, we rejoiced in his newfound salvation.

CHAPTER SIX

God's Way Is Best

A student once asked, "If I give my life to Christ, do I become a puppet?" The answer is a resounding "No!" We never become puppets. We have the right of choice; we are free moral agents. God's Word assures us that He guides and encourages us, but we must act as a result of our own self-will. God does not force us to make decisions.

The more we understand the love, the wisdom, the sovereignty, the grace and power of God, the more we will want to trust Him with every detail of our lives. The secret of the supernatural life is to keep Christ on the throne of our lives and delight ourselves in Him as Lord. We fail in the Christian life when we, as a deliberate act of our will, choose to disobey the leading of the Holy Spirit.

It is a tragedy of the human will that we often think we have a better way than God has for living the Christian life. But do not deceive yourself or allow Satan to mislead you: *God's way is best!*

"Don't be misled," Paul writes to the Ephesians. "Remember that you can't ignore God and get away with it: a man will always reap just the kind of crop he sows! If he sows to please his own wrong desires, he will be planting seeds of evil and he will surely reap a harvest of spiritual decay and death; but if he plants the good things of the Spirit, he will reap the everlasting life which the Holy Spirit gives him.

"And let us not get tired of doing what is right, for after a while we will reap a harvest of blessing if we don't get discouraged and give up" (Galatians 6:7-10, TLB).

What Is God's Will For You?

In my travels around the world, I have found that many Christians are frustrated, defeated and fruitless because they do not understand how to know God's will for their lives. It isn't surprising, therefore, that one of the questions I am most frequently asked is, "How can I know God's will for my life?"

I believe it is the desire of all true Christians to have God guide them in making the many decisions of life — whom to marry, what career to select, whether to make a major purchase, and so on. Consequently, I am convinced that all Christians can know and do God's will, with the result that they can live a supernatural life of meaning and fulfillment. Such a life can be lived by any Christian if only he understands and applies certain simple biblical principles.

First and foremost, we must trust God. We must understand that God's will is the best possible plan for our lives. God is not the vengeful tyrant that some seem to think He is. He is not a cosmic policeman waiting to give us a traffic citation every time we "break the law." The man who has this small view of God tries to get away with everything he can, just as he breaks the speed limit whenever convenient, if he thinks the police are not watching. He cannot love and worship a God whom he cannot trust.

But to trust God requires that we know God. The Bible tells us about God as He really is — a holy, loving, compassionate and wise God and Father; a merciful Savior; an all-knowing and all-powerful, sovereign, gracious God. The man who has this view of God will have no trouble saying, "Lord, I trust You with every detail and area of my life. I will go where You want me to go and do what You want me to do."

Because God is perfect, His plan for you is perfect. He already has considered the many alternatives for your life, so do not attempt to outguess His perfect wisdom and foreknowledge. His plan for you is not only the best of the alternatives; it is also a *perfect* plan!

Second, we must apply the promises of God's Word as they become a reality in our lives, according to Philippians 2:13. "It is God who works in you both to will and to do of His good pleasure" (NAS). Let me explain: When God leads you by His Holy Spirit to do a task, you may be absolutely sure that He will enable you to do what He calls you to do, by providing the ideas, vision, wisdom, power, money, personnel, etc.

We cannot claim God's promises in a general way. We must wait upon the Lord and delight ourselves in Him until a particular promise or promises from God's Word become His Word to us personally.

Do not misunderstand: all of God's Word is holy and inspired and profitable to read, study and memorize, but there are times, as when we wait upon the Lord with prayer and fasting, that He speaks to us in a definite, personal way and uses His Word to tell us what to do.

I live by Philippians 2:13. God speaks to me through giving impressions of His Holy Spirit on my mind. I have never heard an audible word from God, nor do I feel the need for Him to communicate to me in this way. When God tells me to undertake a specific project, I generally follow this procedure to test the impression to see if it is from God or Satan or my own thoughts.

First, I ask, If I follow the impression given will it honor and glorify God?

Second, is it consistent with the written Word of God?

Third, are my motives pure?

Fourth, will it bring blessing to the Body of Christ?

Fifth, I usually ask godly Christians who are Spirit-filled, praying, sensitive people, for their counsel.

As the impression grows with time into a consuming conviction, I proceed to follow God's instructions and leading, even in the face of criticism of men and obstacles of Satan.

"Closed Doors"/Closed Minds

Many sincere people follow various man-made formulas for finding God's will in their lives. As a result, there is much confusion. Some simply leave decisions to chance and not to God's sovereign wisdom.

One of these formulas is the "closed-door" policy; it could just as well be called the "closed-mind" policy! Let me give you an example.

A young seminary graduate was investigating various possibilities of full-time Christian service. He came to see me to discuss our organization. Early in our conversation, I discovered he was following the "closed-door" approach.

The young man told me, "A few months ago, I began to investigate seven opportunities for Christian service. The Lord has closed the door on all but two. If the door to accept a call to a particular church closes, I'll know that God wants me in your organization."

Unfortunately, many sincere Christians follow this unscriptural method, often with most unsatisfactory and frustrating consequences. Don't misunderstand me — God may, and often does, close doors in the lives of believers, even those who are active in Christ's service and are Spirit- filled.

The apostle Paul experienced a "closed-door" situation. The Holy Spirit, according to Acts 16:6-11, forbade Paul's going into Bithynia because God wanted him in Macedonia. I mention this only to illustrate that my reference to "closed door" policies does not preclude such authentic experiences, but refers rather to a careless "hit-or-miss" attitude without careful evaluation of all the issues.

Spirit-Controlled Reasoning

The shortcomings of the "closed door" policy are that

it does not provide for careful, intelligent evaluation of all the factors involved. It is an unscriptural method because it fails to employ the God-given faculties of reason that are controlled by the Holy Spirit.

The "closed-door" policy is wrong, too, because it seeks God's will through the process of elimination rather than seeking God's best directly and first.

Spirit-controlled reasoning, on the other hand, establishes true faith on the basis of fact, emphasizing vital, active faith in God rather than minimizing it.

In making decisions, some sincere Christians rely almost entirely on impressions or hunches. They are afraid that they will grieve the Holy Spirit if they use their God-given ability to think and reason. This, of course, is faulty thinking.

Some Christians assume that God has closed a door simply because they have encountered difficulties. But we must remember that even Spirit-filled Christians who are intent on doing God's will can encounter opposition from Satan, from the world and even from an inner struggle with the old sin-nature. We shall discuss such spiritual conflicts in a later chapter.

The question logically follows, "How do I know whether God is closing the door or I am encountering opposition from Satan, the world or my old nature?"

Let me point out, first of all, that Scripture teaches and experience confirms that God's richest blessings often follow periods of greatest testing. This might include financial needs, loss of health, objections of loved ones and criticism by fellow Christians.

The principle here is that God promises to bless those who are *obedient*, who keep on striving to do His good and perfect will, and thereby demonstrate their faith in His faithfulness. For "without faith, it is impossible to please Him, for he who comes to God must believe that He is, and that He is a rewarder of those who seek Him" (Hebrews 11:6, NAS).

Every significant effort for the Lord that I have been involved in has experienced major — sometimes almost overwhelming — problems and resistance. For example, we experienced such obstacles in establishing our ministry on the campus of the University of California at Los Angeles in 1951. Most Christian groups on campus and many pastors in the area were opposed to our ministry and questioned our motives.

So it has been through the years on campus after campus, in city after city and country after country. We have continued to serve the Lord prayerfully, humbly and as obediently as we have known how, until today we have the privilege of working with tens of thousands of churches and Christian groups of all denominations around the world.

The Holy Spirit enabled us to win their confidence and trust by our actions as well as our words. However, in all honesty, there are still those who question our motives and criticize our efforts.

Should we wait for some dramatic revelation from God of His plan? Should we look for visual proof before taking action? While there are exceptions, God's will is usually determined by faith alone. Faith that comes when God speaks to us from His Word. God's communication to us in the twentieth century is seldom dramatic or unusual.

The Scriptures point this out: "God, after He spoke long ago to the fathers in the prophets in many portions and in many ways, in these last days has spoken to us in His Son, whom He appointed heir of all things, through whom also He made the world" (Hebrews 1:1, 2, NAS).

So if you have been waiting for God to speak to you in a dramatic way, I urge you to follow the scriptural teaching for knowing and doing God's will. Communion with Jesus Christ, obedience to His commands and trusting in His Holy Spirit result in discovering God's will.

No doubt there are areas of your life today in which you are seeking to know God's will. Perhaps they deal with family relationships, moving to a new house, changing jobs, going into full-time Christian work, or any number of things.

Are you willing to trust Christ? To obey His commands? To step out in faith on His promises, in the power and guidance of His Holy Spirit? Are you willing to entrust the outcome to our perfect, loving, all-wise God and Father? If you are, then may I suggest that you follow this scriptural approach to knowing and doing God's will.

Using Our Sound Minds

First of all, let me share with you what I have chosen to call the "Sound-Mind Principle" of Scripture. It has helped many people to discover God's will in their lives.

The apostle Paul wrote to young Timothy, one of his disciples in the faith, "God hath not given us the spirit of fear; but of power, and of love, and of a sound mind" (2 Timothy 1:7, KJ). The sound mind referred to in this verse means a well-balanced mind, under the control of the Holy Spirit — "remade" according to Paul's letter to the Christians at Rome:

"Therefore, my brothers, I implore you by God's mercies to offer your very selves to Him: a living sacrifice, dedicated and fit for His acceptance, the worship offered by mind and heart.

"Adapt yourselves no longer to the pattern of this present world, but let your minds be remade and your whole nature thus transformed. *Then you will be able to discern the will of God, and to know what is good, acceptable, and perfect*" (Romans 12:1, 2, NEB, italics added).

The Sound-Mind Principle is valid only when certain factors exist. By following the procedure below, you will find yourself taking positive actions leading to God's perfect will in your life:

1. *Confess all sin.* There must be no unconfessed sin in your life. Be sure you have applied 1 John 1:9: "If we confess our sins, He is faithful and righteous to forgive us our sins and to cleanse us from all unrighteousness."

2. *Surrender yourself to Christ as Lord and Master.* Your life must be fully dedicated to Christ according to Romans 12:1, 2, above, and you must be filled with the Holy Spirit in obedience to the command of Ephesians 5:18. (You may wish to turn ahead to chapter eight and read how to be filled with the Spirit.)

3. *Ask God to reveal His will to you.* God wants you to know and do His perfect will. If you have confessed all known sins and have surrendered yourself to Christ, then you can ask God to reveal His will to you, knowing by faith in Him and His Word that He will answer:

"And this is the confidence which we have before Him, that, if we ask anything according to His will, He hears us and if we know that He hears us in whatever we ask, we know that we have the requests which we have asked from Him" (1 John 5:14, 15, NAS).

4. *Consult God's Word.* The Bible is God's holy Word and as such "is inspired by God and profitable for teaching, for reproof, for correction, for training in righteousness; that the man of God may be adequate, equipped for every good work" (2 Timothy 3:16, 17, NAS).

Are you seeking God's will with regard to finances? Then consult a good Bible concordance for related verses that deal with "money" and "stewardship."

Are you seeking God's will regarding a health concern? Then look in your concordance for verses that deal with "heal" and "health."

For whatever matter you are seeking God's will, use a concordance to steer you to the appropriate verses in the Bible. Then, as you study the Bible, ask yourself three questions:

First, who is speaking — God, demon, angel or man?

Second, to whom is God speaking? To the nation Israel, to the Gentiles, to the Church, to men in general, or to some individual man or being? Third, how can this verse of Scripture be applied to my own life as not just information, but as God speaking to me personally, to help me do His will?

5. *"Listen" to the Holy Spirit.* Many mature Christians relate that God has led them in certain specific directions by impressions of the Holy Spirit on their minds. As I have already stated, this is often the way God speaks to me. "For it is God who is at work in you, both to will and to work for His good pleasure" (Philippians 2:13, NAS).

"Listening" to the Holy Spirit in this manner can be a valid means of knowing God's will, but only when the certain factors already mentioned are present. Let me summarize them for you. Will the impression you have give honor and glory to God? Is it consistent with the Bible? Are your motives pure? Will it bring blessing to the Body of Christ? Has it received the blessing of godly Christians?

Those who are just beginning to walk daily in the Holy Spirit should not rely on impressions or emotions. You may be misled because a mere hunch or wishful thinking has convinced you that it is the will of God or because of some subtle trickery from Satan himself.

This is why I cannot stress enough the importance of getting to know and respond to the perfect, holy, sovereign mind of God through regular, Spirit-led study and application of His divinely inspired Word so that it becomes God's personal word to you.

6. *Consider godly counsel.* Also prayerfully consider the counsel of mature, dedicated Christians who know the Word of God and are able to relate the proper use of Scripture to your need. However, do not make their counsel a crutch. Although God often speaks to us through other Christians, we are admonished to place

our trust solely in Him.

7. *By faith, follow God's commands.* Once you come to an understanding of God's will in your area of need, by faith be obedient to Him by following His commands and adhering to His guidelines, as written in the Bible. Trust the Holy Spirit to enable you to obey God so that the outcome of your decision and actions will be in accordance with His perfect will.

8. *Confirming circumstances.* When you have followed the above procedure, confirmation of a decision may come in various ways. Usually, the confirmation is a quiet, peaceful assurance that you are doing what God wants you to do, with an expectancy that God will use you to bear fruit.

Remember this: the above procedure for knowing God's will is no guarantee of an easy path to follow. Do not mistake satanic opposition for a door closed by God.

Spirit-filled Christians who are following the guidance of the Holy Spirit will oftentimes encounter difficulties in doing God's will. In fact, as you do God's will, you can *expect* spiritual opposition, but do not be unduly concerned. Keep your eyes on Jesus. He is your life, your peace, your victory. Delight yourself in Him.

As you seek God's will, be alert to these very common self-deceptions: First, do not try to manipulate God into doing *your* will by bargaining with Him or by trying to outfox Him. Second, do not deceive yourself by trying to justify your wants as being God's will.

For the new believer or Christian who is just now desiring to grow into spiritual maturity, the above procedure for knowing God's will is indispensable and needs to be followed often. However, as a person matures in Christ and learns how to walk in the Holy Spirit, day by day, moment by moment, this procedure need not *consciously* be applied so frequently.

As we learn more about the Lord and His commands,

and learn to rely continually on the leading and empowering of His Holy Spirit, we begin to discover that our will is conforming more and more to God's will.

Our goal, therefore, is to mature toward knowing the mind of Christ. Then, when decisions are made, we make them in the knowledge of what Christ would decide. When action is taken, we move in the direction that Christ would go and do the things that He would do.

God's way is best. Knowing and doing His will is the essence of the supernatural life, and the key to supernatural life is in the power and control of the Holy Spirit in our lives. As the following chapters will explain, we are living supernaturally when we are walking in the Spirit.

CHAPTER SEVEN

Walking In The Spirit

My wife, Vonette, and I were wading down a shallow stream in Yosemite Park with our two young sons. Because the rocks were slippery, I was holding my five-year-old, Bradley, by the hand to keep him from slipping on the rocks.

Suddenly Brad did slip, and his feet went out from under him. Fortunately I was holding his hand. I held him firmly until he regained his balance. Had he fallen he could have been seriously injured.

As we continued on our walk, Brad looked up into my face with a radiant expression of gratitude. "Daddy," he said, "I'm sure glad you saved me from falling."

God Holds Us

In the flash of a moment, it was as though God had spoken to me through Brad. I looked upward and said to my Father in heaven, "Father, I'm so glad You have kept me from falling; on thousands of occasions You have kept me from falling."

We walked in silence for a few moments. Then Brad looked up into my face again with that kind of expression that melts the heart of a father. "Daddy," he said, "I'm glad you're holding my hand." This time tears came to my eyes as I said to my Father in heaven, "I'm so glad You hold me by the hand; I'm so prone to fall."

Oh, this supernatural life is wonderful! Exciting! It is filled with adventure for those who let God control their lives — who walk with Him, moment by moment, day by day, allowing Him to "hold their hands."

This personal, intimate walk with Christ, the Savior, Lord and Friend, is what supernatural living is all about.

The Christian life is not always the struggle, the strain, the labor, the self-discipline it is oftentimes pictured so negatively by the typical, misinformed person.

How to Walk in the Spirit

Would you like to know how to experience supernatural living — to walk in the fullness of the Holy Spirit and experience an abundant, purposeful and fruitful life for Jesus Christ? Well, you can!

If you have been living in spiritual defeat — powerless and fruitless, wondering if there is any truth to the Christian life, there is great hope for you. What greater promise could Christ have possibly offered to you than the assurance that you can walk daily in the joy and power of the Holy Spirit and experience His supernatural life.

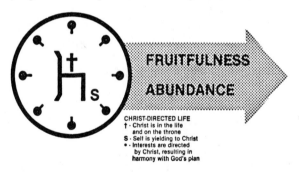

CHRIST-DIRECTED LIFE
† - Christ is in the life
   and on the throne
S - Self is yielding to Christ
● - Interests are directed
   by Christ, resulting in
   harmony with God's plan

Jesus Christ Himself has promised this for you and for everyone who receives Him as Lord and Savior and continues in faith and obedience. Here is Christ's promise to you:

"Truly, truly, I say to you, he who believes in Me, the works that I do shall he do also; and greater works than these shall he do, because I go to the Father. And whatever you ask in My name, that will I do, that the Father may be glorified in the Son. If you ask anything in My name, I will do it" (John 14:12-14, NAS).

Certain basic spiritual truths, when you fully understand and experience them by faith, guarantee you life-changing spiritual benefits, and the guarantee is backed by nothing less than the Word of God. These proven principles can help you to be more consistent in your walk in the Holy Spirit and more effective in your witness for the Savior.

A Supernatural Life

The Christian life, properly understood, is not complex or difficult. As a matter of fact, the Christian life is very simple. It is so simple that people sometimes stumble over its very simplicity. This is because the Christian life is a supernatural life. The only one who can truly live it is the Lord Jesus Christ.

If you try to live the Christian life through your limited human capacity, it *does* become complex, difficult and even impossible to live. But if you invite the Lord Jesus to direct your life, if you know the reality of having been crucified with Christ and raised with Him by faith as a way of life, and if you walk in the light as God is in the light, then the Lord Jesus simply lives His abundant life within you — by the indwelling Holy Spirit — in all of His resurrection power.

This fact was dramatically demonstrated in the lives of the early Christians. When the enemies of the Lord saw the way He was fulfilling His promise in the lives of Peter and John, and observed their boldness and the remarkable quality of their lives, they were amazed at these obviously uneducated, non-professional men and realized what being with Jesus had done for them (Acts 4:13).

This is not to suggest that by walking in the fullness of the Holy Spirit you will have no problems. Poor health, loss of loved ones, financial needs and other such experiences are common to all men. However, many of our problems are self-imposed because of our own carnal, selfish actions.

The spiritual person is spared most of these problems because he allows the Holy Spirit to control his life. But when the problems do come, the spiritual person can face them with a calm and confident attitude because he is aware of the divine resources of God which are available to him to deal with such problems.

This is not simply a matter of positive thinking. Positive thinking is fine, but this life is more than that. We are instructed to cast our cares upon the Lord Jesus because He cares for us (1 Peter 5:7). The spiritual person knows the trustworthiness of God from experience. The Lord becomes the problem-solver, and the trials and burdens of this world are no longer too great for us when He is carrying the load.

This was at the heart of the apostle Paul's moment-by-moment experience. "I have been crucified with Christ; and I myself no longer live, but Christ lives in me. And the real life I now have within this body is a result of my trusting in the Son of God, who loved me and gave Himself for me" (Galatians 2:20, TLB).

Simple and Understandable

Some years ago, while speaking at the University of Houston, I was told about a brilliant philosophy major. He was much older than most of the other students, having spent many years in the military before he returned to do graduate work.

He was so gifted, so brilliant, so knowledgeable that even the professors were impressed by his ability to comprehend quickly and to debate rationally. He was an atheist, and he had a way of embarrassing the Christians who tried to witness to him.

During one of my visits to the university, I was asked to talk with him about Christ. We sat in a booth in the student center, talking about his philosophy of life and the Word of God. It was a very unusual dialog. He successfully monopolized the conversation with his philosophy of unbelief in God.

At every opportunity, I would remind him that God loved him and offered a wonderful plan for his life. I showed him various passages of Scripture, underlining the importance of his turning to God. He seemed to ignore everything I said; there appeared to be no communication whatsoever.

A couple of hours passed, and the hour was late. I felt that there was no need to continue the discussion, and he agreed to call it a day. A friend and staff member who was with me suggested that he would be glad to drop him off at his home on the way to my hotel.

As we got in the car, his first words were, "Everything you said tonight hit me right in the heart. I want to receive Christ. Tell me how I can do it right now." Even though I had not sensed it during our conversation, the Holy Spirit had been speaking to his heart through the truth of God's Word which I had shared with him.

Learn to use the Word of God. Do not try to impress people with your brilliance, your logic, your persuasiveness. Men will usually respond with their arguments against your arguments, but there are no valid arguments against the Word of God when it is presented in the power of the Holy Spirit. That is why it is important to study the Word of God, make it a part of your daily devotions and apply its truths to your daily life and witness.

One school of theology is so "profound," so intellectual that it cannot be understood. It is not only the product of fuzzy thinking; it is also a direct contradiction of Scripture.

Further, certain teaching to which some refer as the "deeper truths" of the Word often leads to a fascination with these "truths," but does not produce holy lives, fruitful witness or a greater love for Christ and commitment to His cause.

The teaching of the Lord was simple and understandable, even though some of the truths He taught were obscure to men whose eyes were spiritually blind. He spoke of the lilies of the field, the sower and the seed, fishing for men, new wine skins, the vine and the branches — simple lessons that were easily understood by His listeners. Jesus communicated with the people. The "multitudes heard Him gladly." They understood Him, and they followed Him.

In a spiritually illiterate world, we must follow the simplicity of our Savior's message and method if we are to communicate His good news to the multitudes. Since God so loves the people of the world, most of whom have little or no knowledge of spiritual truth, and since He gave His only begotten Son to die for our sins that we may have eternal life, it does not seem reasonable to me that one must be a theologian or even a deep student of the Bible (though this is to be desired) before one can experience and share the supernatural life of joy and victory which is our heritage in Christ.

As You Walk in the Spirit

Faith in God and in His promises and obedience to His commands are the only means by which you can live the supernatural life. As you continue to trust Christ, moment by moment, you will begin to experience many wonderful benefits:

Your life will demonstrate more and more of the fruit of the Spirit: "But when the Holy Spirit controls our lives he will produce this kind of fruit in us: love, joy, peace, patience, kindness, goodness, faithfulness, gentleness and self-control" (Galatians 5:22, 23, TLB).

You will be more and more conformed to the image of Christ: "Give your bodies to God. Let them be a living sacrifice, holy — the kind He can accept . . . Don't copy the behavior and customs of this world, but be a new and different person with a fresh newness in all you do and think. Then you will learn from your own experience how his ways will really satisfy you" (Romans 12:1, 2, TLB). "As the Spirit of the Lord works within us, we become more and more like Him" (2 Corinthians 3:18, TLB).

Your prayer life will become more powerful.

Your study of God's Word will become more meaningful.

You will experience His power in witnessing: "But when the Holy Spirit has come upon you, you will receive power to testify about me with great effect" (Acts 1:8, TLB).

You will be prepared for spiritual conflict against the world: "Stop loving this evil world and all that it offers you, for when you love these things you show that you do not really love God; for all these worldly things, these evil desires — the craze for sex, the ambition to buy everything that appeals to you, and the pride that comes from wealth and importance — these are not from God.

"They are from this evil world itself. And this world is fading away, and these evil, forbidden things will go with it, but whoever keeps doing the will of God will live forever" (1 John 2:15-17, TLB).

You will be prepared for spiritual conflict against the flesh: "I advise you to obey only the Holy Spirit's instructions. He will tell you where to go and what to do, and then you won't always be doing the wrong things your evil nature wants you to.

"For we naturally love to do evil things that are just the opposite from the things that the Holy Spirit tells us to do; and the good things we want to do when the Spirit has His way with us are just the opposite of our natural desires. These two forces within us are constantly fighting each other to win control over us, and our wishes are never free from their pressures" (Galatians 5:16, 17, TLB).

You will be prepared for spiritual conflict against Satan: "Let Him have all your worries and cares, for He is always thinking about you and watching everything that concerns you. Be careful — watch out for attacks from Satan, your great enemy.

"He prowls around like a hungry, roaring lion, looking for some victim to tear apart. Stand firm when he attacks. Trust the Lord; and remember that other Christians all around the world are going through these sufferings too" (1 Peter 5:7-9, TLB).

You will experience His power to resist temptation and sin: "Remember this — the wrong desires that come into your life aren't anything new and different. Many others have faced exactly the same problems before you. And no temptation is irresistible.

"You can trust God to keep the temptation from becoming so strong that you can't stand up against it, for He has promised this and will do what He says. He will show you how to escape temptation's power so that you can bear up patiently against it" (1 Corinthians 10:13, TLB).

"For I can do everything God asks me to with the help of Christ who gives me the strength and power" (Philippians 4:13, TLB). (See also Ephesians 1:19-23, 6:10; 2 Timothy 1:7; Romans 6:1-16).

Again, let me say it: This supernatural life is wonderful! As you continue to let God control your life — to walk with His Spirit, allowing Him to "hold your hand," you will experience life's greatest adventure.

Guard Against Emotions

A word of caution is in order. Though emotions are important and valid in the life of the believer, do not seek an emotional or mystical experience, and do not depend on mystical impressions. Be on your guard: emotions and mystical experiences can be a deceptive counterfeit of faith.

Jesus promised, "The one who obeys Me is the one who loves Me: and because he loves Me, My Father will love him; and I will too, and I will reveal Myself to him" (John 14:21, TLB). Valid emotions are the natural result of faith and obedience. To seek an emotional experience refutes the law of faith and grieves the Holy Spirit.

The Word of God must be the basis of your spiritual growth. There is an interesting parallel between the chapter, which admonishes us, "Be filled instead with the Holy Spirit, and controlled by Him," and Colossians 3:16, "Remember what Christ taught and let His words enrich your lives and make you wise" (TLB).

The end result of both letting the Word of Christ dwell in you and being filled with the Holy Spirit will be that you will talk much about the Lord, quoting psalms and hymns and making music in your heart to the Lord.

The Spirit Gives Understanding

It is very important for us to recognize the need of balance between the Word of God and the Spirit of God. The Word of God is closed to our understanding and has little meaning to us apart from the supernatural understanding given by the Holy Spirit. And the Holy Spirit is hindered in speaking clear and life-changing truths apart from the Word of God.

When the emphasis on the ministry of the Holy Spirit

and the Word of God is in proper balance in your life, the result is a life of power and great fruitfulness in which our Savior, the Lord Jesus Christ, is wonderfully honored and glorified.

As you continue then to allow the Holy Spirit to control and empower you, and as you meditate upon the Word of God — hiding it in your heart — your life will express more and more the beauty of Christ and the fruit of the Spirit. These wonderful characteristics of the Lord Jesus Himself, plus fruitful witnessing, indicate that the Lord is actually living His life in and through you.

Moment by Moment

In summary, may I remind you that if you desire to walk moment by moment, day by day, in the fullness and power of God's Holy Spirit, you must:

First, be sure that you are filled with the Holy Spirit, by faith — on the basis of God's *command* to be filled, and by claiming His *promise* that, if we ask according to His will, He will hear and answer.

Second, whenever the Holy Spirit convicts you of sin in your life, confess your sins to God immediately and claim His forgiveness by faith.

Third, be prepared for spiritual conflict. The enemy is a real foe to be reckoned with. The world, the flesh and the devil will assail you.

Fourth, know your rights as a child of God. Our strength must come from the Lord. We must abide in Him.

Fifth, live by faith, drawing daily upon His strength, His wisdom, His power and His love, giving thanks in all things.

As children of God, we should aspire to walk in the Holy Spirit — for several important reasons: first, to please and honor the Lord Jesus Christ, who delights to have fellowship with His children; second, to enjoy a fuller, richer, more exciting, adventuresome life with our

Savior and with others; and third, to be more fruitful in our witnessing for our Savior and Lord.

There are many hindrances to a believer's enjoyment of the supernatural life. We will discuss these in the following chapter. Then we will explore some biblical principles for overcoming these hindrances in the power of the Holy Spirit.

CHAPTER EIGHT

Hindrances To Walking In The Spirit

Sometime ago, a young businessman came to see me. He was very eager to be a man of God. He wanted to know the fullness of the Holy Spirit in his life, but he said that every time he got on his knees to pray, all he could see was the merchandise he had stolen from his employer.

"God doesn't hear my prayers," he lamented. "I feel miserable and don't know what to do."

I suggested he confess his sin to his employer and make restitution.

"I don't have the money to pay for the merchandise I have stolen," he said. "What should I do? I'm afraid to tell my employer what I have done. He could send me to jail."

"The Holy Spirit is convicting you," I told him. "You can never experience the fullness of God's Spirit and you'll never be a man of God or have your prayers answered until you deal with this sin. You must trust the Lord to help you make restitution."

So the next day he went to his employer, confessed he had stolen the merchandise and offered to make restitution. The employer suggested he pay a certain amount each month out of his salary until the debt was paid. The young businessman came immediately to tell me what had happened. "Now God is hearing my prayers," he said. "Now I know I'm filled with the Spirit. My heart is filled with joy and praise to God."

Jesus, on the eve of his crucifixion, told His disciples that it was expedient that He go away, and said, "If you love Me, obey Me; and I will ask the Father and he will give you another Comforter, and he will never leave you" (John 14:15, 16, TLB).

Are you experiencing that supernatural relationship with God that is the work of the Holy Spirit in your life? If not, it could be that you have stifled the Holy Spirit from working in and through your life.

Why Are So Few Living Supernaturally?

Why would a Christian who has experienced the joy of forgiveness that only Christ can give, and has also experienced the joy of His presence, want to reject the will of God and choose to go his own way? Why would a Christian sacrifice the power and dynamics of the supernatural life in order to have his own way? There are several reasons:

Lack of knowledge. Most non-believers, if they knew how to become Christians and if they understood the exciting, adventuresome life which the Lord gives to all who trust and obey Him, would become Christians. Can you imagine an intelligent person saying "No" to Christ if he fully understood how much God loves him and that when he receives Christ his sins are all forgiven, he is given eternal life and he receives a whole new life of meaning and purpose? It is hard to imagine a person saying "No" to such a wonderful life of challenge and adventure, if he *knows* all the facts.

The non-believer who does not know all these things continues to live in disobedience, rejecting God's love and forgiveness. Why? Simply because he does not understand; he has a lack of information.

It is the same with the Christian who is living in spiritual poverty. He continues to live a frustrated, fruitless life. The reason well may be that he just does not understand who the Holy Spirit is and what the supernatural life is all about. But lack of knowledge is not the only obstacle to enjoying the supernatural life.

Pride. This defeating aspect of our human nature has kept many Christians locked out of living supernaturally. Pride is not the same as a healthy love and acceptance of oneself. Pride was the sin of Satan (Isaiah 14:12-14). Pride was the first sin of man, as Adam and Eve wanted to be something they were not. Pride is at the root of most of man's self-imposed estrangement from God. The self-centered, egocentric Christian cannot have fellowship with God, "...for God is opposed to the proud, but gives grace to the humble" (1 Peter 5:5, NAS).

Fear of man. Peer pressure keeps many Christians locked out of the supernatural life. "The fear of man brings a snare" (Proverbs 29:25, NAS). One of the greatest tragedies of our day is the general practice among Christians of conforming to the conduct and standards of a non-Christian society.

Many are afraid to be different; ashamed to witness for Jesus Christ, who loved us and gave Himself for us. Remember, in 1 Peter 2:9 we are told: "But you are a chosen race, a royal priesthood, a holy nation, a people for God's own possession, that you may proclaim the excellencies of Him who has called you out of darkness into His marvelous light."

In the words of the Psalmist, "But His joy is in those who reverence Him, those who expect Him to be loving and kind" (Psalm 147:11, TLB). The Lord said, "For whoever is ashamed of Me and My words, of him shall the Son of Man be ashamed" (Luke 9:26, NAS).

Many Christians are simply afraid to live supernaturally because unspiritual Christians and non-believing friends might think them religious fanatics.

Worldly-mindedness. A love for material things and a desire to conform to the ways of a secular society keep many Christians from discovering the wonder and fulfillment of living supernaturally.

"Stop loving this evil world and all that it offers you, for when you love these things you show that you do not really love God; for all these worldly things, these evil desires — the craze for sex, the ambition to buy everything that appeals to you, and the pride that comes from wealth and importance — these are not from God. They are from this evil world itself.

"And this world is fading away, and these evil, forbidden things will go with it, but whoever keeps doing the will of God will live forever" (1 John 2:15-17, TLB).

A person lives his life, dies and vanishes from the world scene. Every individual should frequently and carefully evaluate how he invests his time, talents and treasure to be sure he is truly living not for worldly values but for the cause of Jesus Christ. "Only one life, 'twill soon be past; only what's done for Christ will last."

"No one can serve two masters; for either he will hate the one and love the other, or he will hold to one and despise the other. You cannot serve God and Mammon. But seek first His kingdom, and His righteousness; and all these things shall be added to you" (Matthew 6:24, 33, NAS).

God is not against material possessions. Be thankful and enjoy them, but do not covet.

Lack of faith. Many Christians basically do not believe in God's trustworthiness. Some of them have been exposed to the truth but, for various reasons, have never been able to comprehend the love of God. They are afraid of Him. They simply do not trust God.

The Bible says, "Without faith (or trust) it is impossible to please Him" (Hebrews 11:6, NAS). Let me use a human illustration. How would you feel if your child were to come to you and say, "Mother, Daddy, I don't love you. I don't trust you anymore"?

Can you think of anything that would hurt you more deeply? I cannot. And yet, by our attitudes and our actions, if not by our words, most of us say that to God. We live as though God did not exist, even though we give lip service to Him. We refuse to believe His promises that are recorded in His Word.

Do you know what I would do if my sons were to express their love for me and their trust in me by saying,

"Daddy, we love you and want to do only that which pleases you"? I would put my arms around them and say, "I love you, too. I appreciate your offer to do anything I want. It is the greatest gift you could give me." Then I would be all the more alert and diligent to demonstrate my love and concern for them.

Is God any less loving and concerned for His children? No. He has proven over and over again that He is a loving God. He is worthy of our trust. Jesus assures us, "If you then, being evil, know how to give good gifts to your children, how much more shall your Father who is in heaven give what is good to those who ask Him" (Matthew 7:11, NAS).

Secret sin. Unconfessed sin keeps many Christians from experiencing the joy of supernatural living. In some situations, God may lead you to make restitution to those whom you have wronged (Matthew 5:23, 24). If so, be obedient to His leading. We may be able to hide these things from our friends and others, but we cannot hide them from God. "Would not God find this out? For He knows the secrets of the heart" (Psalm 44:21, NAS).

Do Not Grieve the Spirit

There are two ways in which we can interfere with the Holy Spirit's work in our lives. The first is mentioned in the book of Ephesians: "Do not grieve the Holy Spirit" (Ephesians 4:30, NAS). The word *grieve* means sadden. Do not *sadden* the Holy Spirit. And how do we sadden Him? By sinning.

As a father of two boys, I was always saddened when I saw either of my sons rebel against their mother and me or against the Lord. But I was deeply grieved when they would continue to sin and not confess it to the Lord. Whenever this would happen, their lives would become so miserable that my heart almost bled for them.

And this is the way that God the Holy Spirit feels about His children. Whenever we commit a sin — and particularly if we continue to live in that sin, without confessing it before Him, the Holy Spirit of our heavenly Father is grieved. He becomes saddened because we are not experiencing the joy of living supernaturally in close fellowship with Him. There is so much that we miss in the way of supernatural living when we grieve the Spirit.

Do Not Quench the Spirit

God has created us to have close fellowship with Him and to bring honor and glory to His Son, Jesus Christ. But when we sin, we not only grieve the Spirit, but we also *quench* Him. Paul wrote to the Thessalonians, "Do not quench the Spirit" (1 Thessalonians 5:19, NAS).

The word *quench,* as used here, is the same word used for putting out a fire. We are not to live in sin or to allow sin to go unconfessed in our lives. If we do, then we put out the Holy Spirit's fire in our lives.

That is what sin can do to the Holy Spirit's influence in our lives. He will remain there, indwelling us, but any evidence of His presence is totally absent, due to unconfessed known sin. His power is no longer effective in our lives. He no longer controls us, because the power of sin has taken over control of our lives. And, since His fire in our lives has been put out, the light of God cannot be seen in our lives.

The Bible tells us, "God is light and in Him is no darkness at all. So if we say we are His friends, but go on living in spiritual darkness and sin, we are lying. But if we are living in the light of God's presence, just as Christ does, then we have wonderful fellowship and joy with each other, and the blood of Jesus His Son cleanses us from every sin.

"If we say that we have no sin, we are only fooling ourselves and refusing to accept the truth. But if we confess our sins to Him, He can be depended on to forgive us and to cleanse us from every wrong. (And it is perfectly proper for God to do this for us because

Christ died to wash away our sins.) If we claim we have not sinned, we are lying and calling God a liar, *for He says we have sinned*" (1 John 1:5-9, TLB, italics added. See also Romans 3:23).

To *confess,* in the original Greek language, means to *agree* with God — in at least two ways: 1. I know that certain attitudes or actions which are contrary to God's Word and will are sinful. 2. I agree with God that Christ's death on the cross has paid the penalty for my sins, according to Colossians 1:13, 14 and Hebrews 10:10. I repent — I change my attitude — toward those sins, and that results in a positive change in my actions.

Unconfessed and Hidden Sin

It is not in the best interest of a person to go to excessive extremes in analyzing his wrongdoings. Once a sin is acknowledged in a person's life, he should confess it to God and, on the promise of 1 John 1:9, believe that it has been forgiven.

At the same time, hidden, secret, unconfessed sins must be dealt with. The Bible is helpful to us in pointing out man's various sins, and the Holy Spirit is quick to convict us concerning any unconfessed sin in our lives. Jesus, according to the promise of 1 John 1:9, will give us the peace and confidence of knowing our sins are forgiven if we will confess them and forsake them.

Seven Things God Hates

The Bible, in many passages, lists the sins that can keep a Christian from experiencing the supernatural life. In the book of Proverbs, we read about the seven things that God hates most:

"Let me describe for you a worthless and a wicked man; first he is a constant liar; he signals his true intentions to his friends with eyes and feet and fingers. Next, his heart is full of rebellion. And he spends his time thinking of all the evil he can do, and stirring up discontent.

"But he will be destroyed suddenly, broken beyond hope of healing. For there are six things the Lord hates — no, seven: haughtiness, lying, murdering, plotting evil, eagerness to do wrong, a false witness, sowing discord among brothers" (Proverbs 6:12-19, TLB).

The Ten Commandments

The Ten Commandments also list the areas of sin which can prevent the Holy Spirit from working in our lives, if we know they exist in our lives, but do not confess them before God. God gave these commandments to Moses and instructed him to present them to the children of Israel:

"Then God issued this edict: 'I am Jehovah your God who liberated you from your slavery in Egypt. You may worship no other god than me. You shall not make yourselves any idols: any images resembling animals, birds, or fish. You must never bow to an image or worship it in any way; for I, the Lord your God, am very possessive.

"I will not share your affection with any other god. And when I punish people for their sins, the punishment continues upon the children, grandchildren, and great-grandchildren, of those who hate me; but I lavish my love upon thousands of those who love me and obey my commandments.

"You shall not use the name of Jehovah your God irreverently, nor use it to swear to a falsehood. You will not escape punishment if you do. Remember to observe the Sabbath as a holy day. Six days a week are for your daily duties and your regular work, but the seventh day is a day of Sabbath rest before the Lord your God.

"On that day you are to do no work of any kind, nor shall your son, daughter, or slaves — whether men or women — or your cattle or your house guests. For in six days the Lord made the heaven, earth, and sea, and everything in them, and rested the seventh day; so he blessed the Sabbath day and set it aside for rest.

"Honor your father and mother, that you may have a long, good life in the land the Lord your God will give you. You must not murder. You must not commit adultery. You must not steal. You must not lie. You must not be envious of your neighbor's house, or want to sleep with his wife, or want to own his slaves, oxen, donkeys or anything else he has" (Exodus 20:1-17, TLB).

Violating a single one of these commandments, knowingly, and not confessing it, can put you on a course of greatly grieving and quenching the Holy Spirit.

Rotten Fruit

In a later chapter, we will discuss what the apostle Paul terms "the fruit of the Spirit": "But when the Holy Spirit controls our lives he will produce this kind of fruit in us: love, joy, peace, patience, kindness, goodness, faithfulness, gentleness and self-control; and here there is no conflict with Jewish laws" (Galatians 5:22, 23, TLB). These are Christlike traits that will become evident in our lives as we walk with the Holy Spirit, moment by moment, day by day. But each of these traits has its own counterpart in the realm of sin — rotten fruit.

In 1 Corinthians 13, the apostle Paul gives us the most beautiful definition of godly love ever written. In that same passage, however, he tells us what love is not: It is not jealousy, bragging, arrogance, unbecoming acts, selfishness, quick-temper, accusation or being prone to rejoice in unrighteousness.

The opposite of joy is sadness, anxiety and bitterness, which lead to depression. The opposite of peace is hostility. Instead of patience, there can be impatience, wickedness instead of goodness, meanness instead of kindness, unfaithfulness instead of faithfulness, pride and self-centeredness instead of gentleness and meekness, and lack of discipline instead of self-control.

Human Nature in the End-Times

Paul writes to Timothy that there will be unprecedented sinfulness in the last days: "But the Holy Spirit tells us clearly that in the last times some in the church will turn away from Christ and become eager followers of teachers with devil-inspired ideas" (1 Timothy 4:1, TLB).

"You may as well know this too, Timothy, that in the last days it is going to be very difficult to be a Christian. For people will love only themselves and their money; they will be proud and boastful, sneering at God, disobedient to their parents, ungrateful to them, and thoroughly bad.

"They will be hardheaded and never give in to others; they will be constant liars and troublemakers and will think nothing of immorality. They will be rough and cruel, and sneer at those who try to be good.

"They will betray their friends; they will be hotheaded, puffed up with pride, and prefer good times to worshiping God. They will go to church, yes, but they won't really believe anything they hear. Don't be taken in by people like that. They are the kind who craftily sneak into other people's homes and make friendships with silly, sin-burdened women and teach them their new doctrines.

"Women of that kind are forever following new teachers, but they never understand the truth just as Jannes and Jambres fought against Moses. They have dirty minds, warped and twisted, and have turned against the Christian faith" (2 Timothy 3:1-8, TLB).

I have listed a number of hindrances to walking in the Spirit, but the list is far from complete. God has given us a mind and conscience through which His Holy Spirit will convict us of all sin in order that we might confess it before God and claim the forgiveness which is already ours through our wonderful Savior and Lord

Jesus Christ.

You may wonder, "Is it necessary for me to gain victory over all of my defeats and frustrations before I can be filled with the Holy Spirit and live supernaturally?" Absolutely not, because as you continue to grow and mature, God will reveal new areas of your life that need to be cleansed and surrendered. Remember, only Jesus Christ can truly and perfectly live the supernatural life.

Just as Jesus is the only one who can forgive your sins, so the Holy Spirit is the only one who can enable you to live supernaturally. The Holy Spirit actually does this as you by faith invite Christ to live supernaturally in you and through you. The apostle Paul talks about this concept in his letter to the Galatian Christians:

"I have been crucified with Christ; and it is no longer I who live, but Christ lives in me; and the life which I now live in the flesh I live by faith in the Son of God, who loved me, and delivered Himself up for me" (Galatians 2:20, NAS).

We have discussed briefly in this chapter how quenching and grieving the Holy Spirit keeps us from living supernaturally. In the following chapters, we will discuss how you can constantly walk in fellowship with Christ and experience the joy of supernatural living.

CHAPTER NINE

The Fullness Of The Holy Spirit

In order to walk in the Holy Spirit, you must be sure that you are filled with the Spirit. God's Word admonishes us, "Be not drunk with wine, wherein is excess; but be filled with the Spirit" (Ephesians 5:18, KJ).

To be filled with the Holy Spirit is to be controlled and empowered by the Holy Spirit. We cannot have two masters (Matthew 6:24). There is a throne, a control center, in every life — either self or Christ is on that throne. This concept of Christ being on the throne is so simple that even a child can understand it.

1. NATURAL MAN
(One who has not received Christ)

"But a natural man does not accept the things of the Spirit of God; for they are foolishness to him, and he cannot understand them, because they are spiritually appraised" (I Corinthians 2:14).

SELF-DIRECTED LIFE
S—Ego or finite self is on the throne
†—Christ is outside the life
●—Interests are directed by self, often resulting in discord and frustration

2. SPIRITUAL MAN
(One who is directed and empowered by the Holy Spirit)

"But he who is spiritual appraises all things . . ." (I Corinthians 2:15).

CHRIST-DIRECTED LIFE
†—Christ is in the life and on the throne
S—Self is yielding to Christ
●—Interests are directed by Christ, resulting in harmony with God's plan

A Family Affair

My wife, Vonette, and I began to teach this simple, basic truth to our sons when they were very young. One evening when we were saying our prayers together, I asked our then eight-year-old son, Zac, "Who is on the throne of your life?" He said, "Jesus." I asked our five-year-old son, Brad, who was on the throne of his life. He too answered, "Jesus."

The next morning, Vonette prepared a special breakfast dish called "egg in a bonnet." It was a delicious, thick piece of French toast with a hole in the middle, and in that hole was a poached egg. As I was enjoying it, I looked over at our little Brad. He was not eating the egg or the toast.

The conversation that followed went something like this:

I said, "Brad, eat your breakfast."

He replied, "I don't want it."

"Of course you do," I said. "You'll enjoy it. Look at me, I am enjoying mine."

"Well," he said, "I don't like it, and I'm not going to eat it."

Being a bit dramatic, Brad began to release a few tears. I had to make up my mind what I was going to do. I could either say to him, "Now, young man, you eat your breakfast or else I will spank you," or "Forget it. I'll eat it myself."

Who's on the Throne?

However, I thought of a better idea. "Brad," I asked, "who is on the throne of your life this morning?" At that, the tears really began to flow. He understood immediately the point I was making. He had learned the concept that Christ must be on the throne; but Christ was not on the throne of his life at that moment.

When he regained his composure, he replied, in answer to my question, "The devil and me." I asked him, "Who do you want on the throne?" He answered, "Jesus."

So I said, "Let's pray," and he prayed, "Dear Jesus, forgive me for being disobedient and help me to like this egg." God heard that prayer, and Brad enjoyed his breakfast. As a matter of fact, he ate it all! You see, he had said he did not like the egg in a bonnet even before he had tasted it.

That evening as we were having our family time of fellowship, Bible reading and prayer, I asked Zac who had been on the throne of his life that day. He said, "Jesus." Then I asked Brad the same question. He replied, "Jesus." "Oh" he added, "except at breakfast this morning."

It is such a simple truth, and yet, in its distilled essence, that is what the supernatural, Spirit-controlled life is all about — *just keeping Christ on the throne.* We do this when we understand how to walk in the control and power of the Holy Spirit, for the Spirit came for the express purpose of glorifying Christ by enabling the believer to live a holy life and to be a productive witness for the Savior.

The key to supernatural living is a life centered in the Holy Spirit of Jesus Christ. This supernatural life is often called the Spirit-filled life or the Christ-centered life. The Spirit-filled Christian is one who, according to Romans 6:11, has considered himself to be dead to sin but alive to God in Christ Jesus. Christ is now at the center of his life; He is Lord.

In order to live supernaturally a Christian also must be dead to self. When he is dead to self, the Lord Jesus Christ, who now has unhindered control of his life, can begin to express His love through him.

Jesus Christ, to whom "all power in heaven and in earth is given," and "in whom dwells all the fullness of the Godhead bodily," can now express that power through the yielded, Spirit-filled Christian.

Christ, who came to seek and save the lost, now begins to seek the lost through the Christian. He directs the Christian's steps to those who are lost and to those who are in need. He begins to use the Christian's lips to tell of His love. His great heart of compassion becomes evident in the supernatural life of the Christian.

Actually, in a very real sense, the Spirit-filled Christian has given up his own powerless, defeated and fruitless life for the supernatural power, victory and fruitfulness of Jesus Christ. This is what we mean by the supernatural life. When a Christian is living supernaturally, he is filled with the Holy Spirit — filled with Jesus Christ, allowing God to work in him and through him.

A Great Adventure

The supernatural life is a great adventure for the Christian. It is a life of purpose and power. The Lord Jesus Christ has given us a promise that, from a human perspective, seems unbelievable: "He who believes in Me, the works that I do shall he do also; and greater works than these shall he do . . . And whatever you ask in My name, that will I do." (John 14:12, 13 NAS).

The Spirit-filled Christian no longer thinks of Christ as his helper to do some kind of Christian task. Rather, he recognizes that Jesus Christ does the work through the Christian. Jesus does not want us to work for Him; He wants us to let Him do His work in and through us.

This is that marvelous, liberating experience that the apostle Paul writes about: "I have been crucified with Christ; and it is no longer I who live, but Christ lives in me" (Galatians 2:20, NAS). The Christian's body now becomes Christ's body to use as He wills; the mind becomes His mind to think His thoughts; the heart now overflows with His love; the will is now controlled by His will; the total personality, time and talents are now completely yielded to His control.

Filled by Faith

How is one filled with the Holy Spirit? We are filled with the Holy Spirit by faith. How did you become a Christian? By faith. "For by grace you have been saved through faith; and that not of yourselves, it is the gift of God; not as a result of works; that no one should boast" (Ephesians 2:8, 9, NAS). "As you therefore have received Christ Jesus the Lord, so walk in Him" (Colossians 2:6, NAS).

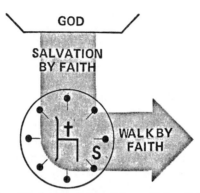

We receive Christ by faith. We walk by faith. Everything we receive from God, from the moment of our spiritual birth until we die, comes by faith. Do you want to be filled with the Holy Spirit? You can be filled right now, whoever you are and wherever you are, by faith.

You do not have to beg God to fill you with His Holy Spirit. You do not have to barter with Him, by fasting or weeping, or begging or pleading.

As a new Christian, I spent long periods of time fasting and crying out to God for His fullness in my life. Then one day I discovered from the Scriptures that "the just shall live by faith" (Romans 1:17, NAS). We do not earn God's fullness. We receive it by faith.

Receive What Is Already Yours

The Christian does not need to beg God for that which is already his. Suppose that you want to cash a check for a hundred dollars. Would you go to the bank where you have several thousand dollars on deposit, place the check on the counter, get down on your knees, and say, "Oh, please Mr. Teller, cash my check?"

No, that is not the way you cash a check. You simply go in faith, place the check on the counter and wait for the money which is already yours. Then you thank the teller and go on your way.

Millions of Christians are begging God, as I once did, for a life of victory and power which is already theirs — an abundant life just waiting to be appropriated by faith. They are seeking some kind of emotional experience, not realizing that such an attitude on their part is an insult to God — a denial of faith, without which we cannot please God.

A Prepared Heart

Though you are filled with the Holy Spirit by faith and faith alone, it is important to recognize that several factors contribute to preparing your heart for the filling of the Holy Spirit.

First, you must desire to live a life that will please the Lord. We have the promise of the Savior, "Blessed are those who hunger and thirst for righteousness, for they shall be filled" (Matthew 5:6, NAS).

Second, be willing to surrender your life to Christ in accordance with the command of God: "And so, dear brothers, I plead with you to give your bodies to God. Let them be a living sacrifice, holy — the kind He can accept. When you think of what He has done for you, is this too much to ask?

"Don't copy the behavior and customs of this world, but be a new and different person with a fresh newness in all you do and think. Then you will learn from your own experience how His ways will really satisfy you" (Romans 12:1, 2, TLB).

A young seminarian came to me for counsel. "The last time you spoke in chapel, you challenged us to be filled with the Spirit by faith," he said. "I did what you told us to do, and nothing has happened to me. You assured us that if we were truly filled with the Spirit, one of the things that would result would be that we would lead others to Christ. Well, I haven't led anyone to Christ since you were here."

I responded by asking him the logical question, "Have

you talked to any non-believers since I was here?"

He said, "No, I haven't."

I explained the obvious: "You can't expect to lead any non-believers to Christ unless you talk to non-believers."

So, there is something more: It is not enough to pray a prayer or go through the ritual of appropriating the fullness of the Holy Spirit. If we expect to lead others to Christ, we must go to non-believers and share Christ in the power of the Holy Spirit. Then we can expect to see results.

I pursued the matter further with my young ministerial student friend: "One of the points I made about heart preparation before you can expect to be filled with the Holy Spirit by faith was that you must surrender your life fully to Christ in accordance with Romans 12:1, 2." Then I asked him, "Did you surrender every area of your life to Christ? Or did you hold something back?"

He paused for a moment, then with some embarrassment said, "Well, in all honesty, there were a couple of areas in my life that I didn't surrender." Then he laughed a bit sheepishly.

"You know very well," I said, "that you cannot be filled with the Holy Spirit unless you allow Him to control every area of your life. You cannot be controlled by self in some area and by the Holy Spirit in others. Either you are controlled totally, completely, irrevocably by the Holy Spirit, or you are not controlled at all."

He said, "I really want to surrender everything to Christ. I want every area of my life to be under His leadership and direction."

At this point, we bowed together in prayer. And this time he met God's conditions, and his life was changed.

It could be that you have gone through the ritual of praying, "Lord, fill me with your Holy Spirit," but you have had your fingers crossed. You didn't really mean it, and you wonder why your life is not different.

It never will be different until you make that full surrender of every area of your life — your home, your social life, your business, your studies, your recreation, your thought life, your attitudes, actions, motives, desires and words.

Confess All Known Sin

Third, if you want to live a Spirit-filled life, you must confess every known sin which the Holy Spirit calls to your remembrance. As we grow in the Spirit, certain sins will become obvious to us that we had not recognized before.

It is as we grow, mature and understand God's Word and God's way that additional sins — sometimes the so-called "refined sins" — become obvious. When they do, we need to be prepared to confess them. God knows that if He were to reveal to us all of our sins while we are still new, baby Christians, we would not be able to handle them.

If you say to an inquirer, "In order to become a Christian you must give up all areas of your life that are wrong — things like smoking, drinking, dancing, attending movies, etc. — the person may well choose to give up the Christian life altogether and say, "It is impossible for me to live the Christian life. I don't have the strength. I guess the Christian life was not meant for me."

But if you help the person to grow in the Spirit through prayer, studying God's Word and fellowship with other believers, putting the emphasis, not on what they give up, but on what they receive as they walk with Christ, they very naturally will mature in Christ and automatically give up those objectionable practices because they want to. Until the caterpillar goes through the metamorphosis it cannot live like a butterfly — no matter how hard it tries. Keep in mind too that you should not be unduly introspective — probing, digging for sins to confess which might result in a superficial, artificial kind of confession.

Jesus promised, "The one who obeys Me is the one who loves Me, and because he loves Me, My Father will love him;and I will too, and I will show Myself to him" (John 14:21, TLB).

Many people have found it helpful to write down all the sins which the Holy Spirit chooses to call to their attention and of which He convicts them. You may wish to do that. Ask the Holy Spirit to reveal unconfessed sins to you, then list them on a sheet of paper.

Next, confess these sins to God in prayer and appropriate forgiveness in accordance with I John 1:9: "But if we confess our sins to Him, He can be depended on to forgive us and to cleanse us from every wrong. And it is perfectly proper for God to do this for us because Christ died to wash away our sins" (I John 1:9, TLB).

After praying, write the word "forgiven" boldly across the sheet of paper. Tear the paper into shreds, and either burn it or flush it down the drain. Never share the list with anyone. When you confess your sins you can know that by faith they have been forgiven, because Christ died and shed His blood to wash away your sins (Colossians 1:13, 14; Hebrews 10).

Again, we are not filled with the Holy Spirit because we desire to be filled, nor because we confess our sins or present our bodies a living sacrifice — we are filled by faith. Desire, confession, presenting are only factors which contribute toward preparing us for the filling of the Holy Spirit by faith.

Command and Promise

There are two very important words to remember. The first is *command*. God commands us to be filled with the Holy Spirit: "Do not get drunk with wine, for that is dissipation, but be filled with the Spirit" (Ephesians 5:18, NAS). Not to be filled, controlled and empowered by the Holy Spirit is disobedience.

The other word is *promise* — that which makes the

command possible: "This is the confidence which we have before Him, that, if we ask anything according to His will, He hears us. And if we know that He hears us in whatever we ask, we know that we have the requests which we have asked from Him" (I John 5:14, 15, NAS).

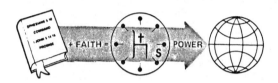

Now, let me ask you: Is it God's will for you to be filled and controlled by Him? Of course, it is. He desires to do this because He loves us. It is God's will because it is His *command*. The wonderful truth is that you can right now ask God to fill you — not because you deserve to be filled, but on the basis of His *command* and His *promise*. It is His love gift to you.

If you are a Christian, the Holy Spirit already dwells within you. Therefore, you do not need to invite Him to come into your life. The Holy Spirit took up residence in your life when you became a Christian and Jesus promised He will never leave you (Hebrews 13:5).

The moment you received Christ, the Holy Spirit not only came to indwell you, but He also imparted to you spiritual life, causing you to be born anew as a child of God. The Holy Spirit also baptized you into the body of Christ (1 Corinthians 12:13) and thereby opened the door for you to enter into supernatural life.

There is but one indwelling of the Holy Spirit, one rebirth by the Holy Spirit and one baptism with the Holy Spirit — all of which occur when you receive Christ. Being filled with the Holy Spirit, however, is not a once-for-all experience.

There are many fillings, as evidenced in the lives of the disciples and recorded in the book of Acts. This fact is also made clear in Ephesians 5:18: "Be filled with the Spirit." In the original Greek writing of this command, the meaning is more clear than that in most English translations. It literally means, "Be constantly and continually filled, controlled and empowered with the Holy Spirit." To do this is to live supernaturally.

Technically, it is not necessary to pray to be filled with the Holy Spirit. There is no place in Scripture where we are told to pray for the filling of the Holy Spirit. We are filled by faith. However, since the object of our faith is God and His Word, I suggest that you claim the fullness of the Holy Spirit in prayer as an expression of your faith in God's command and in His promise. You are not filled because you pray, but because by faith you trust God to fill you with His Spirit.

What About Emotions?

Frequently, during counseling sessions, individuals have come to share their frustration following some kind of deep emotional experience. At the time of the experience, they felt the love and presence of the Lord and the joy of the Spirit. But with the passing of time, they lost that emotion and have tried to repeat the experience. They have come to inquire how they can recapture that experience.

One person shared, "I have gone to all kinds of prayer meetings. I've had people lay hands on me in prayer for God's anointing. I have gone through all kinds of self-imposed disciplines, but I have not been able to recapture that experience."

This is not unusual, but such efforts are to be avoided. As mentioned earlier, the very act of seeking to recapture an experience grieves the Spirit of God; we are to live by faith, not by emotions.

People who attend emotionally charged meetings often reach the point where they need something more dramatic and even ecstatic to satisfy them. In the process, some become hardened and even resort to manufacturing counterfeit experiences. Others have indicated that they have become hypocritical in trying to keep up with those who share dramatic personal experiences.

We are told by specialists that, as one becomes addicted to a drug, his body develops a tolerance to that drug and his craving increases. When this happens, the user must increase the dosage or switch to a more powerful drug.

It is the same with emotional experiences that are of the flesh and not of the Spirit. An "experience addict" encounters frustration and a growing lack of fulfillment. He must therefore satisfy his craving through stronger and stronger emotional experiences. This is the reason the Word of God emphasizes over and over again the importance of faith.

Feelings are valid in their proper place, but they can be deceptive. We are emotional creatures, and there is nothing wrong with emotions that are genuine — the overflow of a full, joyful, grateful heart in control of the Holy Spirit.

Again, Jesus reminds us in John 14:21, "The one who obeys Me is the one who loves Me; and because he loves Me, My Father will love him; and I will too, and I will reveal Myself to him."

To reveal Himself to us means that we have an emotional experience. It may be expressed in different ways, according to our own uniqueness of personality as individuals, but we become aware of the presence of God. Remember, however, these kinds of experiences are always the by-product of faith and obedience. We do not need to seek these experiences; they naturally flow from a life that walks in obedience to the Lord.

When you claim the fullness of the Holy Spirit as a

prayer of faith, do not think that you must have an emotional experience or that something dramatic must happen. How did you receive Christ? Was it because of some emotional pressure brought to bear upon you?

Your emotions may have been involved. But ultimately you became a Christian, not because of your emotional experience, but because of your faith. For the Bible says, "For by grace you have been saved by faith" (Ephesians 2:8, NAS).

The emotions which you experienced when you became a Christian were the *result* of your expression of faith, acted out in obedience to God's command and in trusting Him to fulfill His promise.

The Holy Spirit is not given to us that we might have a great emotional experience, but that we might live supernaturally — holy lives — and be fruitful witnesses for Christ. So, whether or not you have an emotional experience is not the issue.

A Hungry Heart

A medical doctor, the lay leader of a large church, came to me with a very hungry heart. He had met one of our staff members who had recently experienced the fullness of the Holy Spirit in his life and had been dramatically changed as a result.

This staff member was having a powerful impact for the Lord, and the doctor wanted to experience the same kind of power in his life. I asked the doctor if he really desired to be filled with the Holy Spirit — to which he replied that he did.

Then I asked if he were willing to turn from all known sin and surrender the total control of his life to Christ. He assured me that he was, that he was even willing to leave a very lucrative medical practice and go to some remote part of the world as a medical missionary if that was what God wanted. Whatever the cost, he wanted to be a Spirit-filled man — fully surrendered to the Lord.

So I turned to the book of Ephesians and read aloud: "Don't drink too much wine, for many evils lie along that path; be filled instead with the Holy Spirit, and controlled by Him" (Ephesians 5:18, TLB).

"Do you believe it is God's will that you be filled with the Spirit?" I asked.

"Yes," he said, "it is, because He commands me to be filled."

Then we turned to the first letter of John to consider this promise of God: "And we are sure of this, that He will listen to us whenever we ask Him for anything in line with His will. And if we really know He is listening when we talk to Him and make our requests, then we can be sure that He will answer us" (1 John 5:14, 15, TLB).

I asked the doctor, "If we were to kneel here right now and pray, and claim God's promises that if we ask anything according to His will, He will hear and answer us, in reference to your being filled with the Spirit, do you believe He would hear us?"

"Yes," he replied, "God would hear us because I know it is His will."

"Then would He answer; would He fill you with His Spirit?"

He did not answer my question, because by that time he was on his knees, beginning to pray. He claimed by faith the fullness of the Holy Spirit on the basis that God had commanded him to be filled and on God's promise that He would fill him if asked.

There was no emotion, and nothing dramatic happened that I was aware of — except that God heard and answered his prayer. The doctor and I chatted for awhile and rejoiced in the fact that God had heard him.

About six months later, he wrote me a wonderful letter. It was filled with praise and thanksgiving to God. "God has done more in and through my life every day during the last six months than all the rest of my Christian life put together," he said.

I recalled that he was the lay leader in a large Lutheran church, teaching Bible studies, conducting prayer meetings and engaging in all kinds of activities. And now, God was using him in the power of the Spirit. In the past, he had performed in the energy of the flesh.

Have you met God's conditions? Do you "hunger and thirst after righteousness?" Do you sincerely want to be filled, controlled and empowered by the Holy Spirit? To enter into the wonderful experience of the supernatural life? Are you willing to confess all known sin and surrender your life completely to the Lordship of Christ?

If so, I invite you to bow your head and pray this prayer of faith right now. Ask God to fill you with His Spirit and to open the door to supernatural living. Without begging or pleading, just say to God:

"Dear Father, I need You. I acknowledge that I have been in control of my life; and that, as a result, I have sinned against You. I thank You that You have forgiven my sins through Christ's death on the cross and the shedding of His blood for me. I now invite Christ to take control of my life.

"Fill me with the Holy Spirit as You commanded me to be filled, and as You promised in Your Word that You would do if I asked in faith. I pray this in the authority of the name of the Lord Jesus Christ. As an expression of my faith, I now thank You for filling me with Your Holy Spirit and for taking control of my life."

How to Know You Are Filled by the Spirit

Did that prayer express the desire of your heart? Did you ask God to fill you with the Holy Spirit? Do you know that you are now filled with the Holy Spirit? On what authority?

Do not depend on your feelings. The promise of God's Word — not your feelings — is your authority for knowing that you are filled with the Spirit.

The Christian is to live by faith, trusting in the

trustworthiness of God Himself and His Word. This can
be illustrated by a train. Let us call the engine or locomo-
tive *fact* — the fact of God's promises found in His Word.
The coal car we will call *faith* — our trust in God and
His Word. The caboose we will call *feelings*.

You place fuel in the engine and the train runs. However, it would be futile to attempt to pull the train by
the caboose. In the same way we, as Christians, do not
depend upon feelings or emotions, but in order to live
a supernatural life we simply place our faith in the
trustworthiness of God and the promises of His Word.

Feelings are like the caboose — they will come along
in the life of faith and obedience, but we should never
depend on feelings or look for them. As mentioned earlier, the very act of looking for an emotional experience
is a denial of the concept of faith, and whatever is not
of faith is sin.

You can know right now that you are filled with the
Holy Spirit by trusting in God, His command and promise, and you can go through life with that assurance.

In order to walk in the Spirit and live supernaturally,
you must first be sure that you are filled with God's Holy
Spirit. As a Spirit — filled Christian, you can begin this
very moment to draw upon the vast, inexhaustible resources of the Holy Spirit to enable you to live a supernatural life and to share the claims of our Lord Jesus and
His love and forgiveness with people everywhere.

Remember that being filled with the Holy Spirit is a
way of life for those who want to live supernaturally. We
are commanded to be constantly controlled by the Holy
Spirit. Thank Him for the fullness of His Spirit as you

begin each day and continue to invite Him to control your life moment by moment.

With or without an emotional experience, you are now filled with the Holy Spirit and can continue to walk in the fullness of the Holy Spirit by faith as you meet the scriptural conditions outlined in this and the following chapter.

CHAPTER TEN

Spiritual Breathing

A friend who participated in one of our Lay Institutes for Evangelism a few years ago shared with me his experience when he first realized the practical benefits of the biblical concept which I like to call Spiritual Breathing. He had agreed to teach a Sunday school class of young students. But there was one problem: he was apprehensive about the assignment because he had never taught students of that age.

My friend planned to arrive at church early in order to make proper preparation for the arrival of his new class. He had asked his family to be ready to leave the house early on that Sunday morning. As sometimes happens, the family was late in getting ready and, as he sat in the car in the hot sun, he began to resent his family's tardiness. He began to fume and fuss while waiting for them. The longer he waited, the more tense and irritated he became.

Finally, his family loaded into the car. By this time the man was ready to explode with anger. He started to vent his anger, but before he went very far the Holy Spirit reminded him that his attitude and actions were not honoring to the Lord.

Furthermore, he knew that he would be sharing with the children in Sunday school about God's love, forgiveness and patience. By this time, he was well aware that he was in no mood for God to use him.

Changed Attitude

Then he remembered what he had learned about Spiritual Breathing, and he applied it then and there. The result? His attitude was immediately changed, and God was able to use him that morning to introduce several young people to Christ in his Sunday school class. Obviously, he would not have been able to witness effectively to these young people had he continued in his anger, carnality and unrepentant spirit.

Life-Changing Concept

Spiritual Breathing is one of the most important truths of Scripture. The understanding and application of this vital concept has enriched my life as has no other truth. This concept of Spiritual Breathing has been shared with millions of people through our literature program and with those who have been involved in our various student, lay and pastors' institutes of evangelism — always with revolutionary results.

As you walk in the Holy Spirit by faith, practicing Spiritual Breathing, you need never again live in spiritual defeat for more than a few minutes at a time. Spiritual Breathing, like physical breathing, is a process of exhaling the impure and inhaling the pure — an exercise in faith that enables you to experience God's love and forgiveness. This simple, scriptural process must be practiced by the Christian who wants to experience supernatural living.

The moment you invited Christ into your life as Savior and Lord, you experienced a spiritual birth. You became a child of God, and you were filled with the Holy Spirit. God forgave *all* your sins — past, present and future, making you righteous, holy and acceptable in His sight. He did this because of Christ's sacrifice for you on the cross. You were given the power to live a holy life and to be a fruitful witness for God.

Roller Coaster Life

But the average Christian does not understand this concept of Spiritual Breathing. As a result, he lives on a spiritual roller coaster. He goes from one emotional experience to another, living most of his life as a carnal Christian, trying without success to control his own life, experiencing frustration and fruitlessness as a result.

If this is your experience, Spiritual Breathing will enable you to get off this emotional roller coaster and to enjoy the supernatural life. Jesus promised the abundant Christian life when He said, "I came that they might have life and might have it abundantly" (John 10:10b, NAS). As an exercise in faith, Spiritual Breathing will enable you to continue to experience God's love, forgiveness, power and control of the Holy Spirit as a supernatural way of life.

Exhale — Confess

If you retake the throne, the control center, of your life through sin — a deliberate act of disobedience — breathe spiritually. *First, exhale by confession.* Remember, God's Word promises, "If we confess our sins, He is faithful and just to forgive us our sins, and to cleanse us from all unrighteousness" (1 John 1:9, NAS). Confession (*homologeo* in the Greek) suggests agreement with God concerning our sins. Such agreement involves at least three considerations.

First, you must acknowledge that your sin or sins — which should be named to God specifically — are wrong and therefore are grievous to God.

Second, you acknowledge that God has already forgiven you through Christ's death on the cross for your sins.

Third, you repent, which means that you change your attitude, and this results in a change in your conduct. Instead of doing what your old sin- nature — your fleshly self — wants to do, you can now, through the enabling of the Holy Spirit, do what God wants you to do.

Inhale — Appropriate by Faith

Next, inhale by appropriating the fullness of God's

Holy Spirit by faith. Trust Him now to control and empower you according to His *command* to "be filled with the Spirit" (Ephesians 5:18, NAS). In its original meaning, this verse suggests that one is to be constantly and continually controlled and empowered by the Holy Spirit, moment by moment, as a way of life.

Furthermore, according to God's *promise*, He hears us and grants our request because we pray according to His will (1 John 5:14, 15). Continue to claim His love, forgiveness and power by faith and continue to have fellowship with Him, moment by moment.

Through the concept of Spiritual Breathing, God has provided you with a way to get off the spiritual roller coaster of spiritual highs and lows. You can cease to be a carnal Christian and start to live the rest of your life as a Spirit-filled Christian. If you are breathing spiritually — exhaling, confessing your sin, and inhaling, appropriating the fullness of the Holy Spirit by faith — you are a Spirit-filled Christian.

Attitude of Belief

The frustrating and fruitless defeat of living carnally is most often the result of unbelief. You may find yourself back on the spiritual roller coaster, with its ups and downs, from one emotional experience to another, if you develop an attitude of unbelief — when you cease to believe the promises of 1 John 1:9 and 1 Corinthians 10:13:

"No temptation has overtaken you but such as is common to man; and God is faithful, who will not allow you to be tempted beyond what you are able; but with the temptation will provide the way of escape also, that you may be able to endure it."

God's Word also says, "Whatever is not of faith is sin" (Romans 14:23, NAS). If you cease to practice Spiritual Breathing, you will become carnal. You do not become carnal simply by committing one sin or a dozen sins, provided you *sincerely* continue to breathe spiritually.

You will become carnal only when you develop an *attitude* of unbelief and refuse to breathe spiritually.

The angered Sunday school teacher to whom I referred earlier in this chapter applied the concept of Spiritual Breathing to his situation. He exhaled by confessing his anger to the Lord, and he thanked God that he was already forgiven on the basis of Christ's death and the shedding of His blood for our sins. Then he apologized to his wife and children, inhaled by acknowledging the control of the Holy Spirit afresh and went on his way rejoicing.

Thousands of Christians around the world have shared similar experiences of how this concept of Spiritual Breathing has brought unusual blessing to their lives and, through them, to others.

As you exhale and inhale the moment you know that you have sinned, you will recognize greater freedom and power in your life. Simply keep short accounts with God. Do not allow your sins to accumulate.

The Real Evidence

This is not to suggest that we have to sin. As we were reminded from the Epistle of John, "My little children, I am telling you this so that you will stay away from sin. But if you sin, there is someone to plead for you before the Father.

"His name is Jesus Christ, the one who is all that is good and who pleases God completely. He is the one who took God's wrath against our sins upon Himself, and brought us into fellowship with God; and He is the forgiveness of our sins, and not only ours but all the world's.

"And how can we be sure that we belong to Him? By looking within ourselves: are we really trying to do what He wants us to do? Someone may say, 'I am a Christian; I am on my way to heaven; I belong to Christ,' but if he doesn't do what Christ tells him to, he is a liar.

"But those who do what Christ tells them to will learn to love God more and more. That is the way to know whether or not you are a Christian. Anyone who says he is a Christian should live as Christ did" (1 John 2:1-6, TLB).

Discovering Faith and Learning to Grow

In your relationship with the Holy Spirit, you discover that His power is appropriated by faith and that you learn how to grow and mature in the supernatural life by faith.

If you have been walking in the Spirit by faith for many years, your life will probably demonstrate more of the fruit of the Spirit and you will be more effective in your witness for Christ than a believer who has just discovered how to walk in the Spirit.

But, no matter how long you have been walking in the Spirit, there is ample room for continued growth and maturity in Christ. Even the most mature Christians become aware of new areas in their lives that need to be surrendered to the control of the Holy Spirit. When you become aware of such an area of your life — an attitude or action — that is displeasing to the Lord, simply breathe spiritually.

The Spirit Reveals Sin

The Holy Spirit reveals sin in our lives. Whenever the Spirit convicts you about some wrong attitude or action in your life, breathe spiritually, exhaling or confessing the sin, and inhaling as you go on walking in the fullness and control of the Holy Spirit by faith.

Some Christians breathe spiritually faster and more often than others. Exhale only when the Holy Spirit reveals something that needs to be confessed. For some, that will be several or many times each day, while for others it will be only a few times a year.

Temptation and Sin

It should be explained that there is a difference between temptation and sin. Temptation is the initial impression to do something contrary to God's will. Such impressions come to all men, even as they did to the Lord, and they are not sin in themselves. Temptation becomes sin when we meditate on the impression and develop a desire which becomes lust, often followed by the actual act of disobedience.

Yet, this major conflict is largely resolved when we, by an act of the will, surrender ourselves to the control of the Holy Spirit and face these temptations in His power. "Walk by the Spirit and you will not carry out the desire of the flesh" (Galatians 5:16, NAS).

For practical daily living, we simply recognize our weakness whenever we are tempted and practice Spiritual Breathing, trusting by faith that the Lord will take care of the problem for us.

The Line Between Spirituality and Carnality

The question is often asked, "At what point does one who practices Spiritual Breathing become carnal again?" The fact is, one need never be carnal again. As long as a believer keeps on breathing spiritually, there is no need to live a life of defeat. Because the moment you do that which grieves or quenches the Spirit, you simply confess immediately, exhale, then keep on walking in the light as God is in the light.

"But," you may ask, "suppose I don't confess? At what point do I become carnal? Do I become carnal if I commit one sin? Ten sins? Fifty or one hundred sins?"

You become carnal at that point where you cease to believe the truth of 1 Corinthians 10:13, which says, "But remember this — the wrong desires that come into your life aren't anything new and different. Many others have faced exactly the same problems before you. And no temptation is irresistible.

"You can trust God to keep the temptation from becoming so strong that you can't stand up against it, for He has promised this and will do what He says. He will show you how to escape temptation's power so that you can bear up patiently against it" (TLB).

Scripture reminds us that the "righteous man shall live by faith" (Romans 1:17, NAS).

Whenever the believer ceases to live by faith, he becomes carnal. Whenever the believer ceases to claim 1 Corinthians 10:13, he becomes carnal. Let me illustrate. Suppose you are walking in the light as God is in the light, breathing spiritually, and you are tempted to criticize, lie, steal, become immoral or allow yourself to engage in lustful thinking.

The moment the temptation comes and the Holy Spirit says to you that it is wrong, do not continue your present course of thinking or action. You have the authority of God's Spirit to claim I Corinthians 10:13 or, as a free moral agent, you can choose to yield to the temptation. A thought becomes a desire and a desire becomes lust, which is followed by an act, and that act results in sin.

At that point, if you yield to the temptation and do grieve or quench the Spirit as a deliberate act of disobedience, the Holy Spirit will continue to convict you until you repent. If you refuse to repent, you will become carnal.

You will not lose your salvation, but you will lose fellowship with God. At this point, you are in danger of being chastened of the Lord just as a loving father or mother disciplines a child who is disobedient. As King David wrote in Psalm 32, it is necessary when one becomes aware of sin to confess that sin; judgment will not touch him if he does.

Many Christians are sick, many are going through all kinds of adversity, disciplining and chastening because they are living disobedient lives, and they are not really aware what is causing them to experience such difficulty. Never judge another person who is going through difficulty. It may be that his is an experience like Job's.

If you are having difficulty, be quick to look into the mirror of God's Word and ask the Holy Spirit to show you if there is sin in your life for which He might be chastening you. Carnal Christians are always being chastened. There are no happy carnal Christians, and the cause of their unhappiness is their disobedience.

Avoid being introspective. Do not probe within yourself, looking for sin to confess. Believe God and His Word. Do not seek an emotional experience. If you genuinely hunger and thirst after God and His righteousness; if you have confessed your sin, surrendered the control of your life to Christ and asked God to fill you, believe that you are filled by faith on the basis of His promise. God will prove Himself faithful to His promise.

The Christian who does not practice Spiritual Breathing is vulnerable to the ways of the world, the temptations of the flesh and the deceitfulness of the devil. But Spiritual Breathing alone is not enough to combat these hindrances to the supernatural life. The following chapters will discuss ways in which you can properly prepare for spiritual conflict.

CHAPTER ELEVEN

The Holy Spirit Illuminates God's Word

An angry young student leader of a leftist movement approached me after one of my lectures on campus. "I resent your influencing these students with your religious ideas," he said, obviously trying to start an argument.

Instead of responding in kind, I asked him to come to our home for dinner where we could talk quietly and more in depth. He accepted the invitation.

After dinner, we discussed our individual views concerning God and man and the way we felt our ideas could best help man to maximize his potential. He objected when I started to read from the Bible. "I don't believe anything in the Bible," he said.

"Well, if you don't mind," I said, "I would like to read you a few portions of Scripture which will help you better understand why I became a Christian after many years of agnosticism. I didn't believe in God or the Bible either, but something wonderful happened to me to change my thinking — in fact, my whole way of life. These are some of the Scripture passages which made a great impression on my thinking, and I would like to share them with you."

Reluctantly he agreed to listen. So I began to read in Colossians: "[Christ] is the exact likeness of the unseen God. He existed before God made anything at all, and, in fact, Christ Himself is the Creator who made everything in heaven and earth, the things we can see and the things we can't; the spirit world with its kings and kingdoms, its rulers and authorities: all were made by Christ for His own use and glory....

"For God wanted all of Himself to be in His Son....In Him lie hidden all the mighty, untapped treasures of wisdom and knowledge....

"Don't let others spoil your faith and joy with their philosophies, their wrong and shallow answers built on men's thoughts and ideas, instead of on what Christ has said. For in Christ there is all of God in a human body; so you have everything when you have Christ, and you are filled with God through your union with Christ. He is the highest ruler, with authority over every other power" (Colossians 1:15, 16, 19; 2:3, 8-10, TLB).

His attention now riveted, I continued reading from the Scriptures, "Before anything else existed, there was Christ — with God. He has always been alive and is Himself God. He created everything there is — nothing exists that He didn't make.

"Eternal life is in Him, and this life gives light to all mankind. His life is the light that shines through the darkness — and the darkness can never extinguish it.

"God sent John the Baptist as a witness to the fact that Jesus Christ is the true Light. John himself was not the light; he was only a witness to identify it. Later on, the One who is the true Light arrived to shine on everyone coming into the world.

"But although He made the world, the world didn't recognize Him when He came.

"Even in His own land and among His own people, the Jews, He was not accepted. Only a few would welcome and receive Him. But to all who received Him, He gave the right to become children of God.

"All they needed to do was to trust Him to save them. All those who believe this are reborn! — not a physical rebirth resulting from human passion or plan — but from the will of God.

"And Christ became a human being and lived here on earth among us and was full of loving forgiveness and truth. And some of us have seen His glory — the glory of the only Son of the heavenly Father!" (John 1:1-14, TLB).

Next I turned to the book of Hebrews and read: "Long

ago God spoke in many different ways to our fathers through the prophets, telling them little by little about His plans. But now in these days He has spoken to us through His Son to whom He has given everything, and through whom He made the world and everything there is.

"God's Son shines out with God's glory, and all that God's Son is and does marks Him as God. He regulates the universe by the mighty power of His command. He is the one who died to cleanse us and clear our record of all sin, and then sat down in highest honor beside the great God of heaven" (Hebrews 1:1-3, TLB).

And finally, I read, "And who is the greatest liar? The one who says that Jesus is not Christ. Such a person is antichrist, for he does not believe in God the Father and in His Son. For a person who doesn't believe in Christ, God's Son, can't have God the Father either. But he who has Christ, God's Son, has God the Father also" (1 John 2:22, 23, TLB).

After I read each portion of Scripture, my new young friend asked if he could read it himself — then he asked questions. Finally, after reading all of the above passages and several others, his questions were answered.

Before he left that night he wrote in our guest book his name, address and these words: "The night of decision." God the Holy Spirit honored the reading of His Holy, inspired Word, and another person was launched into the great adventure of supernatural living.

The Bible, a supernatural book, without question is the most amazing book in all of history. Individual lives are influenced by it, broken homes are restored, communities and entire countries are changed — wherever this holy, inspired Word of God is read and obeyed.

Great men throughout the history of the Church have applauded the Bible, have read it, believed it and lived their lives by it.

John Quincy Adams, for one, said: "So great is my

veneration for the Bible that the earlier my children begin to read it, the more confident will be my hope that they will prove useful citizens to their country, and respectable members of society."

"Hold fast to the Bible as the sheet-anchor of your liberties," wrote Ulysses S. Grant. "Write its precepts in your hearts, and practice them in your lives. To the influence of this book we are indebted for all the progress made in true civilization, and to this we must look as our guide in the future. 'Righteousness exalteth a nation; but sin is a reproach to any people.'"

Patrick Henry said of the Bible: "There is a Book worth all other books which were ever printed."

"I have always said," wrote Thomas Jefferson, "that the studious perusal of the sacred volume will make better citizens, better fathers, and better husbands."

Immanuel Kant said, "A single line in the Bible has consoled me more than all the books I ever read besides."

And the great emancipator, Abraham Lincoln, wrote: "This great book … is the best gift God has given to man….But for it we could not know right from wrong."

The History of the Bible

The Bible was written by many writers over a period of 1,500 years. It is the all-time, best-selling book. It has been translated into more than 1,200 languages — more than any other book. In fact, organizations such as Wycliffe Bible Translators have developed alphabets for many exotic, verbal-only tongues for the primary purpose of translating the Bible into written form.

But not everyone has accepted the Bible. It has been banned and burned by godless governments down through the centuries.

It is valued by believers above all other material possessions. It has been smuggled into "closed countries" by the millions of copies. Men have paid high prices for it on the black markets of the world. Many have died for it.

What is it about the Bible that has caused it to be the extraordinary book of all time? Jesus spoke to this point: "When the Holy Spirit, who is truth, comes, He shall guide you into all truth, for He will not be presenting His own ideas, but will be passing on to you what He has heard. He will tell you about the future" (John 16:13, TLB).

It was this same Holy Spirit who spoke to the ancient Hebrew prophets, inspiring them in the writing of the Hebrew portion or Old Testament of the Bible. And it was this same Holy Spirit who inspired the many writers of the New Testament with God's truth to be recorded for His people.

A story is told of a young woman who had been informed about a famous novel. She was interested in reading it, but as she began to read the novel, she found it very difficult. She would put it down to read something else, and then she would come back to read it again because her friends said it was an excellent book.

Even with the high recommendations of her friends, the book just did not captivate her. Then one day she met the author. He was very handsome and personable. They became interested in each other, and she fell in love with him.

Now she could hardly wait to read the novel. It was the most exciting book she had ever read, for she had fallen in love with the author.

This is what happens with the Scriptures when we love the Author — the Lord Jesus Christ.

During my years of skepticism and agnosticism, I found the Bible very difficult to read and I believed it was filled with "all kinds of errors and inconsistencies." After becoming a Christian I began to read the Bible again. It was a completely different book, filled with exciting, life-changing truth. All the "errors and contradictions" were gone.

Why the difference? The non-believer or disobedient Christian does not understand spiritual truth (1 Corinthians 2:14). The Spirit-filled believer is taught by the Holy Spirit, who illumines the truth which He revealed to the original authors as recorded in the Bible.

The Inspired Words of God

The apostle Paul wrote to Timothy, "All Scripture is inspired by God" (2 Timothy 3:16, NAS). This word, *inspired*, in the original Greek language in which it was written, means "God-breathed." This means the Bible is God-breathed or God-spoken through those whom He chose to record His words. As a result, the Bible has many benefits.

For example, memorization of Scripture keeps us from sin (Psalm 119:11), gives understanding (Psalm 119:130); and helps our prayers to be answered (John 15:7).

The Bible is devotional in nature in that it can meet our personal needs for comfort (Psalm 43:1-5), courage (Psalm 46:1-11), direction (Hebrews 4:16, James 1:5, 6), peace (Psalm 4:1-8), relief (Psalm 91:1-16, 2 Corinthians 12:8-10), rest (Matthew 11:28-30, Romans 8:31-39), for resisting temptation (Psalm 1:1-6, 1 Corinthians 10:6-13 and James 1:12- 16), and for instruction.

Paul wrote to Timothy, "The whole Bible was given to us by inspiration from God and is useful to teach us what is true and to make us realize what is wrong in our lives; it straightens us out and helps us do what is right. It is God's way of making us well prepared at every point, fully equipped to do good to everyone" (2 Timothy 3:16, TLB).

How Can It Be Understood?

Many people shy away from reading the Bible because they have found it difficult to understand. Now this deserves some discussion. First of all, as we just read in 2

Timothy 3:16, Christians are commanded to study the Bible. We already have discussed that. "God is at work within you, helping you to obey Him, and then helping you do what He wants" (Philippians 2:13, TLB).

Therefore, if God wants you to understand the Bible, you can be sure that He will help you to understand it if you are willing to read and study it with a pure, open heart and mind. This is His command and His promise.

The Holy Spirit will always help Christians whom He fills and controls to understand the truths which He inspired holy men of old to record.

A story is told of a famous actor who was at a party one evening. A clergyman, who was also present, asked him if he would be kind enough to recite the twenty-third Psalm. The actor, a famous and eloquent star of stage and screen, agreed on one condition — that the clergyman, a man in his eighties, who had served God faithfully and humbly for half a century, would also recite the twenty-third Psalm.

The minister agreed, and the actor began to recite the Psalm. Oh, the words came like beautiful music, and everyone was enthralled as he gave that beautiful presentation of Psalms 23. When he finished, there was an enthusiastic response and a standing ovation.

Then the minister stood. He was not polished or eloquent. But as he began to recite the twenty-third Psalm, a holy hush fell over the congregation and tears began to fill their eyes. When he finished, there was no applause — only silence. The actor stood to his feet and said, "I have reached your eyes and your ears, this man of God has reached your hearts."

I think we all admire a life like that — one that so loves God that the Bible has richly penetrated his heart. But you may be saying, "I can't even *begin* to picture myself having such a deep relationship with God. I fall far short of that."

Well, let me ease your mind and tell you that it does

take time. It will not happen overnight, but the more time you spend in God's Word and the more consistently you obey Him, the faster you will grow in your Christian life.

Though I have been a Christian for more than 35 years, I still have much to learn. No, I am not perfect. And I do not ever expect to be — in this lifetime. But I know that the more time I spend with God through reading, studying, memorizing and meditating on His Word, the more I become like Christ, His Son.

By spending time daily in personal Bible reading, your life can change. After reading God's Word consistently for several months, you will be amazed by the things God has done in your life.

How can we understand the Bible? How can we have it reach to our very hearts?

The non-believer and the disobedient carnal Christian have difficulty in understanding the Bible because they must rely on their human faculties in their attempt to understand things that are of a spiritual nature in God's Word.

Paul writes, "But the man who isn't a Christian can't understand and can't accept these thoughts from God, which the Holy Spirit teaches us. They sound foolish to him, because only those who have the Holy Spirit within them can understand what the Holy Spirit means. Others just can't take it in" (1 Corinthians 2:14, TLB).

The Spirit-filled Christian, on the other hand, has the Holy Spirit to give him supernatural insight into the meaning of the spiritual truths of Scripture. "As far as God is concerned there is a sweet, wholesome fragrance in our lives. It is the fragrance of Christ within us, an aroma to both the saved and the unsaved all around us. To those who are not being saved, we seem a fearful smell of death and doom, while to those who know Christ we are a life-giving perfume" (2 Corinthians 2:15, 16).

Do you have difficulty understanding the Bible? If so, it could well be that you have not asked the Holy Spirit who lives within you to help you understand God's Word. Perhaps you have unconfessed sin in your life that is hindering the work of the Holy Spirit. Maybe your faith has not extended to the help of the Holy Spirit in Bible study. Possibly you have lacked the discipline or knowledge of helpful methods for studying the Bible.

In order for you to benefit the most from the study of God's Word, five elements are necessary:

1. There must be no unconfessed sin in your life.
2. You must be filled with the Holy Spirit.
3. You must have a plan for study.
4. You must have certain basic Bible study aids.
5. You should, when possible, have a time and place for studying God's Word.

Now let's examine these requirements in more detail. We discussed the importance of confessing our known sins and appropriating God's forgiveness in chapter nine, "Spiritual Breathing." Always practice Spiritual Breathing when you open God's Word for study.

You Must Be Filled With the Spirit

Since all understanding of the spiritual truths of God, which are entirely contained within the Bible, requires the supernatural assistance of the Holy Spirit, we must approach the study of God's Word in holiness and righteousness. We do this in two ways: First, we claim our right to holiness, not by virtue of anything we have done, but on the basis of what Christ has done and is doing for us:

"This includes you who were once so far away from God. You were His enemies and hated Him and were separated from Him by your evil thoughts and actions, yet now He has brought you back as His friends. He has done this through the death on the cross of His own human body, and now as a result Christ has brought you into the very presence of God, and you are standing there before Him with nothing left against you — nothing left that he could even chide you for" (Colossians 1:21, 22, TLB).

Second, we must confess all our known sins and appropriate, by faith, the fullness of the Holy Spirit, asking Him to give us spiritual insight into the true meaning of God's Word:

"And so, dear brothers, I plead with you to give your bodies to God. Let them be a living sacrifice, holy — the kind He can accept. When you think of what He has done for you, is this too much to ask? Don't copy the fashions and customs of this world, but be a new and different person with a fresh newness in all you do and think. Then you will see from your own experience how His ways will really satisfy you" (Romans 12:1, 2, TLB).

"But if we confess our sins to Him, He can be depended on to forgive us our sins and to cleanse us from every wrong. And it is perfectly proper for God to do this for us because Christ died to wash away our sins" (1 John 1:9, TLB).

Any individual who fasts for a long period of time becomes weakened in his physical body, and ultimately he will die without proper nourishment. Spiritually, the Word of God is the food for our spirit.

When one's physical health deteriorates, one becomes more susceptible to colds and other contagious diseases. A strong healthy body repels the contagious germs. Spiritually the same principle applies. Without regular daily nourishment from the Bible, one will soon become aware that there is not the resistance to temptation.

An individual who is strong and robust in his spiritual walk, mastering the Word of God, praying, walking in the Spirit, is not prone to catch the spiritual diseases that are all around us.

One of the first questions I ask a Christian who comes to me for counsel is this, "Do you know for sure that you are filled with the Spirit? And are you daily reading and studying the Word of God?" If he responds in a negative way to either one of these questions, I can help him discern the answer to his problems quickly.

A pastor I know once delighted in studying and preaching the Word of God. In his earlier days, he was a real soul-winner. But the time came when he no longer spent time reading and studying the Word of God. He became critical, discouraged and pessimistic. Finally, his personal life and family fell apart.

At one point, he told me, he was thinking about committing suicide. I believe he would have been spared all of this heartache, tragedy and sorrow if only he had continued to study the Word of God, to meditate on its truths and obey its commands. As someone wisely said, "Sin will keep you from God's Word, or God's Word will keep you from sin."

Many of the problems we experience in the Christian life are self-imposed. They are the result of carelessness in the way we walk. The promise of God is true; it is sure:

"God is light and in Him is no darkness at all so if we say we are His friends, but go on living in spiritual darkness and sin, we are lying. But if we are living in the light of God's presence, just as Christ does, then we have wonderful fellowship and joy with each other, and the blood of Jesus His Son cleanses us from every sin" (1 John 1:5-7, TLB).

You Must Have a Plan for Studying the Bible

Regular study of God's Word is essential to living supernaturally. It will keep you from sin and better equip you for service.

Numerous Bible study plans and methods are available in published form. Some will help you read through the Bible in one year, while others are expanded to three years. Some are for those who wish to study twice a week; others are designed for those who want to be in the Word daily. Some plans are for individual Bible study and others are for the entire family.

My own approach is to begin each day in prayer and worship of the Lord, listening to a recording of and/or reading His holy Word. A helpful plan for those of you who do not yet have consistent personal devotions can be found in *The 31-Day Experiment*. and in *Faith: A 31-Day Experiment*, both by Dick Purnell. Another excellent series is Irving Jensen's *Do-It- Yourself Bible Studies* on various books of the New Testament. These tools to aid you in Bible study and personal devotions are available from Here's Life Publishers. Pray, asking God to give you discernment as to which of all the available plans He would have you use, remembering that you will never enjoy the supernatural life provided by the Holy Spirit unless you spend considerable quality time in the Word of God.

Method of Study

There are several methods of studying the Bible. One is the *topical* method. *Salvation, the second coming* and *heaven* are examples of topics. To use this method, you will need the help of a good Bible concordance which lists the verses of the Bible by topic.

Another method is to study the Bible by book, by chapter, by paragraph and by verse. I suggest the latter, but seasoning it from time to time with an extra study of topics that are of particular current interest to you.

Three prime aspects of Bible study include *observation* (what does the Bible say?), *interpretation* (what does it mean?) and *application* (what does it mean in my life?).

Here are some important, practical suggestions for your individual devotional reading and study of the Bible:

Prayer

1. Begin with a prayer. "Breathe spiritually," and ask the Holy Spirit to give you an understanding of God's Word.

Observation

2. Keep a Bible study notebook.

3. Read the text slowly and carefully. After reading it, crystallize in your mind what it said. Then read the text again. Enter brief notes in your notebook.

Interpretation

4. Find out the true meaning of the text. Ask yourself these questions, then write the answers in your notebook:

   a. Who or what is the main subject?
   b. Whom or what is he speaking about?
   c. What is the key verse?
   d. What does the passage teach you about Jesus Christ?
   e. Does the passage bring to light personal sin that you need to confess and forsake?
   f. Does the passage contain a command for you to obey?
   g. Does the passage give a promise you can claim?

Of course, not every passage you read will have answers to all these questions.

5. Enter in a "diary" section of your Bible study notebook the practical applications the study has for you, any commands you have by faith determined to obey, and the promises you have claimed by faith.

6. Memorize the Scriptures — particularly key verses. Type or write these verses on cards and carry them with you for frequent reference and memory practice.

Students, place the cards over your study desk. Housewives, place cards above the kitchen sink and on the front of your refrigerator. Businessmen, place a card on your desk or in some other conspicuous location for frequent reference.

A word of caution: keep your priorities straight; do not use company time that should be restricted to work.

Application

7. Obey the commands and follow the instructions you learn in God's Word. Paul told Timothy, "The whole Bible was given to us by inspiration from God and is useful to teach us what is true and to make us realize what is wrong in our lives; it straightens us out and helps us do what is right" (2 Timothy 3:16, TLB).

It is important to remember that one reason God has given us the Bible is to help us live holy, righteous lives. It is for this reason the Bible says, "And remember, it is a message to obey, not just to listen to" (James 1:22, TLB).

Use Good Bible Study Aids

In recent years a number of very helpful Bible study aids have been developed. These include concordances, encyclopedias and Bible dictionaries. The Here's Life edition of the *Open Bible* contains an excellent number of Bible study helps.

Strong's Concordance is helpful in finding the meaning of biblical terms in their original languages.

The New Bible Dictionary (Eerdmans) gives in-depth definitions and historic background to biblical subjects. Bible commentaries can be helpful, too, but use them with discernment, remembering that they are but man's interpretations of God's Word and can be in error.

A Time and a Place for Study

Bible study might seem like considerable hard work

that could take much time. You might not want to use all the methods I have discussed as you begin your Bible study, but rather "work up to it." The important thing is to be in God's Word on a regular basis. I suggest that you set aside a specific time in a place where you can be undisturbed by outside influences for your Bible study.

In my own life, as I have come to know God better and to live more fully in the power and control of the Holy Spirit, my daily devotional Bible reading and study is not a duty or a chore, but a blessing; not an imposition on my time, but an invitation to fellowship in the closest of all ways with our holy, heavenly Father and our wonderful Savior and Lord.

Remember, God delights to have fellowship with you. The success of your time of studying God's Word and time for prayer is not to be determined by some emotional experience which you may have, though this will be your experience frequently, but by the realization that God is pleased that you want to know Him enough to spend time in Bible study and prayer.

A Bible Study Blessing — Right Now

Would you like a special blessing from God right now — a conscious awareness of the indwelling Holy Spirit? Of course you would. So let us look in God's Word for the next few minutes and see what blessings will come our way. But first, let us pray. Breathe spiritually, claiming forgiveness of your sins according to the command and promise of 1 John 1:9. Then, thank the Holy Spirit for filling you and giving supernatural insight into God's Word as you study it.

Now for a few tools. Get your Bible and a pen or pencil. Turn to page ??, and use this chart as we study the Bible, or make your own chart on a separate piece of paper.

Our brief study will be of Psalm 119:9: "How can a

young man stay pure? By reading Your Word and following its rules" (TLB).

Observation: What Do I See?

Observation may be defined as seeing and noting carefully what is contained in a passage of Scripture. It uses the questions, "who?", "what?", "where?", "when?", and "how?"

In verse nine, about whom are we reading? A young man. What are we reading about? Counsel on keeping his life pure. How will he do this? By living his life according to the rules set forth in the Word of God.

Make these entries in your Bible study chart. Now, try this approach on your own, using Matthew 6:19-34.

Interpretation: What Does It Mean?

Interpretation is determining what the author intended to say to his readers. There is only one correct interpretation for any passage. We can ask, "Why?" to help discover the meaning of a passage. For example, "Why did the author describe it this way?"

In Psalm 119:9, we observed a young man, keeping his life pure by living it according to the rules of God's Word. The interpretation therefore is this: A young person can live a pure life by living according to the principles of the Bible.

Make these entries on your Bible study chart. Now practice interpretation on the passage, Matthew 6:19-34, referring to your observation of this passage.

Application: What Difference Does It Make To Me?

Application is determining what things you need to do as a result of learning these truths. There can be many applications for one truth.

In Psalm 119:9, we interpreted this verse to mean that "a young person can live a pure life by living according to the principles of the Bible." Now pray to the Holy Spirit, asking Him to show you how to apply this verse to your life.

Here are some applications a person might perceive:

1. I can live a pure life if I follow God's Word.

2. I will begin today by determining to know His Word and to obey it.

3. I will start a regular, daily, devotional Bible study.

Make these entries on your Bible study chart. Now look at your interpretation of Matthew 6:19-34, and prayerfully consider how the Holy Spirit would have you apply this passage to your life.

By applying the lessons learned from Psalm 119:9 to your own life, you can develop a Bible study plan that is best suited for you. Schedule a plan for regular Bible study, using one of the methods I have suggested in this chapter.

On the following page is reproduced a sample chart that you may wish to use as part of your Bible study program. The "results" column is for you to record the results of making this application in your own life.

For example, still using Psalm 119:9, the typical young person mentioned earlier would enter as a "result": "Began a daily, *devotional* Bible study plan." If this is actually your determination, then enter this in the "results" column of your Bible study chart. If you do not have enough room in the results column, you may wish to make appropriate entries in a "diary" in your Bible study notebook.

Bible study will always remain exciting and relevant to you if you will follow the above procedures. The Holy Spirit will give you such insight into the truth of God's Word that you will eagerly and joyfully look forward to every morning's devotional Bible study.

Regular, meaningful Bible study is foundational to the supernatural life. God's Word is the communications channel through which God speaks to us in the power

There is special, supernatural power in the Bible. Among other great blessings, the Word of God is the sword of the Holy Spirit (Ephesians 6:17). As such, the Bible is the greatest weapon a Christian can have as he encounters spiritual warfare.

Remember, it is impossible to live in the fullness and power of the Holy Spirit and experience the reality of the supernatural life apart from knowledge of and obedience to God's holy, inspired Word.

The Holy Spirit Illuminates God's Word

SAMPLE CHART

Verse and question	Observation	Interpretation	Application	Results

CHAPTER TWELVE

Prepare For Spiritual Conflict

The movie, "Star Wars" — one of the most successful films at the box office in the history of motion pictures — is based on the science-fiction premise that a supernatural force of good and evil can have a strong influence in the affairs of men. The film's hero, young Luke Skywalker, must learn to master the "ways of the force" in order to utilize this supernatural power in his battle against evil Darth Vader, the "black Lord of the Sith," and the sinister powers of the corrupt Empire.

In Frank Allnutt's book, *The Force of Star Wars*, the film is viewed as religious allegory and interpreted from a biblical perspective. The author explains that just as the force is seen to empower Luke Skywalker for action, the Bible teaches that the Holy Spirit, in reality, is the empowering, loving and personal Spirit of God who is the key to the Christian's supernatural life. Just as Luke Skywalker is a soldier engaged in battle against evil forces, so is the Christian a soldier of God in the battle waged against satanic forces.

As Christian soldiers, you and I must recognize our enemies, learn how to prepare for spiritual conflict against them and understand that God has already decreed Christ and His followers as the victors, though the day of final victory is still future — the day when Christ will return bodily to earth.

The Uninformed Soldier

A story appeared in the press about a soldier who had been wounded and separated from the rest of his company in the jungles of a South Seas island. The soldier had to hunt for food, water and shelter, and he was in constant fear of being captured or killed by enemy patrols.

For two years, the soldier avoided his enemy. Finally he stumbled upon some soldiers from his own country near the edge of a village. With joy, he quickly told them his story and asked if the enemy had finally been driven off the island. The men were amazed and saddened by the man's story. They told him that the war had been over for a long time and that his country had won.

This story is similar to what often happens in the life of a Christian. Like the soldier, many Christians are living in defeat and fear because they do not know that victory has been won in the conflict with Satan. Such Christians live in fear of Satan.

They try to fight the battle alone, become separated from God and need fellowship. They feel defeated, frustrated and confused. They can experience freedom when they find out that the war has already been won. Their attitude would change if only they knew that they are already on the winning side. They would be more confident in fighting and would have more confidence in their leaders.

Supernatural Walk — and Warfare

The Bible teaches very clearly that the Christian life is not only a walk, but also a warfare. Many believers do not realize this. They think that living the Christian life means escaping all trials, difficulties and temptations, and they expect to glide through their years on earth with scarcely a problem.

As a matter of fact, we are strangers and pilgrims on this earth (1 Peter 2:11), living in a world ruled by Satan, and we must continually face opposition and difficulty. The Christian life should be a victorious one, but it is not always an easy one.

We must continually be strengthened "in the Lord, and in the strength of His might" (Ephesians 6:10, NAS). We cannot expect to win the battle unless we allow Christ to fight the battle for us through the indwelling power of His Holy Spirit. We have all that it takes to be good soldiers; we have the Holy Spirit of our wonderful Savior and Lord Jesus Christ.

Satan: A Defeated Foe

A young man who came to see me was obviously very distraught and in need of comforting. He wasted no time in getting to the point of the matter.

"I am afraid of Satan," he blurted out.

"Then you must be trying to control your own life," I responded.

My guest looked at me with a puzzled expression as I continued: "You should be afraid of Satan — if you insist on controlling your own life. But if you are willing to let the Holy Spirit control your life, you have nothing to fear because the Bible says, 'Greater is He [the Holy Spirit] who is in you than he [Satan] who is in the world' " (1 John 4:4, NAS).

I reminded my guest that Satan was defeated almost 2,000 years ago when Christ, in fulfillment of prophecy, died on the cross for our sins. Though Satan has great power to influence man, he has only that power which has been granted to him by God. That is why the disciples could pray to God in His sovereignty and power in the face of great persecution and be used by the Lord to "turn the world upside down."

God, Our Protector

God's Word commands us, "Let Him have all your worries and cares, for He is always thinking about you and watching everything that concerns you. Be careful, watch out for attacks from Satan, your great enemy. He prowls around like a hungry, roaring lion, looking for some victim to tear apart" (1 Peter 5:7, 8, TLB).

While Satan's defeat is assured by the very Word of God, he remains a very real foe to reckon with. We need to be alert to Satan's cunning and subtle ways, as well as to his obvious attempts to defeat and destroy us.

Stay Out of the Cage

My friend who was afraid of Satan happened to live in a city which has one of the largest zoos in the world. So I asked him, "What do you do with lions in your city?"

He answered, "We put them in a cage."

"Satan is in a cage," I said. "Visit the lion cage at the zoo and watch a lion pacing impatiently back and forth. He can't hurt you. Even if you go up close to the cage, he still can't hurt you if you are careful.

"But stay out of that cage — don't even stick a hand inside, or you'll be in danger. Get in the cage, and the lion will probably tear you apart. But you have nothing to fear so long as you stay out of that cage.

"In the same way, you have nothing to fear from Satan so long as you stay out of his 'cage' — the world — and depend upon the Holy Spirit and not on your own strength. Remember, Satan has no power except that which God in His wisdom allows him to have."

I repeat: Stay out of Satan's domain — the present world system.

When Satanic Forces Attack

Satan is a created being, and as such can be in but one place at a time. He is unlike God, who is omnipresent, which means He is present everywhere, all the time. Many times people attribute some difficulty in their lives to "satanic attack." In most of these cases it is not Satan who is personally attacking, but rather one or more of his fallen angels, whom we call demons or evil spirits.

Let me tell you about one such incident. It concerns one of the most remarkable young men I have ever met. He was a student at the Massachusetts Institute of Technology, a doctoral candidate with a brilliant mind.

More importantly, he truly loved the Lord with all his heart.

In his studies, however, he came to the conclusion that God had revealed something very special to him. He believed that he had reached the point of sinless perfection in his life. I warned him against this heresy, but he just smiled as though he had some special message directly from God.

After some months, a tragic thing happened. I was visiting Boston, and this young student picked me up at the airport. During our drive into town, he told me how he was going through agony — literal, physical agony. He said it was as though a dagger was being twisted in his back. And he couldn't explain the cause.

"I've gone to physicians and psychologists, but no one can help me," he lamented. "There's no explanation for the pain; there's nothing wrong with me, physically or psychologically. But the pain is so excruciating that I can hardly endure it. I've spent hours in prayer. I've done everything I know to do, and the pain still remains."

I suggested we turn to the Bible, which we did. Then I explained the importance of turning the whole matter over to the Lord. I recalled the Lord's promise of Romans 8:28 and 1 Thessalonians 5:18, then asked him to join me in praising God and thanking Him for this experience.

"This is a satanic attack," I told him, "probably through some psychosomatic kind of reaction."

As we prayed, he experienced relief from the terrible pain that had plagued him.

I asked him to give his testimony that night at a large gathering of a thousand or so people where I was going to speak. He did — a wonderful testimony of victory in Christ.

The Pain Returns

The next morning he came to see me at Harvard

Square, where I was staying for the week-long series of talks. He told me that the pain had returned during the night, and asked that I pray again for him to receive relief. We prayed together, and again the pain went away.

Every day that week he came to me — once, sometimes twice, a day — and each time we prayed, and each time he experienced relief from the pain. Every time we met for prayer I repeated the reminder that God releases His healing power in our behalf when we praise Him, thank Him and worship Him.

Finally, on my last day in Boston before returning to my home in California, he came to see me again. He was in tears because of the great pain he was suffering.

"I'm really in great agony, physically and emotionally," he said, "and I just don't see how I can survive."

Admonishing him in love, I pointed out that even if he were to die from this, he was still to praise God all the way. "You praise God and thank Him through your tears, day and night, until the pain leaves," I told him.

Then we knelt together in prayer. This time, the pain did not subside. But he did leave with the promise to me that he would praise and thank God continually — even if he should die in the process.

He left, and I prayed again for him. Here was this brilliant young doctoral candidate at MIT, who was being devastated by pain. I wanted so desperately to help him but was helpless apart from prayer.

A Welcomed Letter

Some days later, after I had returned to Arrowhead Springs, a letter was waiting for me. It was filled with praise and thanksgiving to God, also containing an explanation of what had happened since we were together. He told the story of how he had returned to his room after our last visit, still suffering excruciating pain, but praising, thanking and worshipping God. The pain only grew worse. For the next two days and nights he prayed continuously, able only to nap once in a while because of the terrible pain.

Then, finally, it was as though God had supernaturally touched him in response to his expression of faith, and the pain suddenly was gone. Obviously, it had been an attack of Satan or one of his demons.

As a result of this young man's healing, he experienced such great joy in the Lord that for two months he button-holed everyone he could on campus — most of them his friends who were Christians, but some who had been living carnal lives and had cold hearts.

"The just shall live by faith," he would tell them enthusiastically. "The reason you're not living a joyful life is because you're not living by faith, you're not praising God, you're not thanking God."

This young man became an instrument of revival at MIT. He had one of the most profound impacts for the faith on that campus. Later, he joined our staff and was mightily used of God. Today, he has a very outstanding ministry of the gospel.

It was through that experience of excruciating pain, for which there was no human explanation and no human solution, that God gave him victory and relieved him from the pain. And it was all because this young man began to realize that he was not sinlessly perfect, and that God simply wanted his praise, thanksgiving and worship.

The Ways of the World

What is the world? "For the whole world system, based as it is on men's primitive nature, their greedy ambitions and the glamour of all that they think splendid, is not derived from the Father at all, but from the world itself" (1 John 2:16, Phillips).

The world has not always been corrupt. God created it perfect and good, and He placed Adam and Eve in authority over it (Genesis 1:28-31). But then Satan tempted Adam and Eve into disobeying God (Genesis 3) and thereby introduced sin into the world, thus usurping their position of authority over the world and everything in it. For this reason, the Bible calls Satan the "god of this world" (2 Corinthians 4:4, NAS).

Adam and Eve, because of their original sin, were separated from fellowship with God, as have been all their descendants throughout history (Genesis 3; Romans 3). But God, in His sovereign mercy, "loved the world so much that He gave His only Son [Jesus Christ] so that anyone who believes in Him shall not perish but have eternal life" (John 3:16, TLB), no longer separated from God, but rather brought into fellowship — a personal relationship — with God (John 1:12).

"For He has rescued us out of the darkness and gloom of Satan's kingdom and brought us into the kingdom of His dear Son, who bought our freedom with His blood and forgave us all our sins" (Colossians 1:13, 14 TLB).

Therefore, as children of God, Christians are no longer in Satan's kingdom living under Satan's authority, but rather they are now members of Christ's kingdom living under God's protective, loving authority. Christians are citizens of heaven (Philippians 3:20) and are not to conform to the evil ways of the world (John 17:14-16; Romans 12:2).

A Subtle Threat

Yet, the world remains a threatening enticement to the children of God. On close analysis we find that the world in some ways today is actually a greater enemy to Christians than it was to first-century believers.

In the time of the apostles, believers faced persecution and even martyrdom. But the ways of the world are more subtle in the twentieth century. True, in many parts of the world today, Christians continue to be persecuted and martyred. But in the free countries, the world has lost its appearance as an enemy.

Instead, we find that the world outwardly professes to embrace Christianity while, in reality, it wages war against believers by tempting them into ineffective living with materialism, immorality, humanistic philosophies and false religions.

The Bible warns us: "Stop loving this evil world and all that it offers you, for when you love these things you show that you do not really love God; for all these worldly things, these evil desires — the craze for sex, the ambition to buy everything that appeals to you, and the pride that comes from wealth and importance — these are not from God.

"They are from this evil world itself. And this world is fading away, and these evil, forbidden things are going with it, but whoever keeps doing the will of God will live forever" (1 John 2:15-17, TLB).

The Church's Finest Hour

Today, because of the subtle ways of the world system, there are perhaps more carnal Christians than at any time in history. But the Bible tells us that the tide will turn, that the Church will soon enter its finest hour.

I believe we are on the threshold of witnessing the greatest spiritual revival in the history of the Church. I believe that the Great Commission will indeed be fulfilled before the return of our Lord Jesus Christ (Matthew 28:19, 20; Mark 13:10).

We are beginning to see the turning of the tide. More and more Christians are discovering how to live supernaturally in the power and control of the Holy Spirit. The gospel is being spread throughout the world by many committed Christians who are determined, by faith, to help fulfill the Great Commission in this generation.

I do not know anyone, however, who loves this world who has ever been used of God in any significant way. There is nothing wrong with money and other material success. However, we are to wear the cloak of materialism loosely. We are to set our affection on Christ and His kingdom, not on the material things of this world.

The Lord left us with this promise: "But take courage; I have overcome the world" (John 16:33, NAS). And the apostle John writes: "For whatever is born of God overcomes the world; and this is the victory that has overcome the world — our faith. And who is the one who overcomes the world, but he who believes that Jesus is the Son of God?" (1 John 5:4, 5 NAS).

Preparing for Battle

The apostle Paul was an aggressive soldier of God who carried the gospel far and wide throughout the known world. He was greatly used of God to expand the territorial borders of Christendom. All that Paul did, he did in the name of Christ and through the power and control of the Holy Spirit.

But there was great opposition to Paul's ministry. Consequently, he always seemed to be in the center of spiritual warfare. He knew his enemies — Satan and the world system — and their subtle, deceiving devices.

Throughout his Christian life, he suffered various kinds of persecutions, including stonings, beatings and imprisonment. In spite of such harsh persecution, Paul could write, "Rejoice in the Lord always; again I will say, rejoice" (Philippians 4:4, NAS).

It was during Paul's imprisonment in Rome, about 61 or 62 A.D., that he wrote to the church at Ephesus. The theme of his letter is supernatural living. In his concluding remarks, he talks about the Christian's spiritual warfare:

"Last of all I want to remind you that your strength must come from the Lord's mighty power within you. Put on all of God's armor so that you will be able to stand safe against all strategies and tricks of Satan.

"For we are not fighting against people made of flesh and blood, but against persons without bodies — the evil rulers of the unseen world, those mighty satanic beings and great evil princes of darkness who rule this world; and against huge numbers of wicked spirits in the spirit world.

"So use every piece of God's armor to resist the enemy whenever he attacks, and when it is all over, you will still be standing up.

"But to do this, you will need the strong belt of truth and the breastplate of God's approval. Wear shoes that are able to speed you on as you preach the Good News of peace with God.

"In every battle you will need faith as your shield to stop the fiery arrows aimed at you by Satan. And you will need the helmet of salvation and the sword of the Spirit — which is the Word of God.

"Pray all the time. Ask God for anything in line with the Holy Spirit's wishes. Plead with him, reminding him of your needs, and keep praying earnestly for all Christians everywhere" (Ephesians 6:10-18, TLB).

Here, Paul tells us that the battle we fight is against Satan and the spiritual forces of wickedness. It is not against other people.

Paul uses the analogy of a Roman soldier's armor to describe the various forms of protection that the Lord has given us against the spiritual forces of wickedness. The armor of protection includes the belt of truth, the breastplate of righteousness, shoes that are the good news or gospel of peace, the shield of faith, the helmet of salvation and the sword of the Holy Spirit, which is the Bible, God's Word.

We are told by Paul that our strength must come from the Lord's mighty power within us. This tells us to trust the Lord to give us the power of His Holy Spirit to resist the enemy. We must always remember this: It is impossible to fight supernatural powers in our own human strength; the battle is God's. If we try in our own strength we are certain to fail.

Examining the Armor

Let us examine in more detail the various parts of the spiritual armor. The Roman soldier was girded or strapped with a belt that measured six to eight inches wide around his waist. Everything he wore was held together by this belt. His skirt was caught up in it to allow freedom of movement, and his sword hung from it. It was the foundational piece of his armor.

When Paul tells us we will need a "strong belt of truth," he means we need to wrap the truth around ourselves. We need to abide in Jesus Christ and the Word of God, and have a growing knowledge and understanding of the Bible and how it relates to our lives.

The breastplate is important because it protects the chest area, especially the heart. The "breastplate of God's approval" helps us to "stand right before God." We identify ourselves with Christ's righteousness, therefore we are righteous. Putting on the breastplate of God's approval helps us to remember where we stand before God and to realize that we already have victory over Satan and the world system.

Paul further says we should "wear shoes that are able to speed you on as you preach the Good News of peace with God." This actually refers to a part of the armor that might be difficult to describe unless we turn to that part of the Old Testament to which Paul was referring: "How beautiful upon the mountains are the feet of those who bring the happy news of peace and salvation, the news that the God of Israel reigns" (Isaiah 52:7, TLB).

This reference to the "happy news" comes from a time when the Jews were taken captive by the Babylonians. The happy news of peace was that the war was over. It came to signify the happy news that a war was over and the victory was won. The happy news in Ephesians is that the battle with Satan has already been won.

Now this passage in Ephesians is not necessarily talking about evangelism, but as we share Christ we have the happy news that the victory over Satan has been won by Christ's death and resurrection.

Once you have put on the shoes of the glad tidings of peace, you will want to tell non-Christians about Jesus Christ and how they can have a personal relationship with Him. Based on the authority of God's Word, you can happily tell them that Christ has victory over troubles, concerns and hurts.

The "shield of faith" described by Paul is one of our most effective pieces of armor. Just as a shield protected a Roman soldier from attacks by his enemies, our faith protects us from attacks by Satan — attacks waged with such spiritual weapons as temptation, impure thoughts, confusion and the like.

Next is the Roman soldier's helmet. This was a hard, solid, impenetrable piece of armor that could not be broken. So when Paul writes about the "helmet of salvation," he refers to the knowledge and facts about the truth of Christ.

Having this protection for our heads means our thoughts are protected from doubt. Being secure in our right relationship with God is our greatest protection. Salvation for the Christian is assured and eternal.

God has promised, "I will never, never fail you nor forsake you." This is why we can say without any doubt or fear, "The Lord is my helper and I am not afraid of anything that mere man can do to me" (Hebrews 13:5b, 6, TLB). He further promises, "No one shall snatch them out of My hand" (John 10:28, NAS).

The "sword of the Spirit — the Word of God" is the only offensive weapon carried by the Christian soldier. It is used to charge against Satan and his evil forces to keep them away. It is also used defensively as protection.

As Satan attacks, we can quote Scripture to defeat

him. When we fill our hearts, minds and mouths with the Word of God, Satan has less opportunity to tempt or attack us.

Now that we have looked at the kind of battle in which we are engaged and the weapons available to us. let us consider how we can use our spiritual weapons—daily.

We can study the Bible by ourselves and in groups so that we will learn what God's Word really says. We can memorize Scripture so that our minds will be filled with it; our lips will be ready to speak it. And we can meditate on God's Word. This simply means to think about different parts of a passage and determine its meaning and application to our lives.

For the Christian who fails to put on his spiritual armor, there can be serious consequences. Without the belt of truth, a Christian will be easily influenced to follow false teaching, to live an ungodly life-style, to believe in wrong doctrine.

Without the breastplate of God's approval, a Christian can live an ungodly life, feel unnecessary guilt and forget that he has the approval of God. Without shoes of the good news of peace, a Christian stands to miss God's blessing by not telling people about Christ.

Without the shield of faith, a Christian can feel discouraged and defeated. His life can become ineffective and impotent in spiritual things, and he will not experience the victory God has provided. Without the helmet of salvation, a Christian will lack security in his relationship with God.

And without the sword of the Holy Spirit, God's Word, a Christian will have no power in his witness. He will experience inability to counsel others effectively. He will lack aggressiveness as a Christian because of lack of confidence in God's Word.

Put on the full armor of God and you too, like Paul, will be protected from the enemy and will be able to "rejoice in the Lord" regardless of your circumstances as you live a supernatural life.

CHAPTER THIRTEEN

The Struggle Within

A native Christian went to a missionary for counsel. He was very much troubled by the spiritual conflict going on within his heart. He wanted to do what God wanted him to do, but he was frequently disobeying God. He found that he was prone to do evil things, even as he did before he became a Christian.

The native described this conflict within himself as a dogfight. He said to the missionary, "It is as though I have a black dog and a white dog inside me fighting each other constantly." The black dog, he explained, represented evil and the white dog represented good.

The missionary asked him, "Which dog wins the fight within you?"

After several moments of silence, the native said, "The dog that wins is the one I tell to 'sic 'em.' "

Man has a free will; he is a free moral agent. As such, he can decide, even as a Spirit-filled Christian, whether he will obey the dictates of the flesh or the leading of the Spirit. Whether he lives a consistent, Spirit-filled life is determined by the frequency with which he says "Yes" to the leading of the Spirit and "No" to the temptations of the flesh.

External forces — outside and inside us — are constantly fighting to win control over us. While we walk around in fleshly bodies here, in Satan's domain, we will never be free from the pressures of these negative forces.

"For we naturally love to do evil things that are just the opposite from the things that the Holy Spirit tells us to do; and the good things we want to do when the Spirit has his way with us are just the opposite of our natural desires. These two forces within us are constantly fighting each other to win control over us, and our wishes are never free from their pressures" (Galatians 5:17, TLB).

131

What a relief it was to me one day when I read in the Bible, "The old sinful nature within us is against God. It never did obey God's laws and it never will" (Romans 8:7, TLB). I had been trying to make myself good enough to please God, but that is impossible.

The Bible says, "The heart is the most deceitful thing there is, and desperately wicked" (Jeremiah 17:9, TLB). Therefore, I cannot hope to make myself good enough to earn God's favor. The only way that I can please God is to trust Him to enable me to be obedient to His will.

Our Two Natures

Someone once said, "We are our own worst enemy." Whether or not he knew he was speaking about a fundamental biblical truth, I do not know. But even if he had never opened a Bible, he surely learned from his own life that the man within, which we call our old sin-nature, is indeed an enemy set against us.

For the Christian, the old sin-nature, if not properly dealt with, can become a major hindrance to living supernaturally. A Christian who, for any variety of reasons (which we shall discuss later), does not properly deal with his old sin-nature is said to be living in a state of *carnality*. This is a graphic metaphor: The unspiritual Christian is said to be living in his flesh, his old sin-nature.

Such a *carnal* Christian is usually a miserable person — even more miserable than the non-believer. Having experienced the joy and blessing of fellowship with God, he has lost present contact and does not know how to recapture that lost fellowship. Sometimes he gives the impression that he does not want to recapture it.

The Carnal Christian

Obviously, the carnal Christian cannot experience the supernatural life. He trusts in his own efforts to try to

CARNAL MAN
(One who has received Christ. but who lives in defeat because he trusts in his own efforts to live the Christian life)

SELF-DIRECTED LIFE
S—Self is on the throne
†—Christ dethroned and not allowed to direct the life
●—Interests are directed by self. often resulting in discord and frustration

SPIRITUAL MAN
(One who is directed and empowered by the Holy Spirit)
"But he who is spiritual appraises all things . . ." (I Corinthians 2:15).

CHRIST-DIRECTED LIFE
†—Christ is in the life and on the throne
S—Self is yielding to Christ
●—Interests are directed by Christ. resulting in harmony with God's plan

live the Christian life. He is either uninformed about, or has forgotten, God's love, forgiveness and power (Romans 5:8-10; Hebrews 10:1-25; 1 John 1-2:3; 2 Peter 1:9; Acts 1:8).

He is on a spiritual roller coaster and goes from one emotional experience to another, frustrated and defeated. He cannot understand himself — he wants to do what is right, but cannot. He fails to draw upon the power of the Holy Spirit to live the supernatural life.

The apostle Paul writes concerning the carnal Christian's dilemma: "I don't understand myself at all, for I really want to do what is right, but I can't. I do what I don't want to — what I hate" (Romans 7:15, TLB).

Some of the Christians at Corinth were living carnal lives and Paul admonished them, "And I, brethren, could not speak to you as spiritual men, but as to men of flesh, as to babes in Christ. I gave you milk to drink, not solid food; for you were not yet able to receive it.

"Indeed, even now you are not yet able, for you are still fleshly [carnal]. For since there is jealousy and strife among you, are you not fleshly, and are you not walking like mere men?" (1 Corinthians 3:1-3, NAS; see also: Romans 7:15-24; 8:7; Galatians 5:16-18).

Some or all of the following traits may characterize the carnal Christian: ignorance of his spiritual heritage, unbelief, disobedience, loss of love for God and for others, poor prayer life, no desire for Bible study, legalistic attitude, impure thoughts, jealousy, guilt, worry, discouragement, critical spirit, frustration, aimlessness.

The person who professes to be a Christian, but who continues to practice sin, should realize that he may not be a Christian at all. We read in the Bible, "By this we know that we have come to know Him, if we keep His commandments" (1 John 2:3, NAS).

"So if we stay close to Him, obedient to Him, we won't be sinning either; but as for those who keep on sinning, they should realize this: They sin because they have never really known Him or become His.... The person who has been born into God's family does not make a practice of sinning, because now God's life is in him; so he can't keep on sinning, for this new life has been born into him and controls him — he has been born again" (1 John 3:6, 9, TLB).

If you have doubts as to whether or not you are a Christian, I suggest you peruse again chapters four and five of this book you are now reading. On the other hand, if you have the assurance of knowing that you are a child of God and that you have eternal life, then re-read chapter nine and begin to practice Spiritual Breathing.

Christian Leaders Are Human, Too

Recently, a young Christian came to inquire, "How do you account for the fact that so many Christian leaders, many of them famous personalities, pastors and heads of Christian organizations, are involved in moral and financial scandals?" He named several well-known pastors and Christian leaders to illustrate his point.

Sadly I acknowledged his statement to be true. It seems as though there is an all-out attack of Satan to destroy the credibility of the Christian message. My explanation to him was that our Lord and the apostle Paul dealt with the same problem because, even though the disciples had been with the Lord Jesus three years or more, Judas betrayed Him and the others deserted Him.

The apostle Paul spoke of several who had deserted him. Those included Demas, who loved the present world (2 Timothy 4:10) and Hymenaeus, Alexander and Philetus who strayed from the truth (1 Timothy 1:18-20; 2 Timothy 2:17, 18).

You see, this conflict goes on in the lives of all Christians — leaders and famous personalities as well as in the life of the new believer. Many times I have prayed, "Oh God, if there is a possibility that I may dishonor Your name by becoming involved in a moral, financial or any other kind of scandal that would discredit my ministry and nullify my love and witness for You, I would rather You would take my life first."

I am sobered by the very thought that having served the Lord for more than 30 exciting, wonderful, fruitful years, I might ever dishonor His name and bring disgrace to His cause. I know what has happened to other brothers — some of whom had apparently at one time been Spirit-filled Christian leaders, and I know that I too could fail the Lord if I do not trust and obey Him. Even the apostle Paul lived in reverential fear that he might dishonor the name and cause of our Lord.

"So be careful. If you are thinking, 'Oh, I would never behave like that' — let this be a warning to you. For you too may fall into sin. But remember this — the wrong desires that come into your life aren't anything new and different. Many others have faced exactly the problems before you. And no temptation is irresistible.

"You can trust God to keep the temptation from becoming so strong that you can't stand up against it, for he has promised this and will do what He says. He will show you how to escape temptation's power so that you can bear up patiently against it" (1 Corinthians 10:12, 13, TLB).

Only one person can help us live holy lives that will honor our Lord, and that is the third person of the Trinity — God the Holy Spirit. As long as we cast our ballot for the Spirit against the flesh we can live every day in the joy, the wonder, the adventure and the power of the resurrection.

The Scripture warns all believers, even those who occupy positions of Christian leadership, that they too could fall. No one reaches the place of spiritual maturity or perfection where he can say, "I don't need the Lord's help any more." We are all dependent on the Lord for our moment-by- moment strength and resistance to temptation. The only one who can enable us to live victorious lives is the Lord Jesus Christ Himself.

And He promises, "I am the light of the world, so if you follow Me you will not be stumbling through the darkness but living light will flood your path" (John 8:12, TLB).

Some Self-Analysis

Perhaps some self-analysis is in order here. Do any of the following apply to you? An exalted feeling of your own importance? Love of human praise? Anger and impatience? Self-will, stubbornness, unteachability? A compromising spirit? Jealous disposition? Lustful, unholy action? Dishonesty? Unbelief? Selfishness? Lack of discipline? Love of money? Love of beautiful clothes? Love of cars, houses and land? If so, it is quite likely that your old sin-nature is in control of your life.

New Master — New Life

The person who walks by faith in the control of the Holy Spirit has a new Master. The Lord Jesus said, "He who does not take his cross and follow after Me is not worthy of Me" (Matthew 10:38, NAS). "Unless a grain of wheat falls into the earth and dies, it remains by itself alone; but if it dies, it bears much fruit" (John 12:24, NAS).

Obviously, you cannot control yourself and be controlled by the Holy Spirit at the same time. Christ cannot be in control if you are on the throne of your life. So you must abdicate — surrender the throne of your life to Christ. This involves faith. As an expression of your will, in prayer, you surrender the throne of your life to Him, and by faith you draw upon His resources to live a supernatural life, holy and fruitful.

The *command* of Ephesians 5:18 is given to all believers — to be filled, directed and empowered by the Holy Spirit, continually, moment by moment every day. And the *promise* of 1 John 5:14, 15 is made to all believers — that, when we pray according to God's will, He hears and answers us.

Or, as I already have explained, if you pray as an expression of your faith to be filled with God's Spirit, He will hear and answer you. He will fill you and keep on filling you. In this way, you will find victory over your old sin-nature, over the ways of the world and over Satan.

CHAPTER FOURTEEN

The Holy Spirit

The Holy Spirit guarantees your rights as a child of God: "He has put His brand upon us — His mark of ownership — and given us His Holy Spirit in our hearts as guarantee that we belong to Him, and as the first installment of all that He is going to give us" (2 Corinthians 1:22, TLB).

And again, in the book of Ephesians: "His presence within us is God's guarantee that He really will give us all that He promised; and the Spirit's seal upon us means that God has already purchased us and that He guarantees to bring us to Himself. This is just one more reason for us to praise our glorious God" (Ephesians 1:14, TLB).

This means that, as children of God, we have the ability to obey God's laws if we are continually filled with the Holy Spirit and refuse to obey the old evil nature within us. Let me illustrate this.

Some time ago, a young Christian came to share his problems. He was very frustrated and confused, and he spoke of the constant defeat and confusion he experienced in the Christian life.

"You don't have to live in defeat," I said to him. The young man registered surprise. "You can live a life of victory, a life of joy, a life of fruitfulness," I assured him. In fact, by the grace of God — and to Him alone be the glory — for more than 25 years as a Christian I do not recall a single hour of broken fellowship with the Lord Jesus."

He was really shocked at that. "You mean you haven't sinned in 25 years?" he asked.

"No, that's not what I mean," I replied. "I have sinned, regrettably I have grieved and quenched the Spirit at times with impatience, anger, or some other expression of the flesh, but when I grieve the Spirit, I know exactly what to do. I confess my sin to God and immediately receive His forgiveness and cleansing, and by faith I continue to walk in the power and the fullness of the Holy Spirit."

This may sound presumptuous and perhaps even arrogant to some, yet this is the heritage of every believer. No one has to live in defeat. Otherwise, all the promises of God to this effect would be nullified. There would be no need for the Holy Spirit.

It is the work of the Holy Spirit to help us, as Paul writes: "So there is now no condemnation awaiting those who belong to Christ Jesus. For the power of the life-giving Spirit — and this power is mine through Christ Jesus — has freed me from the vicious circle of sin and death.

"We aren't saved from sin's grasp by knowing the commandments of God, because we can't and don't keep them, but God put into effect a different plan to save us. He sent his own Son in a human body like ours — except that ours are sinful — and destroyed sin's control over us by giving himself as a sacrifice for our sins. So now we can obey God's laws if we follow after the Holy Spirit and no longer obey the old evil nature within us.

"Those who let themselves be controlled by their lower natures live only to please themselves, but those who follow after the Holy Spirit find themselves doing those things that please God. Following after the Holy Spirit leads to life and peace, but following after the old nature leads to death, because the old sinful nature within us is against God.

"It never did obey God's laws and it never will. That's why those who are still under the control of their old sinful selves, bent on following their old evil desires, can never please God" (Romans 8:1-8, TLB).

On the authority of this and other similar passages of Scripture, you can know that you do not have to live an hour of defeat the rest of your life. God meant for you to live a life of victory, a life of power, love and joy. You can live in the fullness of the Spirit as a way of life if only you know your rights as a child of God and obey the leading of the Holy Spirit.

King David's Experience

King David is an excellent example of victory after defeat. Following his experience of the sins of adultery and murder, he finally came to his senses — like the prodigal son — and confessed his sins to God:

"What happiness for those whose guilt has been forgiven! What joys when sins are covered over! What relief for those who have confessed their sins and God has cleared their record.

"There was a time when I wouldn't admit what a sinner I was. But my dishonesty made me miserable and filled my days with frustration. All day and all night Your hand was heavy on me. My strength evaporated like water on a sunny day until I finally admitted all my sins to You and stopped trying to hide them. I said to myself, 'I will confess them to the Lord.' And You forgave me! All my guilt is gone.

"Now I say that each believer should confess his sins to God when he is aware of them, while there is time to be forgiven. Judgment will not touch him if he does" (Psalm 32:1-6, TLB).

Know Your Rights

In order to live the supernatural life which is available to us through the indwelling Holy Spirit, we need to know our rights as children of God. We need to know our spiritual heritage. We need to know how to draw upon the inexhaustible, supernatural resources of God's love, power, forgiveness and abundant grace.

The first step is to learn everything we can about God.

We also need to know about the nature of man and why he behaves as he does. The best way to learn who God is, who man is and about our rights as children of God is to spend much time — even at the sacrifice of other needs and demands on our schedules — in reading, studying, memorizing, meditating on the Word of God, and in prayer and witnessing.

Paul wrote to the Christians at Rome, "For His Holy Spirit speaks to us deep in our hearts, and tells us that we really are God's children. And since we are His children, we will share His treasures — for all God gives to His Son Jesus is now ours too. But if we are to share His glory, we must also share His suffering" (Romans 8:16, 17, TLB).

Look at what this means to us, both in our lives today and in the age to come. "For God has allowed us to know the secret of His plan, and it is this: He purposes in His sovereign will that all human history shall be consummated in Christ, that everything that exists in heaven or earth shall find its perfection and fulfillment in Him.

"And here is the staggering thing — that in all which will one day belong to Him we have been promised a share (since we were long ago destined for this by the one who achieves His purposes by His sovereign will)" (Ephesians 1:9-11, Phillips).

Every Need Supplied

If we have Christ, we have everything we need. "For I can do everything God asks me to with the help of Christ who gives me the strength and power" (Philippians 4:13, TLB).

We are complete in Jesus Christ; nothing is lacking, nothing remains for us to receive; there is nothing more beyond having the person of Jesus Christ in our lives. This glorious and wonderful truth was expressed by Paul to the Colossian church:

"This is what I have asked of God for you: that you will be encouraged and knit together by strong ties of love, and that you will have the rich experience of knowing Christ with real certainty and clear understanding.

"*For God's secret plan, now at last made known, is Christ Himself.* In Him lie hidden all the mighty, untapped treasures of wisdom and knowledge...just as you trusted Christ to save you, trust Him, too, for each day's problems; live in vital union with Him.

"Let your roots grow down into Him and draw up nourishment from Him. See that you go on growing in the Lord, and become strong and vigorous in the truth you were taught. Let your lives overflow with joy and thanksgiving for all He has done....

"For in Christ there is all of God in a human body; *so you have everything when you have Christ*, and you are filled with God through your union with Christ. He is the highest Ruler, with authority over every other power.

"When you came to Christ He set you free from your evil desires, not by a bodily operation of circumcision but by a spiritual operation, the baptism of your souls. For in baptism you see how your old, evil nature died with Him and was buried with Him; and then you came up out of death with Him into a new life because you trusted the Word of the mighty God who raised Christ from the dead.

"You were dead in sins, and your sinful desires were not yet cut away. Then He gave you a share in the very life of Christ, for He forgave all your sins, and blotted out the charges proved against you, the list of His commandments which you had not obeyed. He took this list of sins and destroyed it by nailing it to Christ's cross" (Colossians 2:2-14, TLB, italics added).

The Spirit of Christ Ministers To Us

Christ's strength is given to you to meet your every

need. How do we receive that strength, that supernatural power? As Christians, we have that potential within us, in the person of Christ's Holy Spirit. But sin hinders the working of the Holy Spirit in our lives.

By confessing all our known sin and appropriating that supernatural power of the Holy Spirit within us, we can, by faith, be filled and continue to be filled with the power of the Holy Spirit. Then, according to God's Word, the Holy Spirit ministers to our every need.

When we by faith are filled with the Holy Spirit, He guides us (John 16:13), empowers us (Micah 3:8), and makes us holy (Romans 15:16 and 2 Thessalonians 2:13). He bears witness in our lives (Romans 8:16 and Hebrews 10:15), comforts us (John 14:16-26), gives us joy (Romans 14:17), gives discernment (1 Corinthians 2:10-16 and 1 John 4:1-6), bears fruit in and through our lives (Galatians 5:22, 23) and gives us spiritual gifts for the building up of the Body of Christ (1 Corinthians 12:3-11).

As our teacher of spiritual truths, the Holy Spirit illuminates our minds with insights into the mind of Christ (1 Corinthians 2:12, 13 and Ephesians 1:16, 17) and reveals to us the hidden things of God (Isaiah 40:13, 14 and 1 Corinthians 2:10, 13).

Do you need Christ's strength in your life? Ask God, for "out of His glorious, unlimited resources He will give you the mighty inner strengthening of His Holy Spirit" (Ephesians 3:16, TLB).

Do you need love? The Lord Jesus Christ is the incarnation of love. Paul writes that our roots may "go down deep into the soil of God's marvelous love; and may you be able to feel and understand, as all God's children should, how long, how wide, how deep, and how high His love really is; and to experience this love for yourselves, (though it is so great that you will never see the end of it, or fully know or understand it)" (Ephesians 3:17-19, TLB)

Do you need peace? Christ is the "Prince of Peace."

"I am leaving you with a gift," said Jesus, "peace of mind and heart! And the peace I give isn't fragile like the peace the world gives" (John 14:27, TLB)

Do you need joy? Christ is joy. Do you need patience? Christ is patience. Do you need wisdom? Christ is wisdom. Are you in need of material possessions so that you can better serve Christ? They are available in Him, for God owns the "cattle on a thousand hills."

All that we need is to be found in Christ and nowhere else. The supernatural life is Christ. Paul experienced the glory of having Christ live in him, meeting all his needs: "I myself no longer live, but Christ lives in me. And the real life I now have within this body is a result of my trusting in the Son of God, who loved me and gave Himself for me" (Galatians 2:20, TLB).

But one cannot know the reality of being identified with Christ unless he is filled — empowered and controlled — by the Holy Spirit, because the Holy Spirit came to glorify Christ: "When the Holy Spirit, who is truth, comes...He shall praise Me and bring Me great honor by showing you My glory" (John 16:13, 14, TLB)›

Knowing Christ Better

Therefore, every Christian should give priority to seeking to know Christ better. We do this largely through spending much time with Him in reading and meditating on His Word, talking to Him in prayer, obeying His commands and telling others about Him.

One cannot really get to know Him well if any one of these four elements is missing from our daily lives. For example, consider and meditate on this exciting passage of Scripture explaining the practical benefits which can be experienced by every believer because of Christ's death for us on the cross.

Paul writes in Romans of our heritage and of what happened to us when we became Christians:

"Adam caused many to be sinners because he disobeyed God, and Christ caused many to be made acceptable to God because He obeyed. The Ten Commandments were given so that all could see the extent of their failure to obey God's laws.

"But the more we see our sinfulness, the more we see God's abounding grace forgiving us. Before, sin ruled over all men and brought them to death, but now God's kindness rules instead, giving us right standing with God and resulting in eternal life through Jesus Christ our Lord.

Sin's Power Broken

"Well then, shall we keep on sinning so that God can keep on showing us more and more kindness and forgiveness? Of course not! Should we keep on sinning when we don't have to? For sin's power over us was broken when we became Christians and were baptized to become a part of Jesus Christ: through His death the power of your sinful nature was shattered....

"Your old evil desires were nailed to the cross with Him, that part of you that loves to sin was crushed and fatally wounded, so that your sin- loving body is no longer under sin's control, no longer needs to be a slave to sin....

"So look upon your old sin nature as dead and unresponsive to sin, and instead be alive to God, alert to Him.... Do not let any part of your bodies become tools of wickedness to be used for sinning; but give yourselves completely to God — every part of you — for you are back from death and you want to be tools in the hands of God, to be used for His good purposes....

"Don't you realize that you can choose your own master? You can choose sin (with death) or else obedience (with acquittal). The one to whom you offer yourself — he will take you and be your master and you will be his slave" (Romans 5:19-21; 6:1-3, 6, 11, 13, 16, TLB).

Oh, how wonderful to know that these members of

our bodies — our eyes, our ears, our lips, our hands, our feet — can be used for the glory of God! When we entrust our entire bodies, our minds and our hearts to Jesus Christ, then, through the indwelling strength and guidance of the Holy Spirit, we begin to exercise our rights as children of God; we begin to live supernaturally.

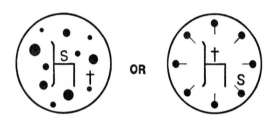

The Balanced Life

Art De Moss, whom I have mentioned previously, was one of the most dedicated and fruitful business executives I have ever known. He had a remarkable *balance* to his Christian life. For example, he gave God the first day of each week, the first hour of each day and the first part of each dollar earned.

Art was one of the most vigorous, zealous, consistent witnesses for Christ I have ever known. I traveled with him on numerous occasions. We would be having lunch or dinner together, when a waitress, the maitre d', or perhaps an acquaintance who recognized one of us would come to the table to talk. Within seconds, Art would be talking about that person's relationship with Jesus Christ. Many times, I have personally seen these people respond to Art's witness by expressing their desire to receive Christ.

It was the balance of Art's life that helped him to give

priority to evangelism, discipleship and helping to fulfill the Great Commission. Art had a vision for the world, and he invested his life and his resources in helping to accomplish that goal.

It is impossible to walk vigorously and contagiously in the Holy Spirit without spending time, unhurried time, in fellowship with the Lord in His Word — in prayer and in listening to Him for His directions for your daily activities as a basis for your daily witness for Christ.

On the other hand, apart from the regular sharing of your faith in Christ with others, Bible study and prayer alone can often lead to a spiritually frustrating, powerless and stagnant life.

After many years of working with thousands of Christians, I am convinced that a person cannot enjoy the supernatural life — which is a believer's heritage in Christ — apart from the proper balance between Bible study, prayer and sharing Christ with others out of the overflow of an obedient, Spirit-filled life. We need to be able not only to experience this great adventure with Christ ourselves, but also to share this good news with others.

A word of caution and reminder is in order at this point. We become spiritual and experience power from God and become fruitful in our witness as a result of *faith* and faith alone. The Bible clearly teaches that the "just shall live by faith" (Romans 1:17, KJ). However, it is equally important to know that works are the *result* of faith, and unless there are "good works" there is not "faith," for "faith without works is dead" (James 2:17, KJ).

The Results of Faith

Many Christians are confused on this point. They think of works (Bible study, prayer and other spiritual disciplines) as the *means* to, rather than the *result* of, the life of faith. They spend much time in Bible study and prayer.

They may even attempt to witness for Christ and to obey the various commands of God, thinking that by these means they will achieve supernatural living. But they remain defeated, frustrated, powerless and fruitless.

They feel that their problem is that they must not be doing enough, so they spend even more time in prayer and Bible study — all to no avail and leading to even greater frustration and defeat.

Bible study, prayer, witnessing and obedience are the *result* of the life of faith, not the *means* to it.

As you are filled with the Holy Spirit, the Bible becomes alive, prayer becomes vital, your witness becomes effective and obedience becomes a joy. Then, as a result of your obedience in these various areas, your faith grows and you become more mature in your spiritual life.

The Bible says, concerning the life of Abraham, "You see, he was trusting God so much that He was willing to do whatever God told him to; his faith was made complete by what he did, by his actions, his good deeds" (James 2:22, TLB).

Yes, Bible study, prayer and obedience are important, *vitally important*, but they should be regarded as the result — the overflow — of the life of faith, not as the means to faith. To live supernaturally is to live by faith in the faithfulness of God and the trustworthiness of His holy, inspired Word.

CHAPTER FIFTEEN

The Supernatural Power Of Faith

Occasionally, I hear people say that "Bill Bright is a man of great faith." The statement is made because our ministry frequently is involved with many thousands of churches of all denominations and other Christian organizations in gargantuan undertakings — massive worldwide programs of evangelism and discipleship in which we have by faith trusted God for the salvation of millions of souls.

At first I trusted Him for one soul, then six, then ten souls, then hundreds, thousands, millions and most recently, for a billion souls for Christ in the next ten years.

These goals are not built on careless presumptions or figures plucked out of the air in some kind of a mystical, emotional, spiritual experience, but they are based upon my confidence in the sovereignty, holiness, love, wisdom, power and grace of the omnipotent God whom I serve — and upon His gracious blessing upon past efforts that have been undertaken for His glory and praise. No credit should be given to me or to the ministry of which I am a part, but only to the One in whom I place my faith.

Faith must have an object, and the object of my faith is God and His inspired Word. The right view of God generates faith. Faith is like a muscle: it grows with exercise. The more we see God accomplish in and through our lives, the more we can be assured that He will accomplish as we trust and obey Him more.

There is nothing mysterious about faith. It is simply a matter of getting to know the God whom we worship, His holy inspired Word, claiming His promises, expecting the results of those promises, claimed by a life that lives in faith and obedience.

At one time in my life, I had little faith, as stated earlier. I could believe God only for small things, but with the passing of time, my knowledge of God has increased. My confidence in God and His Word has grown so that now I believe Him for great and mighty things.

Indeed, I now believe Him for the saturation of the entire world with the gospel, the necessary billions of dollars to make it possible, and the training of tens of millions of Christians to perform the task. But, it is not because of me or our devoted, consecrated staff now serving in more than 150 countries. It is because of my growing knowledge of and therefore trust in — God, and the fact that He chose to use us.

You see, God has not changed; He is the same yesterday, today and forever. The God to whom I prayed for little things is the same God to whom I now pray for great and mighty things. He has deigned to use human vessels.

Get to know God, master His Word, trust Him for great and mighty things and expect those things to happen. Faith unlocks the door to the supernatural resources of God. The eleventh chapter of Hebrews lists faith's hall of fame:

"These people all trusted God and as a result won battles, overthrew kingdoms, ruled their people well, and they received what God had promised them; they were kept from harm in a den of lions, and in a fiery furnace.

"Some, through their faith, escaped death by the sword. Some were made strong again after they had been weak or sick. Others were given great power in battle. They made whole armies turn and run away" (Hebrews 11:33, 34, TLB). Among these great warriors of faith were Abel, Enoch, Noah, Sarah, Jacob, Moses and Abraham.

Romans 4:20-23 records a model in faith. "But

Abraham never doubted. He believed God, for his faith and trust were strong, and he praised God for this blessing before it even happened. He was completely sure that God was well able to do anything He promised. And because of Abraham's faith God forgave his sins and called him just and good.

"Now this wonderful promise — that he was accepted and approved through his faith — wasn't just for Abraham's benefit. It was for us, too, assuring us that God will accept us in the same way He accepted Abraham — when we believe the promises of God Who brought back Jesus our Lord from the dead. He died for our sins and rose again to make us right with God, filling us with God's goodness" (TLB).

Live By Faith

How sad to see wonderful, sincere Christians who have been deceived by a wrong emphasis on emotions. I know of nothing that has caused so much defeat among Christians. We do not live by feelings — "we live by faith," the apostle Paul reminds us (Galatians 3:11, NAS). "Without faith it is impossible to please Him" (Hebrews 11:6, NAS). And this faith is a gift of God (Ephesians 2:8) that comes to us from the Holy Spirit (Galatians 5:22).

Valid emotional feelings are simply the by-product of faith and obedience. There is nothing wrong with feelings. Thank God we have them! Do not be ashamed of or minimize feelings, but do not seek them, either. Never emphasize them out of balance. To seek an emotional experience is contrary to God's command for us to live by faith. Not only that, it is an insult to God. Let emotions find their proper place in your relationship with Christ as you live in faith and obedience.

The apostle John records the words of Jesus who explained that the most valid way to have an emotional experience is to be obedient to Him. He said, "He who has My commandments, and keeps them, he it is who loves Me, and he who loves Me shall be loved by My Father, and I will love him, and will disclose (make real) Myself to him" (John 14:21, NAS).

One of the greatest acts of obedience is to live a holy life and share Christ with others in the power of the Holy Spirit. Matthew 4:19 records the Lord's command and promise: "Follow Me and I will make you fishers of men." Again, in John 15:8, we read of Christ's great concern for our faithfulness to perpetuate the evangelism which He began.

Since He came to seek and to save the lost and has commissioned us to witness for Him, nothing could please the Savior more. If you want a valid, vital, exciting awareness of Christ in your experience, begin to share Christ with others as a way of life as you walk in the Spirit.

Emotional Counterfeits

Avoid man-made emotionalism that is generated by resorting to tricks and manipulations of individuals. Many such emotional experiences are a counterfeit of the genuine experience which can be yours through obedience to Christ, as Lord and Savior.

We live according to God's promise, trusting in the integrity of God Himself. As we have already discovered, faith must have an object. And the object of our faith as Christians is God and His Word. God has proven Himself to be worthy of our trust.

Thousands of promises for us are contained in God's Word, and no Christian has ever found any one of them to be untrue. When God says something, you can stake your life on the fact that whatever He says is true. You can know that He will not fail you.

Give Thanks By Faith

God promises us: "All things work together for good

to those who love God, to those who are called according to His purpose" (Romans 8:28, NAS). Do you believe this promise of God? If so, you logically acknowledge the reasonableness of this command of God, too: "In everything give thanks; for this is God's will for you in Christ Jesus" (1 Thessalonians 5:18, NAS).

Have you learned to say, "Thank You, Lord," when a loved one dies? "Thank You for all the years together." Do you thank God when your body is wracked with pain? "Thank you for sparing my life." When you receive a "Dear John" letter ending a love relationship? "Thank you that you know the future." When you have financial reverses? When you fail an exam? When you are unemployed? Do you thank God when you are discriminated against personally, religiously, racially or because of your sex or age?

You may say that only a fool would give thanks to God under such circumstances. No, not if all things really do work together for good to those who love God, to those who are called according to His purpose.

If God has commanded us to give thanks, there is a reason for it. Let me assure you, as one who has had more than 25 years of experience in this area, this is one of the most exciting lessons I have ever learned — the lesson of saying "Thank You" when things go wrong, as well as in response to God's many gracious gifts and blessings.

A Better Plan

Before I made this discovery, I used to lose my patience when things did not go my way. I would often force open those "closed doors," if necessary. And, if they did not open before me, I tried to break them down. I was often tense inside and impatient with others who did not agree with me. Then I discovered what a fool I was.

Oh, how tragically we can injure our brothers and sisters in Christ with our impatience, our criticism, our thoughtlessness. Christians often act this way and the entire body of Christ suffers as a result.

But God has given us a better way. We can relax. We can say "Thank You" when the whole world is crumbling down around us, because our God is sovereign and all-powerful. He holds the world in His hands, and we can trust Him. He loves us. And He promises to fight for us.

He has commanded us to cast all of our cares upon Him, for He cares for us (1 Peter 5:7). He personally visited planet earth and took upon Himself our sins. Now, He is waiting to bless and use us. But He cannot bless and use us if we are carnal, worried and unbelieving. He will not bless and use us if we complain, criticize and find fault with Him and others whom He commands us to love.

When Difficulties Come

A pastor once came to me for counsel because of a conflict he was having with his church board. As a result of their rift, he had become embittered, resentful and fearful that he might lose his ministry. His anxiety had become so bad that he developed ulcers, and he had become totally ineffective as a pastor.

As this troubled pastor related how the conflict with his board had developed, it became apparent to me that he had lost his trust in God's will and ability to work in his life and in the lives of his board members. So I shared with him two vital passages of Scripture.

The first was the promise of Romans 8:28: "And we know that all that happens to us is working for our good if we love God and are fitting into His plans" (TLB).

The second verse was 1 Thessalonians 5:18: "No matter what happens, always be thankful, for this is God's will for you who belong to Christ Jesus" (TLB).

A Lack of Trust

The pastor admitted that he had not been trusting

God to work out this particular situation for the good, nor had he thanked the Lord for His many blessings in spite of the difficult time he was going through.

I explained to the pastor that it really did not matter whether or not the board was wrong in their position in this instance, but that he, the pastor, was wrong for his resentment and bitterness toward them.

Then I asked him if he would like to pray with me and by faith claim the promises of the Scripture. He said, "Yes," so we knelt and prayed. As he prayed from the depths of his heart, tears began to stream down his face. He confessed to the Lord his lack of trust and his un-thankfulness, and asked God to forgive him and to restore fellowship between them — with his board members as well.

A Miracle

When the pastor came to see me the next morning, he had a radiant smile on his face.

"I slept peacefully last night for the first time in months," said. "God has truly worked a miracle in my life."

God can work in your life the same way he worked in that pastor's life. Whatever may be your experience, God is waiting to help you. Do you have resentment, bitterness, fear or anxiety in your life? Are you having difficulty in your family relationships or with other Christians or non-believers? If so, are you willing to say to the Lord, "I know that all things do work together for good to those who love You and for those who are called according to Your purpose. And I do, by an act of my will by faith, demonstrate that I trust You by saying, 'Thank You,' even in the midst of my present circumstances."

While writing this chapter, a Christian business executive came to me in tears. The doctor had just discovered that the executive's loved one had a brain tumor and advised an immediate operation. My visitor had heard me speak on the importance of "giving thanks in all things" and had come for prayer.

We knelt together and thanked and praised God by faith. Neither one of us felt "joyful." In fact, we were both weeping, but we knew that God honors faith and there is no better way to tell God we trust Him than to praise and thank Him — even when our hearts are broken.

My friend and his family are willing to trust their loved one in the hands of our loving heavenly Father who makes no mistakes.

Those are but two examples. Hundreds of similar stories could be told of Christians whose lives have been transformed by learning the simple lesson of saying "Thank You" in all things.

The Ministry at Stake

Though I have shared this story before, it is worth telling again because it was such a dramatic experience in my life and so important to our ministry.

Some years ago, when there was a desperate need for more than a half million dollars toward the purchase of Arrowhead Springs, the Campus Crusade for Christ international headquarters, the future of a great worldwide ministry was at stake. Because of a technicality, our financial world had crumbled and there appeared to be no hope. The whole ministry was in danger of being destroyed, and my own reputation would be shattered.

When word came to me from a friend that the money which we had been promised was no longer available, I fell to my knees and prayed, "Lord, what am I to do?" Opening my Bible to look for help and assurance, I was reminded that all things work together for good to those who love God; that the just shall live by faith. Too, I read the command from God to give thanks in everything.

God Is Faithful

So, in obedience to His command, I thanked God for what had happened. Through my tears, I thanked Him that in His wisdom and love He knew better than I what should be done, and that out of this chaos and uncertainty would come a miraculous solution to our problem. There on my knees, while I was still giving thanks for this great disappointment, God began to give me the genuine assurance that this miracle was really going to happen. Within ten days, God did provide an almost unbelievable solution to our problem — a miracle. He demonstrated once again that, when we trust Him, He is faithful and worthy of our trust.

Trust God More

One of the greatest lessons I have learned — one of the greatest privileges of my life — is to trust God. I encourage you to major in learning how to walk by faith. I am still learning, and I am confident that one day I shall be able to trust God for infinitely greater things than I am now able to trust Him for.

What a great opportunity is ours to walk with the King of kings every day of our lives, from the time we awaken in the morning until we go to bed at night.

For many years, it has been my practice to begin my day the night before by reading God's Word and meditating upon the attributes and trustworthiness of our wonderful Lord before I go to sleep at night. Then throughout the night watches, when my subconscious mind takes over, I am thinking about Christ. So when I awaken in the morning, my first thoughts are of Him.

Usually a Psalm of praise is in my heart and on my lips, with an attitude of thanksgiving: "Oh, Lord, I thank You that I belong to You. I thank You that You live within me, and I thank You that You have forgiven my sins. I thank You that I am Your child.

"Now, as I begin this day, as I continue throughout the day, I invite You to walk around in my body, to love with my heart, to speak with my lips and to think with my mind.

"I thank You that, during the course of the day, You promised to do greater things through me than You did when You were here on the earth. By faith, I acknowledge Your greatness, Your power, Your authority in my life, and I invite You to do anything You wish in and through me for Your own great glory."

Then I would drop to my knees, as a formal act of acknowledging His lordship. That begins the day right, walking in the fullness of His power. Oh, what an adventure awaits those who trust in the Lord and obey His commands!

In the words of the Psalmist, "Oh, the joys of those who do not follow evil men's advice, who do not hang around with sinners, scoffing at the things of God: But they delight in doing everything God wants them to, and day and night are always meditating on His laws and thinking about ways to follow Him more closely.

"They are like trees along a river bank bearing luscious fruit each season without fail. Their leaves shall never wither, and all they do shall prosper" (Psalm 1:1-3, TLB).

Moment By Moment

In summary, may I remind you that if you desire to live supernaturally, to walk moment by moment, day by day, in the fullness and power of God's Holy Spirit, you must:

First, be sure that you are filled with the Spirit, by faith — on the basis of God's command to be filled and by claiming His promise that, if we ask according to His will, He will hear and answer.

Second, be prepared for spiritual conflict. The enemy is a real foe to be reckoned with. The world, the flesh and the devil will assail.

Third, know that the Holy Spirit guarantees your rights as a child of God. Our strength must come from the Lord. We must abide in Him.

And finally, live by faith, drawing daily upon His strength, His wisdom, His power and His love, giving thanks in all things.

Do you want to live supernaturally but lack the faith to trust the Holy Spirit to empower you and control you? Faith, while a gift of God (Ephesians 2:8), is also mentioned in the Bible as part of the fruit of the Spirit (faithfulness) (Galatians 5:22). Thus, it is a Christian trait that can be developed in a day-to-day, moment-by-moment walk with the Holy Spirit.

CHAPTER SIXTEEN

Fruit Of The Spirit

One morning, as I was speaking to our new staff on the importance of being filled with the Spirit, I explained that the power of God is available to them by faith, even as new Christians, to be witnesses for Christ. However, they should not expect to become mature Christians the moment they claim by faith the fullness of the Spirit.

The growth of the Spirit and the maturing of the fruit in the life of the believer (Galatians 5:22) takes time, much like our physical lives. We are born babies, and we are not even able to take care of ourselves.

A good example of this concerns our older son, Zachary. When he was only a few days old, my wife, Vonette, asked me to watch him. She left, and I sat down beside the bed where little Zachary lay.

Being very tired and afraid that I would go to sleep, I took the baby in my arms so he would not roll off the bed while I was asleep. Then I went to sleep with him in my arms.

Later, when Vonette came back, she laughed at how naive I was. Here was Zachary, just a baby, who had neither strength nor ability to move one inch from where he had been laid. He couldn't possibly have fallen off the bed.

As Zachary grew older, he was able to roll over, then sit up. After several months he could crawl. Then he made attempts to stand, and he would fall and pick himself up and hold on to the side of the crib. When he reached the place where he could take a step or two, we were elated at his progress.

Finally, he could walk across the room from Vonette's protective arms to my protective arms, and we were ecstatic. Soon he began to walk more steadily, and finally he learned to run. Now as a grown man, Zachary runs several miles a day.

We start out as babies, grow into childhood, young adolescence, and finally into mature adults — *physically*.

In like manner, we start out as spiritual babies and grow through childhood, adolescence and into spiritual maturity. The process is different in the life of each believer, and the time schedule is not the same for any two believers. In fact, tragically, most Christians today identify themselves with the believers in Corinth, referred to in 2 Corinthians 3 as "baby Christians."

The Joy of First Love

Oftentimes, new Christians are even more contagious and more convincing than they are later, after they have been influenced by some of the older Christians who have become carnal and lost their joy and their first love.

The fruit of the Spirit is something that is produced and developed with time, and it matures with experience as the Christian learns to trust and obey God and learn the truths of the Scriptures.

Many Christians, especially the newly born, are unable to love, unable to experience joy and peace consistently. They stumble and fall like a young child learning to walk. They do not understand that this is natural for a new, baby Christian. They become discouraged and sometimes give up.

"I can't live the Christian life," they say. "I may as well just forget it." Actually, new Christians who have these problems are simply experiencing what every normal new Christian goes through. But this is not to say that we should do nothing about it.

We should never be satisfied with remaining babies, or being carnal. Whenever there is obvious sin in our lives, it must be confessed, and whenever we become consciously aware that we are not controlled by the Spirit, we should breathe spiritually.

At the same time, we should not be impatient with our immaturity. We should never compare our spirituality with someone who may have walked with the Lord for a longer period of time.

When we do fail to exercise those mature qualities of love, joy, peace, patience, goodness, kindness, faithfulness, gentleness and self-control, we should not give up. Rather, we should simply turn more quickly to the Lord for His supernatural strength that is always available, asking Him to enable us to live the kind of life He has called us to live.

Then, we need to be patient with ourselves and not be influenced by circumstances, but keep our eyes on the Lord, drawing on the supernatural power of the Spirit and claiming the promises in His inspired Word.

My saintly mother, who lived to be 93 years of age, became a Christian when she was 16. Immediately, she determined to become a woman of God with the help of the Holy Spirit. Through the years, as I observed her attitudes and actions closely, I never heard her say an unkind or critical word, nor did I see her do anything that reflected negatively on the Lord.

As a result, my life has been affected in a very positive way. There is no question in my mind that everything God has done and ever will do in and through me will, in no small measure, be a result of those unique, godly qualities of my mother, especially her prayers.

Yet, in today's world, there is considerable criticism of the woman who finds her fulfillment as a wife, mother and homemaker, as though such roles are demeaning to the woman. The popular thought is that there is something better — such as a professional career.

I would not minimize that there are gifted women who should be involved in business and professional life, but in most cases this would be a secondary role compared to the privilege of being a mother, especially a godly Christian mother in whose life the fruit of the Spirit is demonstrated.

What I can say about the qualities of my mother, I believe that my sons could say about their mother, for Vonette has demonstrated those same godly, Christlike qualities as a mother — and to me as a wife. Her prayers, her example and her influence will no doubt be to our sons the same kind of inspiration that the life of my mother has been to me.

These two examples underscore a wonderful, basic truth of supernatural living: As we continue to live supernaturally, walking in the power and under the guidance and control of the Holy Spirit, the personality and character of Christ become more and more a part of us, expressed in what we say and in what we do. This obvious change in our lives is the practical proof that we are children of God and that we are filled with His Spirit.

The Single Fruit

The Christlike qualities seen in spiritual Christians are referred to in the Bible as the "fruit of the Spirit." The apostle Paul explains, "When the Holy Spirit controls our lives He will produce this kind of fruit in us: love, joy, peace, patience, kindness, goodness, faithfulness, gentleness and self control" (Galatians 5:22, 23, TLB).

Technically, this passage is constructed in the original Greek language to mean there is a *single* fruit of the Spirit — *love*. This love, however, is manifested in our attitudes and actions as joy, peace, patience, kindness, goodness, faithfulness, gentleness and self-control.

Literally, the verse could be translated: "When the Holy Spirit controls our lives, He will produce this kind of fruit in us: love, joy-love, peace-love, patience-love, kindness-love, goodness-love, faithfulness-love, gentleness-love and self-control-love."

The Open Bible explains in the notes to Galatians 5:22: "The fruit of the Spirit is love. Only as we live in love can we fulfill the will of God in our lives. The believer must become love-inspired, love-mastered and love-driven. Without the fruit of the Spirit (love), we are just a religious noise.

"The fruit of the Spirit is love, and it is manifested in joy, peace, patience, kindness, goodness, faithfulness, gentleness and self-control:

"Joy is love's strength.

"Peace is love's security.

"Patience is love's endurance.

"Kindness is love's conduct.

"Goodness is love's character.

"Faithfulness is love's confidence.

"Gentleness is love's humility.

"Self-control is love's victory.

"Against such things there is no law.

"A Holy Spirit-controlled man needs no law to cause him to live a righteous life. The secret of a Spirit-controlled life is found in dedication to God. Put your all on the altar (Romans 12:1), and the Holy Spirit will fill your heart with the love of God."

As pointed out earlier, these manifestations of love are the *result* of being filled with the Holy Spirit by faith, and not the *means* of becoming Spirit-filled. This is to say that you cannot become Spirit-filled and live the Christian life by *trying* in your inadequate human strength to be a holy and righteous person.

Many *non*-Christians live fine, moral, ethical lives. But only Christ in you — His indwelling Holy Spirit — can enable you to live supernaturally and to produce spiritual fruit.

Strength in Christ

The apostle Paul says, "I want to remind you that your strength must come from the Lord's mighty power within you" (Ephesians 6:10, TLB). Jesus Christ, in all of His mighty resurrection power, lives in all of us who have become children of God through faith in Christ (Romans 8; Ephesians 1:19-25; Colossians 1:27-2:10). We do not have any strength in ourselves.

As a young man in college and later in business, I used to be very self- sufficient — proud of what I could do on my own. I believed that a man could do just about anything he wanted to do through his own effort, if he were willing to pay the price of hard work and sacrifice, and I experienced some degree of success.

Then, when I became a Christian, the Bible introduced me to a whole new philosophy of life — a life of trusting God for His promises. That new life of faith in God replaced my old life of self-sufficiency. It took me a while to see the fallacy and inadequacy of trying to serve God in my own strength and ability.

Now, I realize how totally incapable I am of living the Christian life — how really weak I am in my own strength, and yet how strong I am in Christ. We do not lay aside our God-given gifts and talents. We give them back to Him in service.

As Paul says, "I can do all things through Him (Christ) who strengthens me" (Philippians 4:13, NAS). "God has not given us a spirit of fear; but of power, and of love, and of a sound mind" (2 Timothy 1:7, KJ).

In John 15, the Lord stresses the importance of drawing our strength from Him: "Take care to live in Me, and let Me live in you. For a branch cannot produce fruit when severed from the vine. Nor can you be fruitful apart from Me. Yes, I am the vine; you are the branches. Whoever lives in Me and I in him shall produce a large crop of fruit. For apart from Me, you can't do a thing" (John 15:4, 5, TLB).

In our own strength we are helpless, powerless. We are like branches cut off from the vine if we try to live our lives in our own strength and ability, but God gives ability empowered by Him and stretched by Him. If we abide in Christ and He abides in us, it is His life-giving power that is expressed through us and enables us to live and witness for Him.

According to the Lord Jesus, the only way we can show that we are truly following Him is to produce fruit, which includes introducing others to the Savior as well as living holy lives. And the only way we can produce fruit is through the indwelling power of the Holy Spirit.

In the next several chapters, we will look at the many Christlike characteristics which are available to the Christian who lives supernaturally, under the guidance and empowering of the Holy Spirit.

CHAPTER SEVENTEEN

Love: God's Greatest Gift

A dear friend and Christian leader hated and resented his father, who was an alcoholic. Through the years, my friend had been humiliated and embarrassed by his father's conduct. He wanted nothing to do with him.

As he grew more and more mature in his faith, and the Christlike qualities began to develop in his life, he began to realize that his attitude toward his father was wrong. He knew well that God's Word commanded him to love and honor his mother and father, with no conditions.

Then he began to comprehend and experience the truth of loving by faith after a message he had heard me give. As a result, he went to his father and, as an act of the will, by faith — because at that point he did not honestly feel like doing so — he expressed his love. He was amazed to discover that his father had been hurt for years because he had sensed that his son had despised and rejected him.

When the son began to demonstrate love for him — to let him know that he cared for him, whether he drank or did not drink — this prompted the father to commit his life to Christ and to trust Him to help him overcome the problem which had plagued him most of his life. Through this new relationship with the Lord, he became a new creature and was able to gain victory over the addiction to alcohol several years before he died, a dramatic example of the power of love.

Love Never Fails

Everybody wants to be loved. Most psychologists agree that man's greatest need is to love and be loved. No barrier can withstand the mighty force of love — God's love. Love never fails!

One reason that love never fails is because love is reciprocal, as in the case of the young man who began to express love to the hard heart of his father, and the father began to reciprocate by expressing love. He loved his son — and others — and, in his efforts to demonstrate his love with God's love, he sought to overcome the evil habit that had kept him in bondage for many years. Love is reciprocal!

If you have problems with any person, I can assure you that if you begin to love him by faith and have opportunity to demonstrate that love in a practical way, you will soon gain a friend.

What is Love?

Three Greek words are translated by the one English word, *Love*. *Eros* is a word that suggests sensual desire. It does not appear in the New Testament. *Phileo* is used for friendship, or love for one's friends or relatives, and conveys a sense of loving someone because he is worthy of our love. *Agape* (ah-*gop*-ay) is God's love — the purest, deepest kind of love — expressed not through mere emotions, but as an act of one's will.

It is God's supernatural love for us revealed supremely through the Lord's death on the cross for our sins and the supernatural love He wants to produce in us, and through us to others, by His Holy Spirit. *Agape is love because of the character of the person loving, rather than because the object of that love is worthy. Oftentimes it is love "in spite of" rather than "because."*

A New Commandment

The Lord Jesus gave to His disciples — and through them to us and to all believers — a new commandment: "Love each other just as much as I love you" (John 13:34, TLB). What kind of love?

Agape — God's love.

It is the very same love that God the Father expresses for His only begotten Son, the Lord Jesus Christ. It is the very same love that Jesus demonstrated by dying on the cross for us, for our sins. It is this same divine, supernatural, unconditional, everlasting, unchangeable love that God offers to us and which He commands us to have for one another.

This promised love is not merely an emotional experience. It is a divine, supernatural power originating with the Father and coming from Him to the Son through the ministry of the Holy Spirit to us and to the world.

The Importance of Love

bThe apostle Paul, through the inspiration of the Holy Spirit, underscores the importance of *agape* love in his first letter to the Corinthian Christians. In this remarkably beautiful passage of Scripture, Paul reminds us that, apart from love, we can do nothing of real value for God or man.

Paul writes, "If I had the gift of being able to speak in other languages without learning them, and could speak in every language there is in all of heaven and earth, but didn't love others, I would only be making noise.

"If I had the gift of prophecy and knew all about what is going to happen in the future, knew everything about everything, but didn't love others, what good would it do? Even if I had the gift of faith so that I could speak to a mountain and make it move, I would still be worth nothing at all without love.

"If I gave everything I have to poor people, and *if I were burned alive for preaching the Gospel but didn't love others, it would be of no value whatever*" (1 Corinthians 13:1-3, TLB, italics added).

No matter what we do for God and for others, it is of no value unless we are motivated by God's love — for God and for others.

But what is the *agape* love? How does this kind of supernatural love express itself?

Love Is. . .

Paul continues by describing this kind of love as the greatest thing in the world. "Love is very patient and kind, never jealous or envious, never boastful or proud, never haughty or selfish or rude.

"Love does not demand its own way. It is not irritable or touchy. It does not hold grudges and will hardly even notice when others do it wrong. It is never glad about injustice, but rejoices whenever truth wins out.
b"If you love someone you will be loyal to him no matter what the cost. You will always believe in him, always expect the best of him, and always stand your ground in defending him.

"All the special gifts and powers from God will some-day come to an end, but love goes on forever. . . . There are three things that remain — faith, hope and love — that keep on forever; but the greatest of these is love."

Through the heart and pen of the apostle Paul, the Holy Spirit goes on to admonish us, "*Let love be your greatest aim*" (1 Corinthians 13:4-14:1, TLB, italics added).

Every person needs to know five things about love: first, God loves you; second, you are commanded by God to love; third, you cannot love in your own strength; fourth, you can love with God's love; and, fifth, you can love by faith.

God Loves You

God loves you with *agape* love — the love described in 1 Corinthians 13. He loves us so much that He sent His Son to die on the cross for us, that we might have everlasting life (John 3:16).

"His love is not based on performance. Christ loves

us so much that, while we were yet sinners, He died for us" (Romans 5:8, NAS). His love for us is *unconditional* and *undeserved.*

God loves us *in spite of* our disobedience, our weakness, our sin and our selfishness. He loves us enough to provide a way to eternal life (which we can actually live supernaturally right now).

The cross clearly demonstrates the highest expression of unconditional love. From the cross Christ cried out, "Father, forgive them for they know not what they are doing" (Luke 23:34, NAS).

If God loved those of us who are sinners that much, can you imagine how much He loves those who are His children through faith in Christ and who seek to please Him?

Never forget: God's love for you is perfect and complete. Nothing you could ever do would cause God to love you more or less.

God's Love is Constant

The early Christians endured persecution, hardships and unbelievable suffering. Yet Paul wrote to them, "Who then can ever keep Christ's love from us? When we have trouble or calamity, when we are hunted down or destroyed, is it because He doesn't love us anymore? And if we are hungry, or penniless, or in danger, or threatened with death, has God deserted us?

"No, for the Scriptures tell us that for His sake we must be ready to face death at every moment of the day — we are like sheep awaiting slaughter; but despite all this, overwhelming victory is ours through Christ who loved us enough to die for us.

"For I am convinced that nothing can ever separate us from His love. Death can't, and life can't. The angels won't, and all the powers of hell itself cannot keep God's love away.

"Our fears for today, our worries about tomorrow, or

where we are — high above the sky, or in the deepest ocean — nothing will ever be able to separate us from the love of God demonstrated by our Lord Jesus Christ when He died for us" (Romans 8:35-39, TLB).

Such love is beyond our ability to grasp with our minds, but it is not beyond our ability to experience with our hearts. God's love is unconditional and it is constant — because He is perfect and therefore His love is perfect, too.

Command to Love

The Scriptures tell of a certain lawyer who asked Jesus, "Sir, which is the most important command in the law of Moses?" Jesus replied, "'Love the Lord your God with all your heart, soul and mind.' This is the first and greatest commandment. The second most important is similar: 'Love your neighbor as much as you love yourself.' b"All the other commandments and all the demands of the prophets stem from these two laws and are fulfilled if you obey them. Keep only these and you will find that you are obeying all the others" (Matthew 22:36-40, TLB).

Why Love God?

The question may come to your mind, "Why does God want our love?" From a human standpoint, this could appear selfish and egotistical. But God in His sovereignty and love has so created man that he finds his greatest joy and fulfillment when he loves God with all his heart and soul and mind and his neighbor as himself.

Early in my Christian life, I was troubled over the command to love God so completely. How could I ever measure up to such a high standard? Two very important considerations have helped me to want to love and please Him completely.

First, the Holy Spirit has filled my heart with God's

love, as promised in the Scriptures: "For we know how dearly God loves us, and we feel this warm love everywhere within us because God has given us the Holy Spirit to fill our hearts with His love" (Romans 5:5, TLB).

Second, by meditating on the wonderful things God has done and is doing for me, I find my love for Him growing. I love Him because He first loved me (1 John 4:19).

We are to love God. We are to love our neighbors. We are to love our enemies. We are to love our family members. And, we are to love ourselves with God's kind of love.

Loving God First

Since the greatest commandment is to love God, we are to give Him our first love, never allowing anyone or anything to come before Him. But, supernaturally, we are to express *agape* love to others — a love no less in its quality and magnitude than that which we express toward God. In the same way, God loves all His children perfectly: He loves you and me just as much as He loves His Son, the Lord Jesus Christ (John 17:23).

The person who has not yet learned to love God and to seek Him above all else and all others is to be pitied. Such a person is only denying himself the blessings that await all who love God with all their heart, soul and mind.

Love Demonstrated

This deep insight into the love and trustworthiness of God was revealed to John, the beloved apostle, as recorded in his first letter in the Bible:

"We know how much God loves us because we have felt His love and because we believe Him when He tells us that He loves us dearly. God is love, and anyone who lives in love is living with God and God is living in him.

"And as we live with Christ, our love grows more perfect and complete; so we will not be ashamed and embarrassed at the day of judgment, but can face Him with confidence and joy, because He loves us and we love Him too. We need have no fear of someone who loves us perfectly; His perfect love for us eliminates all dread of what He might do to us.

"If we are afraid, it is for fear of what He might do to us, and shows that we are not fully convinced that He really loves us. So you see, our love for Him comes as a result of His loving us first" (1 John 4:16-19, TLB).

Loving Your Neighbors

It is natural for us to fulfill the command to love our neighbors as ourselves if we truly love God with all our heart, soul and mind. If we are properly related to God, vertically, we will be properly related to our fellow man, horizontally.

The apostle Paul explains this by saying, "If you love your neighbor as much as you love yourself, you will not want to harm or cheat him, or kill him or steal from him. And you won't sin with his wife or want what is his, or do anything else the Ten Commandments say is wrong.

"All ten are wrapped up in this one, to love your neighbor as you love yourself. Love does no wrong to anyone. That's why it fully satisfies all of God's requirements" (Romans 13:9, 10, TLB).

It is love for God and for men that results in righteousness, in fruit and in glory to Christ.

Love Your Enemies

Jesus said, "There is a saying, 'Love your friends and hate your enemies.' But I say: 'Love your enemies! Pray for those who persecute you!' In that way you will be acting as true sons of your Father in heaven.

"For He gives His sunlight to both the evil and the good and sends rain on the just and on the unjust too. If you are friendly only to your friends, how are you different from anyone else? Even the heathen do that" (Matthew 5:43-45, 47, TLB).

You may rightly ask, "How does loving our neighbors relate to the problems of war, race, capital and labor?" The answer is so obvious and simple that we have missed it in our frenzied quest for solutions.

When Christians begin to act like Christians and love God, love their neighbors as themselves, love their enemies and especially love their Christian brothers — regardless of color, race or class — we will see society change for the better. Then the world will marvel when they see our loving attitudes and actions, "How those Christians *love* everyone!"

Love Yourself

Some people have difficulty understanding God's command to love our neighbors as ourselves. They wonder what it means to love ourselves. The Scriptures warn against those who in the last days will be lovers of themselves rather than lovers of God (2 Timothy 3:2-4).

Obviously these two portions of Scripture are talking about different kinds of love. The love referred to in 2 Timothy applies to the natural and the carnal men who, in arrogance and pride, seek their own interests contrary to the will and way of God.

Agape love — God's love — enables the Christian to apply the truths of 1 Corinthians 13 to his own life, even as he applies them toward his neighbors. Since God is patient and kind and forgiving toward us, we should also be patient and kind and forgiving toward ourselves and our neighbors, as we are enabled to be by His power.

Many students and older adults I counsel with are not able to accept themselves. Some are weighted down with guilt because of unconfessed sins. Others are not reconciled to their physical handicaps or deformities. Still others feel inferior mentally or socially.

My counsel to such people is this: God loves you and accepts you as you are. The love of Christ shed abroad in our hearts by the Holy Spirit enables us to love ourselves as God made us — being thankful for ourselves, loving ourselves unconditionally as God does, loving others unconditionally. Then we should focus our love and attention on Christ and on others; begin to lose ourselves in service for Him and for our fellow man.

Love Your Family

The great tragedy of many families is that resentment, bitterness and hate overtake their members like an all-consuming cancer, ultimately destroying the unity among husband, wife and children.

Love of the husband and wife for each other, and of parents and children for one another, is so basic that it should not need to be mentioned. Yet, sadly — and alarmingly — children are alienated from their parents, and marriages are ending in divorce, in greater numbers today than in any time in history.

Why? Because of financial problems. Because of sexual maladjustment. Because of differences in philosophy of living. And the list of excuses goes on and on. But these are really only the symptoms. The true cause is lack of love for one another.

God's kind of love is a unifying force. Paul admonishes us to "put on love, which is the perfect bond of unity" (Colossians 3:14, NAS), that our "hearts may be encouraged, having been welded together in love" (Colossians 2:2, NAS). Only God's universal love can break through the troublesome barriers that are created by human differences.

Only a common devotion to Christ — the source of love — can ease tension, erase mistrust, encourage openness, bring out the best in people and enable them to serve Christ together in a more fruitful way.

A mother shared how the discovery of learning to love enabled her to be more patient and kind to her husband and children. "The children were driving me out of my mind with all of their childish demands. I was irritable with them and, because I was so miserable, I was a critical and nagging wife. No wonder my husband found excuses to work late at the office. It is all different now; God's love fills our home."

A husband reported, "My wife and I have fallen in love all over again, and I am actually enjoying working in my office with men whom I couldn't stand before I learned to love."

You Can't Love in Your Own Strength

Just as surely as "those who are in the flesh (carnal persons) cannot please God" (Romans 8:8, NAS), we in our own strength cannot love as we should. This absence of the practice of God's love is widespread. Many of us refuse to love certain other people. We love only those who are easy to love.

Why can't we love the ones who are unattractive, or peculiar, or grouchy, or disagreeable or who don't love us? Because in our natural ability, we have neither the power nor the motivation to love them.

We cannot demonstrate *agape* love, God's unconditional love for others, through our own efforts. How many times have you resolved that you would love someone? How many times have you tried to manufacture some kind of positive, loving emotion toward someone for whom you felt nothing?

It is impossible, isn't it? In your own strength it is not possible to love with God's kind of love. By nature, we are not patient and kind. By nature, we are jealous, envious and boastful. We are proud, haughty, selfish and rude and we demand our own way.

We could never love others the way God loves us. But when Christ comes into our lives and we become Christians, God gives us individually the equipment to be a different kind of person.

With the motivation, He also gives us the ability. He provides us with a new kind of love altogether.

Love With God's Love

It was God's kind of love that brought us to Christ. It is this kind of love that is able to sustain and encourage us each day. Through His love in us, we can bring others to Christ and minister to fellow believers as God has commanded.

God's love was supremely expressed in the life of Jesus Christ. We have a perfect, complete picture of God's kind of love in the birth, personality, teachings, life and death and resurrection of His Son.

How does this love enter our own lives? It becomes ours when God comes to indwell us with His Holy Spirit the moment we receive Jesus Christ. The Scriptures say, "We feel this warm love everywhere within us because God has given us the Holy Spirit to fill our hearts with His love" (Romans 5:5, TLB).

God is Spirit and the "fruit of the Spirit is love" (Galatians 5:22, NAS). When we are controlled by the Holy Spirit, we can love with God's love.

But how do we make love a practical reality in our lives? How do we love? By resolutions? By self-imposed discipline? No. The only way to love is explained in my final point.

You Can Love By Faith

Everything about the Christian life is based on faith. We love by faith just as we received Christ by faith, just as we walk by faith and just as we are filled with the Holy Spirit by faith.

If the fruit of the Spirit is love, we may logically ask if it is not enough to be filled with the Spirit. This will be true from God's point of view, but it will not always be true in our actual experience.

Many Christians have loved with God's love and have demonstrated the fruit of the Spirit in their lives, who have not consciously or specifically claimed His love by faith. Yet, without being consciously aware of the fact, they were indeed loving by faith and therefore did not find it necessary to claim God's love by faith as a specific act.

The Bible reminds us, "Without faith it is impossible to please Him" (Hebrews 11:6, NAS). Obviously there will be no demonstration of God's love where there is no faith.

Power to Love

Do you have difficulty in loving others? Jesus reminds us in the gospel account of John of the importance of loving one another: "And so I am giving a new commandment to you now — love each other just as much as I love you. Your strong love for each other will prove to the world that you are My disciples" (John 15:34, 35, TLB).

Therefore, we know that it is God's will — even *His command* — for us to love. We also know that He would not command us to do something that He will not enable us to do.

In 1 John 5:14, 15, God *promises* that if we ask anything according to His will, He hears and answers us. Relating this promise to God's *command*, we can claim by faith the privilege of loving with His love.

God has for us an unending supply of *agape* love — His divine, supernatural love. It is for us to claim, to grow on, to spread to others and thus to reach hundreds and thousands with the love that counts, the love that will bring them to Jesus Christ.

In order to experience and share this love, we must claim it by faith; that is, trust His promise that He will give us all we need to do His will, on the basis of His command and promise.

Begin to Love

You can begin right now to love by faith. Make a list of people you do not love, and begin to love them by faith. Maybe you yourself will be on the list! Have you thought of applying the truths of 1 Corinthians 13 to yourself by faith?

Ask God to enable you to see yourself as He sees you. You have no reason to hate yourself when your Creator has already forgiven you and demonstrated His unconditional love by dying for you.

If Christ is in you, you are *complete*, because Christ Himself *is* perfect love, perfect peace, perfect patience, perfect kindness. He is all goodness, and He is *in you*.

Whenever Satan tries to attack you by reminding you of sins which you have already confessed, or by magnifying your weaknesses and shortcomings, claim in faith the forgiveness and righteousness of God and thank Him that on the authority of His Word, you do not have to be intimidated by Satan's accusation.

Thank Him that you are a child of God, that your sins are forgiven. Thank God that Satan has no control over you except that which is allowed by God (Acts 4:28). Then cast this care on the Lord as we are commanded to do in 1 Peter 5:7.

Pray for Others

Perhaps your boss, a fellow employee, your children, your father or mother is on your list of hard-to-love-and-pray-for people. Ask the Holy Spirit to fill you with Christ's love for all of them.

The next time you meet them, draw upon God's limit-

The next time you meet them, draw upon God's limitless, inexhaustible, overwhelming love for them by faith. Watch God work through you. Watch Him use your smile, your words, your patience to express His love for the individual in question. You can love without necessarily liking certain personalities, habits and attitudes.

Why not make this prayer your own: "*Lord, you would never have commanded me to love had You not intended to enable me to do so. Therefore, on the authority of Your command for me to love and on the authority and promise of Your Word that You will hear and answer when I pray according to Your will* (1 John 5:14, 15), *I appropriate right now Your love — the 1 Corinthians 13 kind of love — for You, for all men and for myself, by faith.*"

Remember that we love by *faith*. By faith, we can claim God's love step by step, person by person. "The fruit of the Spirit is love." Like fruit, love grows. To produce fruit requires a seed, then a flower, then pollination, then some warm sun and refreshing rains, and even some contrary winds.

So in daily life, your love will be warmed by joy, watered by tears, spread by the winds of circumstances. God uses all that we experience to work His will in our lives. He is the one who makes our love grow. It is a continual, ever-increasing thing.

As Paul writes, "May the Lord make your love to grow and overflow to each other and to everyone else" (1 Thessalonians 3:12, TLB).

CHAPTER EIGHTEEN

Joy: Love's Strength

Recently, I was explaining to a group of Christians the meaning of Proverbs 15:13-15: "A happy face means a glad heart, a sad face means a breaking heart. When a man is gloomy, everything seems to go wrong and when he is cheerful everything seems to go right" (TLB).

The apostle Paul tells us the source of joy is the Holy Spirit (1 Thessalonians 1:6). So if a man is filled with the Spirit, he will have a joyful heart. When we are filled with the Spirit, we will express love by singing and making melody in our hearts to the Lord. A happy heart will inevitably express a joyful countenance (Ephesians 5:18-21).

If we don't have a joyful, peaceful countenance, there is reason to question whether we have a loving, joyful heart. And if we do not have a loving, joyful heart, it is not likely that we are filled with the Spirit.

One of the Christian leaders listening to me approached me later. He just happened to have a very somber, stern countenance. He explained to me that this was a new concept to him, and since he was reared in another culture, he felt that his somber countenance was a cultural thing.

We analyzed the Scripture together and concluded that culture has nothing to do with this. If we truly understand the Spirit-filled life, whatever our cultural background, the joy of the Lord will flow from us — from our "innermost being shall flow rivers of living water" (John 7:38, NAS).

Not a trickle — *rivers* of living water — a force from God so powerful that damming it up only gives it greater strength potential, often manifested in impulsiveness. Since God is willing to let such a river of His power and love flow from us, we can claim by faith a radiant countenance that will communicate to the observer a peace, a tranquility, a joy, a happiness that could not be communicated apart from faith.

The Bible has much to say about the fruit of the Spirit, joy-love. In the words of Nehemiah, "The joy of the Lord is your strength: you must not be dejected and sad" (Nehemiah 8:10, TLB).

And in Psalm 32 we read where King David says, "My dishonesty made me miserable and filled my days with frustration. All day and all night Your hand was heavy on me. My strength evaporated like water on a sunny day" (Psalm 32:3, 4, TLB).

A person who has a negative spirit has less energy and less strength than the man who has a joyful spirit. "The joy of the Lord is my strength!" If I get up in the morning with a negative attitude about what might happen during the day, it is not likely to be a good day at all.

I should greet the Lord with a joyful, happy, grateful, thankful heart — "Good morning, Lord!" rather than, "Oh, Lord, it's morning!" I should do this regardless of how I may feel, no matter if I am physically sick or have had news of tragedy. I do this not through mere positive thinking, but on the authority and promise of the Word of God. "Rejoice!" writes Paul, "again, I will say rejoice!" (Philippians 4:4, NAS).

This is a command, not a suggestion. God, through the inspired pen of Paul, tells us to rejoice, regardless of our circumstances. If we determine to rejoice and to saturate our minds with only good things and the blessings of God, then the truth of that Proverb, "The joy of the Lord is our strength," becomes reality.

Conversely, if we allow our actions to respond to a negative attitude, "I don't feel good, I am tired," it is likely we will be tired.

One of the directors of a major Christian ministry, who heard me speak on this subject, came to share, "You have just touched a very responsive chord in my life. I have developed a habit of going around saying that I am tired; I am always tired. I get up tired; I go to bed tired."

Sometime later he contacted me. "When I heard you speak on the subject, I began to realize that it was sin for me to yield to the way I feel. So I determined to rejoice, recognizing that I have available to me the supernatural power of God to live above my circumstances.

"I began to do what you suggested. I began to recognize that I need not be tired, that I had tremendous, supernatural strength available to me, but I wasn't drawing from that strength. Now, I no longer feel tired: I have a new, fresh strength — a new enthusiasm from the Holy Spirit."

At the same time, of course, reason dictates that there are occasions when one must "come apart and rest awhile" — as Jesus did — or come apart. Maintaining proper balance in one's life is an essential discipline.

Enthusiasm is an interesting word. It comes from two Greek terms — *en* and *theos*. It means to be *in God*. If I know that Christ is in me and I am in Him, if I rightly understand my Christian heritage, my rights as a Child of God, my identification with Christ and the role of the Holy Spirit in my life, I can — as an act of the will-say I am going to be the kind of person God has called me to be; I am going to be enthusiastic. I am going to be joyful — not as a result of positive thinking but of supernatural thinking.

Supernatural Thinking

There is a difference between positive thinking and supernatural thinking. Cou'e, the French philosopher, coined the phrase, "Every day in every way I am becoming better and better." But it is said that he committed suicide. There is a difference when one thinks supernaturally. We don't think positively so that we can know Christ better; we come to know Christ better, which results in supernatural thinking. The basis of our thinking is God's Word; supernatural thinking is based upon the attributes of God.

When a man says, "I am going to be enthusiastic, by faith, as an act of the will," or "I am going to rejoice, by faith, as an act of the will," he is simply drawing upon that which is already his as a child of God. In supernatural thinking, we apply the promise of God that if we ask anything according to His will, He will hear and answer us (1 John 5:14, 15).

Some well-known Christian leaders emphasize "positive thinking" and "possibility thinking." They are men whom I greatly admire and with whom I agree basically, because the Christian life is a positive life. The Bible says, "As a man thinketh in his heart so is he" (Proverbs 23:7, KJ).

From a possibility thinking point of view, the average Christian does not begin to claim even a small percentage of what he has the possibility of being and doing for God. But I prefer to use what I believe to be the more scriptural definition of the Christian life — supernatural thinking, which is in reality both *positive* thinking and *possibility* thinking as well.

As Jesus said, "The works that I do shall he do also; and greater works than these shall he do, because I go to the Father. And whatever you ask in My name, that will I do" (John 14:12, 13, NAS). "As a man thinketh in his heart, so is he" (Proverbs 23:7, KJ).

Out of a supernatural relationship with a supernatural God, we can begin to think supernaturally as it relates to the fruit of the Spirit and to all of our relationships in the Christian life.

Jesus said, "I have told you this so that you will be filled with my joy. Yes, your cup of joy will overflow! I demand that you love each other as much as I love you" (John 15:11, 12, TLB).

CHAPTER NINETEEN

Peace: Love's Security

Recently, Arthur DeMoss, one of my very best friends, passed away. He was a man of God who had influenced the lives of tens of thousands of people for Christ. God had richly blessed Art financially and enabled him to build one of the leading insurance companies of America. For many years, he and his wife, Nancy, have hosted large groups — up to a thousand people — at evangelistic dinner meetings in their home, where thousands of people were introduced to Christ through the years.

When Art went to be with the Lord, it was a result of a very unexpected heart attack. All of us were shocked. The word reached me in Austria, where I was meeting with our European staff. Immediately, I flew back to the States for the memorial service.

As I participated in that service, I looked over the large audience, about half of whom had been introduced to Christ through the ministry of this man whom they had come to honor. In the crowd, I saw one face that stood out — a face that was the most radiant of all. It was Art's widow, Nancy. She was sitting in the front row with their seven children. Her radiant countenance was a demonstration to me of the supernatural joy and peace which God gives in such times of extreme grief.

Nancy and Art were the greatest of lovers and friends. They had been deeply in love since their courtship and were almost inseparable — whether in the building of the business, in the rearing of their family or in their joint venture of evangelism. Yet, in this, Nancy's greatest sorrow, the evidence that she was filled with the Spirit radiated from her countenance. She was experiencing the supernatural peace of God — love's security, which is available to all of God's children.

Peace: Knowing God Is in Control

In the course of my responsibilities and privileges as the director of a large organization, word reaches me almost daily of a fellow worker or one of his family who is ill, who has died or who is faced with major problems and needs. I find myself on the telephone often praying with people who have experienced tragedy, heartache and sorrow.

Even with broken hearts and through tears, there are those who witness to the special, supernatural peace that is granted by the Holy Spirit in times of great adversity and tragedy. It is a peace that comes by trusting our sovereign, loving heavenly Father.

The Supernatural Source of Peace

Galatians 5:22 tells us that peace is an aspect of love that we exhibit in our lives when we are filled with the Holy Spirit. In this sense, peace comes from the Holy Spirit. But, actually, all three members of the Trinity are the source of a Spirit-filled Christian's peace.

"Don't worry about anything," Paul writes in his letter to the believers in Philippi. "Instead, pray about everything; tell God your needs and don't forget to thank Him for His answers. If you do this you will experience *God's peace*, which is far more wonderful than the human mind can understand. His peace will keep your thoughts and your hearts quiet and at rest as you trust in Christ Jesus" (Philippians 4:6, 7, TLB, italics added).

Peace-love, as an aspect of the fruit of the Spirit, has its source in the person of Jesus Christ. His is a supernatural peace that non-believers cannot know and experience. "I am leaving you with a gift," promised Jesus, "peace of mind and heart! And the peace I give isn't fragile like the peace the world gives. So don't be troubled or afraid" (John 14:27, TLB).

Worldly Kinds of Peace

Peace is a common word in the world. And there are many kinds of peace. There is international peace, and we hear much about man's attempts to bring lasting peace to the Middle East and other troubled spots in the world. There is national peace, and we in the United States have experienced this, to some degree, since our Civil War. However, civil and domestic peace is often shattered even today by outbreaks of civil disobedience stemming from racial hatred, social injustices and rebellion against civil authorities.

There also is what the late theologian, Francis Schaeffer, termed "personal peace." He spoke of the peace that the natural man strives for, a peace whose creed is "me-ism," a peace that places self before anyone and everyone else, including God. Personal peace — thus defined — is one of the greatest sins in America today, a sin of epidemic proportions that is threatening the very future of our republic. Rightly defined, personal peace is the glorious heritage of every Spirit-filled Christian.

Not all peace is true peace — even by the world's standards. Peace agreements often are entered into by nations when one or more have absolutely no honest intention of keeping their end of the agreement. The result is hypocritical peace and false peace.

The Bible says that in the end times the Antichrist will "guarantee" a peace between Israel and her enemies, only to break the treaty himself after three-and-a-half years.

Supernatural Peace

But the supernatural peace-love that God ordains for us, that Jesus gives to us, that the Holy Spirit guarantees and makes real within our hearts and souls, is a peace that truly goes beyond what the human mind can understand — it is that wonderful.

Do you realize that, on the basis of God's Word, the only peace that will ever really be peace is that peace which comes from God? No nation, of itself, no matter how militarily strong, will ever be able to keep the peace; no individual, no matter how brilliant and friendly, will ever be able to keep a true and lasting peace.

No matter how sincere you might be, no matter how hard you endeavor to keep peace in your own life, you will ultimately fail without the supernatural peace that comes only from Christ and is made real and meaningful only in the lives of Christians who are Spirit-filled. Sinful man is not given this peace and will never know and experience it(Isaiah 48:22; 59:8).

How can a Christian experience this kind of peace? Paul explained this in his letter to the Romans: "So now, since we have been made right in God's sight by faith in His promises, we can have real peace with Him because of what Jesus Christ our Lord has done for us" (Romans 5:1, TLB). The disobedient, carnal Christian cannot experience this peace — only the Spirit-filled Christian.

CHAPTER TWENTY

Patience: Love's Endurance

During my college days, I was not a believer. Only in retrospect can I appreciate in some measure the testimony of one of my professors who was the head of the education department. He and his wife were devout Christians. They had a mongoloid child, whom they took with them wherever they went, and I am sure that their motivation for doing so — at least in part — was to give a testimony of the fruit of the Spirit, patience-love (Galatians 5:22, 23).

They loved the child dearly and felt that God had given them the responsibility and privilege to rear the child personally as a testimony of His grace, rather than placing her in a home for retarded children. The Bible teaches us that God never gives us a responsibility, a load or a burden without also giving us the ability to be victorious.

This professor and his wife bore their tremendous burden with joyful hearts. Wherever they went, they waited on the child, hand and foot. Instead of being embarrassed and humiliated, trying to hide the child in the closet, they unashamedly always took her with them, as a witness for Christ and as an example of His faithfulness and sufficiency.

They demonstrated patience-love by drawing upon the supernatural resources of the Holy Spirit in their close, moment-by-moment walk with God. Because of the working of the Holy Spirit in their lives, they were able to bear their trials supernaturally without grumbling or complaining. This is not to suggest that every dedicated Christian couple would be led of God to respond in the same way under similar circumstances. In their case their lives communicated patience.

The Source of Patience

The apostle Paul wrote to the Romans, revealing that God is the source of patience: "May God who gives patience, steadiness, and encouragement help you to live in complete harmony with each other — each with the attitude of Christ toward the other" (Romans 15:5, TLB).

Then, in Paul's second letter to the Thessalonians, he cites Jesus as an example of patience: "And may the Lord direct your hearts into the love of God and into the steadfastness (patience) of Christ" (2 Thessalonians 3:5, NAS).

There is a remarkable quality about supernatural patience-love: it is most often accompanied by another aspect of the fruit of the Spirit — *joy* (Colossians 1:11). My college professor and his wife not only demonstrated the patience of Christ in the care and love for their mongoloid child, but they also did it with a joy that could come only from the Holy Spirit.

How to Have Patience

The story is told of an impatient man who prayed and kept praying for God to grant him the virtue he so desperately needed. "Lord, give me patience — right now!" he prayed.

Patience, however, is a virtue that is developmental in nature, to a large degree. It develops out of a good heart and a godly attitude (Luke 8:15). It is spawned sometimes during times of tribulation (Romans 5:3, 4) and testing of faith (James 1:3). By His Spirit, God often produces patience without the need of tribulation. Remember, it is a fruit of the Spirit.

Paul writes, "If we must keep trusting God for something that hasn't happened yet, it teaches us to wait patiently and confidently" (Romans 8:25, TLB). So patience comes from hope and trust in God. And finally, we learn patience through the study and personal application of God's Word in our lives (Romans 15:4).

The Destroying Power of Impatience

Without patience, a person can thwart the will of God by acting prematurely. How many times have we "gotten ahead of the Lord" in our actions or decision making?.

Impatience also has a destroying power in relationships. I am convinced that many divorces could be avoided and many lost jobs could otherwise have been held if only the people involved had known and demonstrated God's gift of patience-love.

A Christian family was struggling with the trials of being parents (they had four young children — two of them in diapers). One day the wife, who was frustrated to her wits' end, came to me for spiritual counsel. As she phrased it, she was at the point of losing her sanity.

How could she cope with rearing her children? She told how angry she got with the children when they disobeyed her. In fact, she indicated there were times when she feared she might physically harm her children, though she loved them dearly.

How could she cope with this problem? She needed the fruit of the Spirit, patience-love. And the only way she could obtain such patience was by faith, confessing her sins and appropriating the fullness of the Holy Spirit. This she began to do, continually. Today, she is a woman of godly patience, and being a parent has become a joyful privilege for her.

Patience: We All Need It

All of us need Christ's patience, regardless of who we are or in what circumstances we find ourselves. Patience is granted to us by the grace of God through the Holy Spirit. It is produced by faith as a fruit of the Spirit, and it is granted in times of great crises (Luke 21:15-19), in dealing with church situations (2 Corinthians 12:12), in opposing evil (Revelation 2:2), for soundness of faith (Titus 2:2) and in waiting for the return of Jesus Christ (James 5:7, 8).

To have patience is a biblical command. "Be patient with each other," writes Paul (Ephesians 4:2, TLB). God would not command us to be patient if He did not intend to give us the gift of patience through His Holy Spirit. The principle here is a simple one: whenever patience is needed, by faith confess your sins and ask the Holy Spirit to grant it to you.

As we live day by day, moment by moment, in the power and control of the Holy Spirit, learning to give more and more of ourselves as living sacrifices to Christ, then the fruit of the Spirit, love — and its manifestation of patience, will become more and more evident in our lives, inwardly and outwardly to others.

CHAPTER TWENTY-ONE

Kindness: Love's Conduct

Several years ago, my wife and I were writing training materials on social etiquette for our co-workers. The materials dealt with how to be a good host or hostess, how to be a witness for Christ as a guest, how to demonstrate gratitude when you are invited to a home, how to write notes of appreciation for hospitality given and how to send small gifts expressing thanks for favors.

As we labored over the work, it occurred to us that, though the instruction should be given, we could not effectively legislate good manners. We realized that good manners are the by-product of the Spirit-controlled life. If a person demonstrates the fruit of the Spirit, he will automatically be considerate of others. He will learn to do the right things. He will want to be kind and gracious.

Friendship Toward Others

Kindness, in simplest terms, is showing genuine friendship to others. The apostle Paul writes, "We try to live in such a way that no one will ever be offended or kept back from finding the Lord by the way we act, so that no one can find fault with us and blame it on the Lord.

"In fact, in everything that we do, we try to show that we are true ministers of God. We patiently endure suffering and hardship and trouble of every kind" (2 Corinthians 6:3, 4, TLB).

Paul continues, "We have been kind, and truly loving and filled with the Holy Spirit. We have been truthful, with God's power helping us in all we do. All of the godly man's arsenal — weapons of defense, and weapons of attack — have been ours. We stand true to the Lord whether others honor us or despise us, whether they criticize us or commend us. We are honest but they call us liars" (2 Corinthians 6:6-8, TLB).

Christian Kindness in Society

Most institutions of learning, hospitals, homes for unwed mothers, skid- row missions, rehabilitation centers for drug addicts and alcoholics — social welfare institutions of all types — have had their origin in Christian kindness and compassion. More recently, however, secular society has built hospitals and schools.

But even now, through compassion and kindness, God has motivated groups outside the Christian community to undertake such projects. Many times, this is the result of the inspiration of individuals who are Christians — or non-believing leaders who have been influenced by godly mothers and fathers.

Women's Rights

In the time of Christ, a woman was treated like chattel property. She could be abandoned at will, if the woman displeased her husband. He could simply tell her to go home to her father, and she had no recourse. This was true even of Judaism and certainly of the Roman pagan world. Woman was little more than a sex object or a piece of property.

But Christ put an end to all of this by His example and by His teachings, by His resurrection and by the indwelling Holy Spirit in the life of the believer. Woman was liberated from that bondage. The present militant advocates of women's rights are for the most part people who profess no faith in God. They ignore the fact that Jesus Christ is the greatest liberator of women — and men as well — of all the centuries.

No liberty is possible without Christ, and there is no liberty that is not available in and through Christ. Man is admonished to love his wife as Christ loved the church.

This is the highest possible expression of love — that a man would actually give his own life to enhance and protect the life of his wife.

Throughout history, the kindness of God and the goodness of God have been demonstrated by those who have been followers of Jesus Christ in changing the course of history. Out of the great revivals of England under the influence of John Wesley, came dramatic social reforms.

Abolition of slavery came under the leadership of William Wilberforce, who was influenced by John Wesley. Children's rights were protected, as well, through child labor unions and child labor laws. The first labor unions were organized by a group of ministers who had been influenced by John Wesley.

All of these are practical applications of the Spirit-filled life that demonstrate the fruit of the Spirit, not only in the individual life, but also as that single life influences the whole of society.

Supernatural Kindness

Kindness is one of the attributes of God (Nehemiah 9:17, Isaiah 54:8, 10). It has been demonstrated perfectly to the world through the person of our wonderful Savior and Lord, Jesus Christ. "And now God can always point to us as examples of how very, very rich His kindness is, as shown in all He has done for us through Jesus Christ" (Ephesians 2:7, TLB).

"What a friend we have in Jesus," goes the wonderful old hymn. Kindness- love, like the other manifestations of the fruit of the Spirit, is developed in time through walking in the Spirit and through right relationships.

In the book of Proverbs, we read that a prime virtue of a wife is kindness: "When she speaks, her words are wise, and kindness is the rule for everything she says" (Proverbs 31:26, TLB). It would be a wonderful tribute to the glory of Jesus Christ if it could be truly said that all His children speak words that are wise, and that kindness is the rule in all they do.

The story is told about two Japanese farmers. Every day, one of them would haul pails of water up the steep slope to his terraced field and irrigate his meager crop. The second farmer tilled the terrace just below, and he would poke a hole in the dyke and let the other farmer's water run down into his field.

The first farmer was upset. Being a Christian, he went to his pastor and asked for advice. The pastor told him to keep on watering as before and to say nothing. So, the farmer returned to his fields and the watering of his crop, but the farmer below him continued to drain off his water. Nothing had changed.

After a few days, the first farmer went to his pastor again. The pastor told him to go a step further — to water his neighbor's crop! So the next day, the farmer brought water to his neighbor's field and watered the crops. After that, he watered his own field.

This went on for three days, and not a word was exchanged between the two farmers. But after the third day, the second farmer came to the first farmer and asked, "How do I become a Christian?"

Jesus is quoted, "There is a saying, 'Love your friends and hate your enemies.' But I say: Love your enemies!… If you are friendly only to your friends, how are you different from anyone else? Even the heathen do that. But you are to be perfect, even as your Father in heaven is perfect" (Matthew 5:43-48, TLB).

Do you hate your neighbors and love only your friends? Do you want to show a supernatural kindness-love toward everyone you encounter? Humanly speaking, it is an impossibility. But for the child of God, showing supernatural kindness is a Christlike characteristic that you can develop as you walk in the Holy Spirit.

CHAPTER TWENTY-TWO

Goodness: Love's Character

Recently I met a prominent man who had been an avowed atheist all his life. In fact, he was dedicated to destroying the faith of all those who believe in God. He told me about a dramatic change in his life. He had experienced a personal encounter with God and had made Jesus Christ his Lord and Savior. As we talked, the story of his life began to unfold.

Prior to becoming a Christian, he had been a very nervous and deeply insecure person. He once smoked several packages of cigarettes a day and drank heavily.

Then he related how, following his conversion to Christ, his nervousness and insecurity began to leave him. He stopped smoking and drinking — not because of any legalistic do's and don'ts, but because the void in his heart for so many years, which had caused him to be nervous and insecure, was now filled — filled with the Holy Spirit of Jesus Christ.

My heart was bursting with joy over the testimony of this one-time atheist. Today, praise God, this man is using his influence to help others discover that same life-changing encounter with God that he has experienced.

The Greatest of Virtues

Sir Francis Bacon said, "Of all virtues and dignities of the mind, goodness is the greatest, being the character of the Deity; and without it, man is a busy, mischievous, wretched thing."

From Bad to Good

Natural man has an evil nature. None of us has to probe very deeply into the depths of our old nature to see the potential evil that lurks inside. So how can a man like the one-time atheist make the transition from being basically bad to good? Believe me, it is not humanly possible.

Let me give you a hint: to be good, literally, means "to be like God." Man cannot be "like God" by his own doing; it can come about only through the supernatural ministry of the indwelling Holy Spirit.

My friend, the former atheist, is experiencing goodness in his life because Christ now dwells within him in the person of the Holy Spirit. He has been born again with a new, Christlike nature. The good we see in him is the good of Christ within him. He is exhibiting the fruit of the Holy Spirit, goodness-love.

"God is light and in Him is no darkness at all," we read in 1 John 1:5. And Paul writes, "Because of this light within you, you should do only what is good and right and true" (Ephesians 5:9, TLB).

Do you want the goodness of Christ in your life? All that is of the highest ethical and moral value? If you know Christ and are indwelt by His Holy Spirit, then the goodness of Christ is in you right now.

As you grow in Christ and walk day by day, moment by moment in His Holy Spirit, the fruit of the Spirit, goodness-love, will become more and more evident in your life — to you and to those around you. Right now, you can confess your sins and appropriate Christ's forgiveness and goodness by praying in faith, based upon the command and promise of 1 John 1:9.

A word of caution: goodness is a Christian trait that develops in proportion to your maturity in Christ. Do not be discouraged when you fail God; do not give up. Simply practice spiritual breathing and, by faith, believe that Christ is at work in your life, making you more the kind of person He wants you to be.

CHAPTER TWENTY-THREE

Faithfulness: Love's Confidence

As I have previously shared, there was a time when I prayed that God would enable me to reach one soul for Him, and He answered that prayer by leading me to one person whose heart He had prepared. Now I pray for a billion souls and, by faith, I believe that a billion will be harvested for the glory of God.

God has not changed; I have changed.

I believe that God deals with us in a similar way with regard to spiritual fruit. As we continue to trust God to develop in us all the various love traits, He honors that faithfulness because we are obeying Him by doing what He commands us to do.

A Living Reality

Faithfulness is that trait of the fruit of the Holy Spirit (faithfulness-love) that makes faith a living reality every day in the life of the believer who is living supernaturally. As we continue to walk in the power, love and wisdom of the Holy Spirit, we learn to develop greater confidence in the Lord Jesus Christ, in His Word, in our rights as children of God and in the power and ability of the indwelling Holy Spirit to empower and control our lives.

Faithfulness can be compared to an athlete's conditioning. A marathon runner does not begin training by running great distances. Instead, he starts with short runs. Then, as his body becomes more conditioned, he increases the distance of his runs until he reaches the full distance of the marathon.

Faithfulness in the life of a Christian also develops over an extended period of time spent in "conditioning." As we learn to trust God in small things, our faith grows and grows until we are able to trust Him in greater things.

In the parable of the talents, the Master said to His servant, "Well done, good and faithful slave; you were faithful with a few things, I will put you in charge of many things, enter into the joy of your master" (Matthew 25:21, NAS).

God rewards us for our faithfulness, and each time we see Him respond favorably to our faithfulness, He reaches out to us through His Holy Spirit and gives us an increase in faith through which to trust Him for even greater things.

Your Faith Thermometer

If there were such an instrument as a "faith thermometer," at what level would your faithfulness register? Hot? Lukewarm? Cold?

Jesus said to the church in Laodicea: "'I know you well — you are neither hot nor cold; I wish you were one or the other! But since you are merely lukewarm, I will spit you out of my mouth!'" (Revelation 3:15, TLB)

Again, I ask, where does your faithfulness register on that faith thermometer?

Jesus continued, "You say, 'I am rich, with everything I want; I don't need a thing!' And you don't realize that spiritually you are wretched and miserable and poor and blind and naked.

"My advice to you is to buy pure gold from me, gold purified by fire — only then will you be rich.... I continually discipline and punish everyone I love; so I must punish you, unless you turn from your indifference and become enthusiastic about the things of God" (Revelation 3:17, TLB)

"America! I Hardly Know You!"

The greatest tragedy in the history of nations is happening right here in America. Here we are, a nation founded by Christians, a nation founded upon godly principles, a nation blessed beyond all the nations of history for the purpose of doing God's will in the world. And yet, this once proud, Christian nation has succumbed to the subtle devices of Satan. It has become materialistic and humanistic.

Granted, the opinion polls show meteoric growth in the number of people in America who claim to be born-again Christians. But where does their faith register on the faith thermometer? How committed and mature are they?

America is a modern-day Laodicea. Many have lost that first love, and many have become lukewarm. Like the harlot of Babylon in Revelation 17, we have taken the material blessings that God has given us for His work of evangelism and discipleship in the world and have spent them on ourselves for our own self-gratification.

We have adorned ourselves with precious jewels. We have spent exceedingly beyond our needs for material things of every type and description. We have lost sight of the reason why God has blessed us so abundantly.

God have mercy on us if we, like the harlot of Babylon, continue to turn our back on God and continue to follow lustfully after material things until we find ourselves in the very clutches of anti-Christian tyranny.

Has the Fire Gone Out?

Who is to blame? The government? Big business? Let me tell you where the blame lies.

America is where she is today because too many Christians have quenched the Holy Spirit in their lives. Too many Christians have put out the fire of the Holy Spirit within themselves because they never knew and understood the Spirit-filled life. Again I ask you, where does your faithfulness register on the faith thermometer? Are you only lukewarm for Christ?

By faith, after being filled with the Spirit you can fan the fire of the Holy Spirit so that it will burn fiercely within you. As the fire burns hotter and hotter, so will the light of Christ shine brighter and brighter in you and radiate from you. By that light, the Holy Spirit of Christ will guide your steps and light your path. You will indeed be as a light unto the world.

I urge you now, before it is too late in your life, before it is too late in the short life of our young, beloved country, to begin to trust God in small things — in all things. Begin to flex your faith muscles. Begin to live supernaturally in the power and control of the Holy Spirit.

CHAPTER TWENTY-FOUR

Gentleness: Love's Humility

J. C. Penney, founder of the department store chain that bears his name, was a man of tremendous ability and strength. I had a surprise meeting with this giant in the world of business some years ago when I was a young businessman.

On that particular day, I had traveled to the California Institute of Technology for an appointment with Dr. Robert Milliken, then president of the university and a Nobel Prize-winning scientist. Shortly after our meeting began, J.C. Penney arrived, also to visit with Dr. Milliken and to tour the Cal Tech facilities.

Well, there I was, a young businessman, a young Christian sitting and talking with two of the great men of the world. As I sat there, I was impressed with the fact that they were two of the most humble and gentle men I had ever met.

After a time, a guide came to take them on the tour and they both invited me to accompany them. Being sensitive to the situation, I declined, of course, not wanting to impose upon their important time together. But I was deeply impressed by the fact that these two great men would receive me, an unknown, so warmly and graciously.

Purifying Fires

Through the years, I have found that many leaders in the world of business, in professional life, and in government and education are people who, in the process of becoming leaders, have gone through the purifying fires of trials and tribulations. Those experiences molded these leaders into humble, gentle, approachable people.

On the contrary, it is often most difficult to communicate with the young, inexperienced subordinates whose egos have been inflated because they are a part of the life of a great man. Consequently, they throw their weight around obnoxiously with considerable arrogance.

In my witnessing experiences I have found that, as I talked to many of these leaders about Christ, they are like children in their response. In fact, they are far more open to the gospel than are most of the men on skid row — the alcoholics and drug addicts with whom I worked very closely for several years as a young Christian.

You would think these "down-and-outers" would be more humble, but because of pride they oftentimes are hardened and unresponsive. The same sun hardens clay and melts wax. Adversity humbles some and hardens others.

The word *gentleness* in the original Greek language has the thought of mildness combined with tenderness, meekness and humbleness. The word does not suggest weakness, spiritlessness or timidity.

The Humility of Christ

Non-believers can, of course, and often do, show a degree of gentleness in their relationships with others. But the gentleness of which I write here is a kind that the world cannot know in the way a Christian can.

This gentleness is that part of the fruit of the Holy Spirit called gentleness-love. It is the gentleness and humility of Christ in the lives of all God's children who are Spirit-filled.

Jesus said, "'Wear My yoke — for it fits perfectly — and let Me teach you; for I am gentle and humble, and you shall find rest for your souls; for I give you only light burdens' " (Matthew 11:29, 30, TLB).

Paul's Example

The apostle Paul was a man who had undergone almost every imaginable kind of trial and tribulation for his faith. Yet he was one of the most gentle and humble servants of Christ we read about in the Bible. His great love for his fellowmen led him to teach others to be more Christlike.

In his letter to the Colossian church, he writes, "Since you have been chosen by God who has given you this new kind of life, and because of His deep love and concern for you, you should practice tenderhearted mercy and kindness to others.

"Don't worry about making a good impression on them but be ready to suffer quietly and patiently. Be gentle and ready to forgive; never hold grudges. Remember, the Lord forgave you, so you must forgive others" (Colossians 3:12, 13, TLB).

In his letter to Timothy, Paul encouraged this young pastor, his son in the faith, "Oh, Timothy, you are God's man. Run from all these evil things and work instead at what is right and good, learning to trust Him and love others, and to be patient and gentle" (1 Timothy 6:11, TLB).

Blessed Are the Gentle

The Lord said, "Blessed are the gentle, for they shall inherit the earth" (Matthew 5:5, NAS).

Who are the gentle? In the above passage, Jesus is referring to those who walk with Him in the fullness of His Holy Spirit. He is referring to those in whose lives is seen the fruit of the Spirit — particularly love demonstrated through gentleness of mind and spirit and in relationship with other people.

It is these same gentle people who will someday inherit the earth. The whole earth and everything in it belongs to God. The day is coming when Christ will return in glory and honor and power to judge the wicked and to reward His saints for their works of faith. As joint heirs with Christ, we will be given the earth and all that is in it.

Meanwhile, we are in the world (though not of it), and we are told — by Christ as recorded in Matthew 11:29, and by Paul in Colossians 3:12 and 1 Timothy 6:11 — to be gentle. We are to be humble before all men — not because it is religious protocol, but because Christ who lives within us is humble.

The "Golden Rule"

J.C. Penney, a devout Christian, to whom I referred earlier, built one of America's leading businesses on the principle of the Golden Rule, "Do unto others as you would have them do unto you." He and other gentle men have developed tenderness and sensitivity to others through their years of maturing, and so should we as Christians seek to develop gentle spirits through the trials and tribulations that God permits us to go through.

Do you lack gentleness in your life? Do you have a tendency to be arrogant, proud, boastful? Are you overbearing or even coarse and rude with others?

By faith you can become a gentle person. By faith you can confess your sins and know that they have been forgiven. By faith you can appropriate the filling of the Spirit of Christ.

The Lord has commanded us to be gentle people, so by faith we can ask for that portion of the fruit of the Spirit — gentleness-love — and know that He is changing us for the better.

But, as I have cautioned with regard to other Christlike traits, this is one which usually develops over an extended period of time, usually through the maturing process that can come only with time and trials and sometimes tribulation. Pray that God will give you patience with yourself as you mature into the gentle and humble person He wants you to be.

CHAPTER TWENTY-FIVE

Self-Control: Love's Victory

Recently I talked with a man and a woman who had been plagued all their lives with the problem of overweight. They shared how their self-images had deteriorated severely. They had lost self-confidence and were constantly plagued with guilt every time they looked in the mirror. They made resolution after resolution and tried diet after diet, all to no avail.

Then one day, in the reading of Scripture, they were gripped with the realization that their bodies are the temple of the living God and that, as such, it was dishonoring to the Lord to continue to be overweight. So for the first time in their lives they began to pray, "O God, please help us. We have tried and failed, again and again. Now You must help us. Through the enabling of the Holy Spirit, we invite You to control our appetites. *You* help us to be more careful in choosing the kind and quantity of food we eat."

In answer to their prayers of faith, God enabled them to discipline themselves. Over a period of time, they were able to slim down so that they could look in the mirror and with great joy and thanksgiving to the Lord acknowledge that His Holy Spirit had enabled them to lose weight.

Disciplining Myself

I do not criticize those who are overweight; I have had a problem of weight control for more than 30 years. I know how important discipline is, and for many years I have disciplined my eating habits. For example, I seldom eat anything that contains sugar. Obviously, I forego the many delicious desserts that I could enjoy so much.

Also, as a matter of spiritual discipline, I fast for approximately 32 hours each week, during which time I drink only distilled water and consume no food. Though my motives are for spiritual benefits, there are also physical benefits.

In my travels throughout the world, I am hosted by men and women who want me to enjoy the delicacies of their country. This has reminded me to be very careful about what and how much I eat.

At almost any Christian gathering, a good percentage of the people are overweight. The temple of God — their bodies — is being abused. But this is only symptomatic of a generally undisciplined life.

I have found in my own experience that the temptation of overeating — gluttony — causes me to relax my discipline in other areas of life. But when I am self-controlled in the areas of food and exercise, I find that I am drawn closer to Christ and am more sensitive to the leading of the Spirit.

Disciplined Living

Since the beginning of our ministry, I have often been asked, "How do you account for the fact that there are so many gifted, dedicated, able people in the organization?"

My response is that no one would join us with our meager, modest salaries — and with the necessity of raising their own support — unless they were willing to discipline themselves and put aside worldly ambitions, dreams and aspirations that feed the ego. Any person who joins the staff must humble himself and live a life of discipline and self-control, with, of course, the help of the Holy Spirit.

Consequently, many people of only modest ability join the staff, but go on to become outstanding, gifted and effective people. Why? Because they have learned the secret of discipline, of self-control. I am also frequently asked, "How do staff members live so well on such modest incomes?"

The fact of the matter is that most of our staff do live very well. They dress nicely, live in nice homes, have good cars — and the only explanation is that they have learned to discipline their material appetites. They invest their money where it accomplishes the most for the glory of God and their own blessing, instead of wasting it on extravagant things.

"Greatest Living Woman"

Vonette and I had the privilege of sharing our lives with Dr. Henrietta Mears for 10 years. Dr. Mears was one of the most outstanding women in the Christian world. Dr. Billy Graham often referred to her as "the greatest living woman of her time." As director of education at the First Presbyterian Church of Hollywood, she influenced the lives of thousands of young men and women. Vonette and I are both indebted to her and grateful for her influence in our lives.

Henrietta Mears lived in a palatial home, owned priceless antiques and dressed beautifully. Most people assumed that she was a woman of great wealth. Actually, she was a person of relatively modest means. She simply knew how to take her modest earnings and savings and maximize their investment.

For example, she would advise young people, "Do not eat in expensive restaurants where you spend excessively except on rare occasions. Instead, prepare your own lunch, and over a period of a year you can save enough money by not eating out to take a trip around the world and enrich your spirit, your soul and your cultural sensitivities. Or you can use the money you save to buy something which will enhance the beauty of your home or person."

Discipline-Love

We see disciplined people all around us in this world.

Athletes discipline themselves to strict training, soldiers are drilled in military discipline, artists and writers are disciplined to sharpen their talents through dedicated practice. But, on the other hand, we see many examples of lack of discipline in the lives of many people around us.

Whether a person is a Christian or non-believer, it seems that self-control is a quality of character that is, for most people, a difficult conquest. Yet we are told in the Bible that the Spirit-filled Christian will exhibit self-control as a part of the fruit of the Spirit, which is love.

This discipline-love or self-control-love applies to the spirit, the mind and the body of every believer. We are to exercise self-control in each of these areas. To fail to do so is to quench and grieve the Holy Spirit.

An overweight person, because he cannot control his appetite, quenches and grieves the Spirit. A gossip who cannot control his tongue quenches and grieves the Spirit. A student who fails to study adequately because of poor discipline quenches and grieves the Spirit. Many pages would be required to list all the ways in which lack of self-control quenches and grieves the Holy Spirit.

Spirit, mind and body — these are the three aspects of our being over which we are told to practice self-control.

Disciplining the Spirit

What is man's spirit? It is his immaterial being — man without his body, if you will. The Bible gives many characteristics of the spirit of man. It is that which communicates with the Spirit of God.

Man's spirit is the center of emotions (1 Kings 21:5), the source of passions (Ezekiel 3:14) and the cause of volitions — exercise of the will (Proverbs 16:32). Our spirit is subject to divine influence while housed in our mortal body (Deuteronomy 2:30 and Isaiah 19:14), and leaves the body at the time of physical death (Ecclesiastes 12:7 and James 2:26).

You and I know from experience that it is not easy to discipline our emotions, our passions or our self-will. In fact, apart from God's help, it is an impossibility. The Bible describes the disciplining of the spirit as a great conquest: "He who is slow to anger is better than the mighty, and he who rules his spirit, than he who captures a city" (Proverbs 16:32, NAS).

But the spirit is not all that requires disciplining.

Disciplining the Mind

Our mind is that part of us with which we think, reason, remember, have feelings, desires, generate thoughts and spawn intention. All of these areas of the mind are to be disciplined. And minds *can* be disciplined — but only in the power and control of the Holy Spirit.

The information that goes into the mind has great influence on our spirits, our bodies and our thought processes. Saturating our minds with lustful, pornographic materials — literature and films, for example — can never reap godly results.

The Bible says that the mind of natural man is essentially disgusting (Ezekiel 23:17-22), despiteful (Ezekiel 36:5), depraved (Romans 1:28), hardened (2 Corinthians 3:14), hostile (Colossians 1:21) and defiled (Titus 1:15).

In contrast, the Scriptures show that the mind of the Christian is willing (1 Chronicles 28:9), is at peace (Romans 8:6), is renewed (Romans 12:2), can know Christ's mind (1 Corinthians 2:16) and can be obedient (Hebrews 8:10).

Our minds are susceptible to the influence of our old sin-nature and, as such, can pose some dangers to us. As soon as we get out of step spiritually with the Holy Spirit and get our focus off the Lord, our minds begin give us trouble.

The Bible shows some of these dangers to us: Our cause us to worry (Luke 12:29) and have doubt

(Romans 14:5). The unfortunate results of letting a mind slip into carnality can cause disunity among believers (Romans 12:16), a spiritual struggle within (Romans 7:23, 25), and our growing weary (Hebrews 12:3).

This last point, I believe, may speak to a common cause of depression among Christians. They allow their minds to dwell on ungodly thoughts and/or over-intros-pection. But through self-control, through discipline of the mind, a Spirit-filled Christian need not be bothered by mental weariness, depression or over-introspection.

Paul writes: "I advise you to obey only the Holy Spirit's instructions. He will tell you where to go and what to do, and then you won't always be doing the wrong things your evil nature wants you to.

"For we naturally love to do evil things that are just the opposite from the things that the Holy Spirit tells us to do, and the good things we want to do when the Spirit has His way with us are just the opposite of our natural desires" (Galatians 5:16, 17 TLB).

Disciplining the Body

Every summer Campus Crusade conducts training sessions at the Colorado State University in Fort Collins, Colorado. In addition to the several thousand Campus Crusade staff people who attend, thousands of other people are also on the campus attending music work-shops, summer school, numerous conferences and meet-ings.

Throughout the day, from early morning till late at night, the campus is alive with people jogging, roller-skating, playing tennis, walking and taking part in other physical activities. These people are disciplining their bodies, keeping them in good physical tone.

Yet, I also notice many other people seem to lack in terest in their physical well-being, evidenced by thei smoking, drinking alcoholic beverages and use of narc tics. A stroll down the sidewalks of this beautiful camp can be disappointingly revealing.

The body of the Christian is the temple of the Holy Spirit and of God (1 Corinthians 6:19 and 1 Corinthians 3:16, 17). For this reason, God asks us to present our bodies as "living sacrifices," holy and righteous, for God could dwell in no less a temple.

The bodies of all believers, collectively, are the members — arms and legs, for example — of Christ's body. As the Body of Christ, you and I are the instruments through which the Holy Spirit ministers to Christ's Church and to the world.

These then — spirit, mind and body — are the elements of ourselves which the Bible says we are to control.

Through the years, I have discovered that the best method of self-control is to allow the Holy Spirit of Christ to control my life — completely and without reservation. The Christ-controlled life is a holy and righteous life.

The life controlled by self — outside of Christ — is a life that is hindered by fleshly lusts (1 Peter 2:11), the tongue (Psalm 39:1, 2), strong drink (Proverbs 23:29-35), sexual sins (1 Thessalonians 4:3, 4), the influence of unclean spirits (Mark 5:2-16) and self-centeredness (Proverbs 25:28).

Fit for Ministering

Recently I was watching a Christian program on television. The main speaker was at least 100 pounds overweight. His stomach actually drooped over his belt, and his jowls shook as he spoke. I was repulsed by his appearance, especially since he presented himself as a minister f Jesus Christ.

ꓱurely everything he says is minimized by the fact ⁀he is obviously undisciplined in his appetite and ⁀ses credibility with the masses. This is not to criticize a brother, but only to point out that ꓶ is essential if we are to minister most effec- .ꓵe Lord.

An undisciplined Christian cannot be a very effective Christian in anything he does. Likewise, a group of undisciplined Christians — the Church — cannot effectively fulfill the Great Commission. As someone has said: "Those who wish to transform the world must be able to transform themselves." This transformation is the result of trusting and obeying God.

If we as Christians do not discipline ourselves, God through His sovereign chastening will discipline us through many trials and tribulations. America is lavishing its vast resources of money on itself, and hoarding its manpower and technology. As a result, America is presently experiencing unparalleled economic, social, political and military problems — problems that I believe are due to God's chastening, because He loves us and wants to help us become what He created us to be.

God is preparing His people for a great effort of evangelism and discipleship that will enable His Church to help fulfill the Great Commission. I believe that we shall see this accomplished in our lifetime. After that, Christ will return to earth for His Church.

Preparing for Christ's Return

"But the day of the Lord will come like a thief," writes Peter, "in which the heavens will pass away with a roar and the elements will be destroyed with intense heat, and the earth and its works will be burned up. Since all these things are to be destroyed in this way, what sort of people ought you to be in holy conduct and godliness, looking for and hastening the coming of the day of God" (2 Peter 3:9-11, NAS).

What sort of people ought we to be as we await the return of Christ? Peter answers his own question: "Dear friends, while you are waiting for these things to happen and for Him to come, try hard to live without sinning; and be at peace with everyone so that He will be pleased with you when He returns. And remember why He is waiting. He is giving us time to get His message of salvation out to others" (2 Peter 3:14, 15, TLB).

Peter is saying that we are to be disciplined Christians, living lives of holiness in obedience to God. We are to be Spirit-filled Christians, and our lives are to produce the fruit of the Spirit. We are to be witnessing and discipling as we go throughout the world.

Mastering Self-Control

How do we become self-controlled? Self-control begins when we surrender ourselves to the control of the Holy Spirit.

"But when the Holy Spirit controls our lives He will produce this kind of fruit in us: love, joy, peace, patience, kindness, goodness, faithfulness, gentleness and self-control" (Galatians 5:22, TLB).

How can we come to know and experience the love of God in our lives? How can we truly have joy-love, peace-love, patience-love, goodness-love, kindness-love, faithfulness-love, gentleness-love and discipline-love?

We begin, as Lobstein suggested, by totally yielding ourselves by faith to Christ: "He died once for all to end sin's power, but now He lives forever in unbroken fellowship with God. So look upon your old sin nature as dead and unresponsive to sin, and instead be alive to God, alert to Him, through Jesus Christ our Lord.

"Do not let sin control your puny body any longer; do not give in to its sinful desires. Do not let any part of your bodies become tools of wickedness, to be used for sinning; but give yourselves completely to God — every part of you — for you are back from death and you want to be tools in the hands of God."

A "Living Sacrifice"

"And so, dear brothers, I plead with you to give your

bodies to God. Let them be a living sacrifice, holy — the kind He can accept. When you think of what He has done for you, is this too much to ask?

"Don't copy the behavior and customs of this world, but be a new and different person with a fresh newness in all you do and think. Then you will learn from your own experience how His ways will really satisfy you" (Romans 12:1, 2, TLB).

Someone has said, "The trouble with living sacrifices is that they keep crawling off the altar." That may be true. We "crawl off the altar" when we sin, and the only way to put self back on the altar is to breathe spiritually — confess our known sins in accordance with the promise of 1 John 1:9 and appropriate the fullness of the Holy Spirit as we are commanded to do by faith (Ephesians 5:18). When we do this, we will be living supernaturally and our lives will produce the fruit of the Spirit in great abundance.

Only by being filled with the Spirit, and thus realizing the fruit of the Spirit, can spiritual gifts be effectively utilized in witnessing and building up the Body of Christ.

CHAPTER TWENTY-SIX

Gifts Of The Holy Spirit

My library contains numerous books on the subject of the gifts of the Holy Spirit. Most of these books I have read with great interest over the years — some of them, totally or in part, many times.

Most of these books contain lists of the gifts of the Spirit, with accompanying definitions of varying length and depth. Interestingly, no two lists are identical, and, while some definitions seem to agree, others vary considerably.

Here are some examples. Dr. Charles Caldwell Ryrie, respected scholar and theologian, in his book, *The Holy Spirit*, lists 14 spiritual gifts. Dr. Peter Wagner, also a respected scholar and theologian, lists 27 gifts in his book. And most other writers number the gifts somewhere in between.

An Infinite Mixture

Dr. Wagner suggests the list of spiritual gifts is "open-ended." He writes, "There are gifts mentioned in Ephesians that are also mentioned in Romans, and some in Romans mentioned in 1 Corinthians, and some in 1 Corinthians mentioned in Ephesians. Apparently, they are not intended to be complete catalogs of gifts that God gives. And one could surmise that if none of the three lists is complete in itself, probably the three lists together are not complete" (*Your Spiritual Gifts*, page 62).

William Fitch writes that the Holy Spirit has blessed the Church with "an almost infinite mixture of gifts" (*The Ministry of the Holy Spirit*, page 32).

With so diverse and vast a subject to cover, it is no wonder that people become confused by reading books and listening to numerous speakers talk on the subject.

It is complicated all the more by the presence of man's natural talents and abilities.

Spiritual Gifts and Natural Abilities

Often I have been asked, "What is the difference between a spiritual gift and natural ability?" Well, the difference is not always clear. Keep in mind, though, that spiritual gifts as well as natural abilities come from God.

Whether a certain ability you have is the result of being spiritually gifted or naturally talented really is not that important. What matters is that you develop that gift or ability to its fullest potential through the control and empowering of the Holy Spirit and through much hard work, and that you use it according to God's will and for His glory.

Unlimited Power

As I have prayerfully studied the Scriptures, I have come to the conclusion that any listing of spiritual gifts would indeed be incomplete and would be placing limitations on the sovereign power of God to grant special abilities to His children. Where would such a list end?

The more closely we analyze the nature of spiritual gifts, the longer the list becomes. Consider, for example, the gift of evangelism.

Does a person who has never witnessed for Christ to a group of more than three people necessarily have the same abilities as a "mass meeting evangelist," such as Billy Graham? Consider, too, those who primarily communicate the gospel not so much verbally as they do in written form.

For instance, Frank Allnutt's evangelistic books that tie in with "Star Wars" and other popular movies and themes have communicated the gospel to hundreds of thousands, many of whom would never listen to Billy Graham or attend a church service. Does Frank have a special ability to evangelize? Or to write? Or both?

In each of these cases, the special ability of evangelism appears to have been granted in a unique way. The purpose of the gift is the same, but the method of communicating the gospel is different in each case, and therefore different abilities are required. So you see, if we wanted to project a list of spiritual gifts that far, we could add the gifts of "mass meeting evangelism," "personal evangelism" and, perhaps, "journalistic evangelism."

Uniqueness of Spiritual Gifts

Paul said the Church is like the physical body of Christ, with each member performing a special function in coordination with the entire body:

"Yet, the body has many parts, not just one part. If the foot says, 'I am not a part of the body because I am not a hand,' that does not make it any less a part of the body. And what would you think if you heard an ear say, 'I am only an ear, and not an eye'? Would that make it any less a part of the body?

"Suppose the whole body were an eye — then how would you hear? Or if your whole body were just one big ear, how could you smell anything?

"But that isn't the way God has made us. He has made many parts for our bodies and has put each part just where He wants it. What a strange thing a body would be if it had only one part! So He has made many parts, but still there is only one body.

"The eye can never say to the hand, 'I don't need you.' The head can't say to the feet, 'I don't need you'" (1 Corinthians 12:14-21, TLB).

Within the Body of Christ, each of us has a unique function. True, two people might have similar functions — just as a body has two hands that function similarly. But those two hands are not identical. Just try to wear a lefthand glove on your right hand! The hands have similar functions, not identical functions. You and

I might have similar abilities, but we are not identical. We are unique creations of God.

Therefore, we should not look upon our abilities with pride or be boastful of them. On the other hand, we should not be envious or look with disdain on others because of their different abilities.

It is important to point out that each of us receives at least one spiritual gift from the Holy Spirit: "Now God gives us many kinds of special abilities" (1 Corinthians 12:4, TLB). "The Holy Spirit displays God's power through each of us as a means of helping the entire church" (1 Corinthians 12:7, TLB).

Defining the Gifts

Since it is beyond the scope of this book to delve at length into the nature of specific gifts, in the appendix are some general definitions for those gifts mentioned in the following passages: 1 Corinthians 12, Romans 12 and Ephesians 4.

In 1 Corinthians 12, the following spiritual gifts are mentioned: wisdom, knowledge, faith, healing, miracles, prophecy, discerning of spirits, tongues, interpretation of tongues, apostleship, teaching, helping and administration.

Romans 12 adds, without repeating those mentioned above, these gifts of the spirit: leadership, exhortation, giving and mercy.

Ephesians 4 mentions four church offices: apostle, prophet, evangelist, pastor-teacher. Those who are called by the Lord to any church office can be assured that the Holy Spirit will enable them through special gifts to carry out the responsibilities of that office:

"For I can do everything God asks me to with the help of Christ who gives me the strength and power.... And my God shall supply all your needs according to His riches in glory in Christ Jesus" (Philippians 4:13 TLB, 19, NAS).

The Purpose of Spiritual Gifts

"Why is it that He gives us these special abilities to do certain things best? It is that God's people will be equipped to do better work for Him, building up the Church, the body of Christ, to a position of strength and maturity; until finally we all believe alike about our salvation and about our Savior, God's Son, and all become full-grown in the Lord — yes, to the point of being filled full with Christ" (Ephesians 4:12, 13, TLB).

From the above passage of Scripture, we see that each of us has the obligation first of all to *use* our gifts in a scriptural way. We would be poor stewards of what the Holy Spirit has given us if we ignored the special abilities He has given to us.

Next, we must use our gifts to glorify Christ — not to glorify ourselves, or to glorify some other person, or even to glorify the gift itself. In the first letter of Peter, this is explained for us:

"Are you called to preach? Then preach as though God Himself were speaking through you. Are you called to help others? Do it with all the strength and energy that God supplies, so that God will be glorified through Jesus Christ — to Him be glory and power forever and ever" (1 Peter 4:11, TLB).

Second, we have the obligation to use our spiritual gifts in a scriptural manner to help equip others for Christian service. The apostle Paul writes that spiritual gifts are given "for the equipping of the saints for the work of service, to the building up of the body of Christ" (Ephesians 4:12, NAS).

It is important for us always to exercise our gifts in the power and control of the Holy Spirit — never through our own, fleshly efforts. It is possible for a Christian with, say, the gift of teaching, to exercise that gift while in a carnal or unspiritual state. When that happens, the shortcomings of our old nature hinder the effectiveness of the gift in such a way that Christ is discredited and the saints divided in their witness for Him.

But a Spirit-filled Christian — one who has confessed all known sin in his life and has by faith appropriated the filling of the Holy Spirit — will exercise his spiritual gift apart from his fleshly ability, because he is allowing the Holy Spirit to control and empower him. When this happens, then Christ is glorified and the saints are built up in the faith as a body.

The Unity of the Body

"We are all parts of one body," writes Paul in his letter to the Ephesians. "We have the same Spirit, and we have all been called to the same glorious future. For us there is only one Lord, one faith, one baptism, and we all have the same God and Father who is over us all and in us all, and living through every part of us" (Ephesians 4:4-7, TLB).

As we fellowship together in our common bond in Christ, building up one another through the scriptural use of our spiritual gifts, we "become more and more in every way like Christ who is the Head of His body, the Church. Under His direction the whole body is fitted together perfectly, and each part in its own special way helps the other parts, so that the whole body is healthy and growing and full of love" (Ephesians 4:15, 16, TLB). In this way our Lord is pleased and glorified.

Shared Through Love

While the Christians at Corinth possessed all the spiritual gifts (1 Corinthians 1:7), they were not glorifying Christ or building up one another. Instead, they were glorifying themselves, glorifying their special gifts, and exercising their gifts in the flesh instead of in the power and control of the Holy Spirit.

Time and again the apostle Paul stressed to the Corinthians that an atmosphere of godly love — *agape* love — must prevail or else the exercising of their gifts would be fruitless. Nowhere is this truth more eloquently stated by Paul than in the thirteenth chapter of First Corinthians to which I have already referred.

In verse one, Paul teaches regarding the use of the gift of tongues: "If I speak with the tongues of men and of angels, but do not have love, I have become a noisy gong or a clanging cymbal" (NAS).

Next, Paul expands the admonition to include other gifts: "If I had the gift of prophecy and knew all about what is going to happen in the future, knew everything about *everything*, but didn't love others, what good would it do? Even if I had the gift of faith so that I could speak to a mountain and make it move, I would still be worth nothing at all without love. If I gave everything I have to poor people, and if I were burned alive for preaching the Gospel but didn't love others, it would be of no value whatever" (1 Corinthians 13:2, 3, TLB).

"Pursue love," Paul emphasizes in the next chapter, "yet desire earnestly spiritual gifts" (1 Corinthians 14:1, NAS). Paul is speaking about *balance* here — balance between the exercise of spiritual gifts and our love relationship with Christ and our brothers and sisters in Christ.

He is cautioning us not to emphasize gifts over love. We are to fellowship in love and in *unity* in the common bond of having Christ as our Savior and Lord, and not on the basis of any particular spiritual gift, doctrine or anything else that would tend to focus on our differences and thus *separate* us.

Christians are to aim for spiritual *equality* with one another, not spiritual *sameness*. Our gifts may differ, but the Giver is the same for us all:

"Now God gives us many kinds of special abilities, but it is the same Holy Spirit who is the source of them all. There are different kinds of service to God, but it is the same Lord we are serving.

"There are many ways in which God works in our lives, but it is the same God who does the work in and through all of us who are His. This Holy Spirit displays God's power through each of us as a means of helping the entire Church" (1 Corinthians 12:4-7, TLB).

This principle of spiritual equality, not sameness, is derived from Paul's second letter to the Corinthians, in which he writes: "At the present time your plenty will supply what they need, so that in turn their plenty will supply what you need. Then there will be equality" (2 Corinthians 8:14, NIV).

Not one of us is a total body within himself: collectively we are the body of Christ. The hand can accomplish only certain kinds of functions. The eyes cannot physically grasp objects, but they can see them. The ears cannot transport the body like feet can, but ears can hear many sounds. The hand needs the eye, and the eye needs the hand. All parts of the body need each other in order to function as a healthy body. Are the parts the same? No. Do they have equality? Yes!

We have briefly discussed in this chapter the purposes of spiritual gifts. In the next chapter we will look at spiritual gifts and how they relate to our individual spiritual maturity.

CHAPTER TWENTY-SEVEN

Spiritual Gifts And Spiritual Maturity

A friend once asked me, "Are all the spiritual gifts for today?" and "How can I discern my spiritual gifts?" He had been reading a number of books with conflicting views on gifts and had heard sermons — some encouraging him to discover his gifts and others saying the gifts are not for today. He was woefully confused.

I shared with this friend that I have been a Christian for 35 years and have known the reality of the fullness of the Spirit for almost 30 years. I explained that I have seen God do remarkable — even miraculous — things in and through my life throughout the years. Yet, I have not gone to great lengths to know my gifts, because I believe that whatever God calls me to do He will enable me to do if I am willing to trust and obey Him, work hard and discipline myself.

The Holy Spirit obviously controls and distributes all the gifts. So when I am filled, controlled and empowered with the Holy Spirit, I possess all of the gifts potentially. God could give me any gift I need.

Gifts: Instantaneous and Developmental

I went on to tell my young friend that some of the gifts of the Spirit are supernatural enhancements of abilities common to all men — like *wisdom*. Other gifts — such as healing — are granted by the Holy Spirit to only a select few.

But the gifts differ in another way, too. Some are *instantaneous*, and others are *developmental* in nature. The gift of tongues at Pentecost was *instantaneous*, while the gifts of preaching and teaching are more *developmental*.

The developmental gifts are developed by the Holy Spirit within us over a period of time, just as the fruit of the Spirit are, and usually require some hard work on our part in the process. One is not born into the spiritual kingdom a mature Christian, for the fruit of the Spirit — which is love in its various aspects of joy, peace, patience, kindness, goodness, faithfulness, gentleness and discipline — is developed in time as we walk and work in faith and obedience.

Prepared for Service

With this in mind, we need to understand and remember that whatever God calls us to do He will enable us to do. Again, however, three elements play a part in the developmental gifts: the empowering of the Holy Spirit, dedicated work on our part and an appreciable amount of time over which the work of the Holy Spirit coupled with our efforts bring about a degree of maturity in our lives and the use of the particular gifts God has given us.

The apostle Paul explains this wonderful truth: "For it is God who works in you, both to will and to work for His good pleasure" (Philippians 2:13, NAS).

God's Holy Spirit is at work in our lives, empowering and controlling us — but we must, as a matter of our own wills, consecrate our lives to God and oftentimes work hard and long, with wisdom, power and the enabling of the Holy Spirit to accomplish what God calls us to do.

A Gifted Preacher

The late Dr. William Evans, famous Bible teacher and pulpit orator, was one of the most eloquent preachers I have ever heard. He serves as an example of a person who developed his spiritual gift.

Dr. Evans believed that he had been called of God to

be a preacher. But he spoke in a high, squeaky, English cockney accent that was not particularly pleasant to the ear and certainly not conducive to preaching the most "joyful news ever announced."

So when young Evans told Dwight L. Moody (under whose ministry he had become a Christian) about his calling to be a preacher, Moody unhesitatingly advised him, "Forget it! You don't have the ability to speak, and no one would listen to you."

But William Evans determined that he would become a great preacher for the glory of God. So, like Demosthenes of old, he began to practice speaking with pebbles in his mouth and to practice deep diaphragm breathing. After several years, he developed a deep, resonant, bass voice — one of the most beautiful speaking voices I have ever heard. Wherever he went, congregations would pack the pews to hear him preach.

William Evans was an example of Philippians 2:13 in action. Did he have the spiritual gift of preaching? Of course he did! But it did not come to him overnight. He had to work long and hard, by faith and in the power of the Holy Spirit to develop his spiritual gift.

As stated earlier, God gives each of us at least one spiritual gift (1 Corinthians 12:4), and we are obligated to be good stewards of our spiritual gifts.

Unbalanced Emphasis on Spiritual Gifts

While some Christians are remiss in not using their spiritual gifts for the glory of God and the building up of the body of Christ, all too many are actually quenching the Spirit in just the opposite way — by overemphasizing spiritual gifts.

Many Bible teachers and pastors believe, as I do, that there is a general overemphasis or unbalanced emphasis today on spiritual gifts. Among them is Dr. Gene Getz, professor at Dallas Theological Seminary and founding pastor of the Fellowship Bible Church of Dallas.

For many years, Dr. Getz strongly emphasized in his teaching that Christians should endeavor to discover their gifts. But now, instead, he stresses the concept of "body maturity." His teaching now emphasizes the proper balance of faith, hope, love and the qualities of leadership as explained in the Scriptures — particularly in 1 Timothy 3 and Titus 1.

In his book, *Building Up One Another*, Dr. Getz discusses the reasons why he feels the discovery of one's spiritual gifts has been overemphasized. These can be summarized in three points: *confusion, rationalization* and *self-deception*.

He believes that teaching on the discovery of spiritual gifts can be *confusing* when Christians are told to seek certain spiritual gifts when, in fact, they might already have those gifts or may never be granted them by the Holy Spirit.

A wrong emphasis on gifts can lead to *rationalization*. A person might decline to fulfill his obligations to others because he does not believe that he has a particular spiritual gift. For example, we often hear stories of individuals who make no effort to share Christ with others because they do not believe they have the gift of evangelism. Other Christians refuse to teach Sunday school classes at their churches because they believe they do not have the gift of teaching.

The truth is that such people are not taught the developmental nature of some spiritual gifts. A person might have the gift of evangelism, only he may never have learned how to share the gospel clearly with others. Another person might have the gift of teaching but perhaps has never taken the opportunity or time to develop teaching skills.

The contrary is true as well: some people can be *self-deceived* into believing they have a certain spiritual gift when they actually have never been empowered with such a gift. One reason for such self-deception is that some people are looking for instant, effortless maturity in Christ. They want maturity *now*, without the "bother" of hard work over an extended period of time.

A Timely Process

Do we think and act like mature children of God at the time of conversion? Hardly! But with the empowering and control of the Holy Spirit, coupled with our determination to live obedient, consecrated lives, with much discipline and hard work we mature in Christ over a period of time.

Lane Adams, a gifted teacher, writer and former pastor of the Second Presbyterian Church of Memphis, Tennessee, and a former Billy Graham associate, speaks about this maturing process in his widely read book, *How Come It's Taking Me So Long to Get Better?* He writes:

"There will be little argument about spiritual birth or spiritual maturity, but almost no one seems to take seriously the intermediate stages demanded by the analogy of physical and spiritual life paralleling one another in a developmental process. While avoiding the absurdities inevitably involved in pressing the analogy too far, I do believe that for every stage of physical development there seems to be a corresponding stage of spiritual development.

"Thus, in the process of time, utilizing God's appointed means of grace — the Word, prayer and sacraments — the inquirer moves through these various stages: from the nursery to the kindergarten into the primary and junior stages of life, through the area of agonizing spiritual adolescence, into young adulthood, and finally into maturity."

The apostle Paul serves as an example of one who developed extraordinary abilities through the power of the Holy Spirit. Paul did not become a great teacher overnight. It took years of hard work and, at first, the results were not encouraging. At the beginning, even the disciples would not accept Paul or his teaching (Acts 9:26).

Paul actually had been a believer for some 18 years before he began to have a major impact on the world for Christ. The first three years were spent in Damascus and the Arabian Desert. His first trip took him to Jerusalem for 15 days. Then he was in Tarsus for 14 years, followed by a year in Antioch.

Lane Adams, in reflecting on Paul's 18 years of development, writes, "I shrink inside when I think of the times I have mounted the pulpit, recited the conversion experience of the apostle Paul, and then indicated that he went out and turned the world upside down for Jesus Christ *immediately*.

"This simply was not the case. There is a difference of opinion among scholars concerning New Testament dating, but it seems rather plain that many years went by before the Holy Spirit laid the dramatic burden on Paul as a missionary of the cross" (*How Come It's Taking Me So Long to Get Better?* page 91).

A Matter of Faith

My advice to you is this: if you strongly desire to serve the Lord in some particular way — such as teaching, ask the Holy Spirit in faith to empower you to become an effective teacher. Now, it may be that the Holy Spirit will see fit to make you a great teacher overnight, but this is most unlikely. So if it does not happen, do not be discouraged. Have faith!

Continue to ask and believe that the Holy Spirit will make you an effective teacher of the Word of God and *work hard to develop teaching skills and methods*. Be prepared to sacrifice. And be patient — it might take considerable time before anyone will even listen to you.

But, by all means, have faith that the Holy Spirit will bestow spiritual gifts upon you, though they might be developmental in nature and you might have to work hard and long to develop your gift. The Bible reminds us that "faith without works is useless" (James 2:20, NAS).

Now if we are unique members of the body of Christ, if each of us possesses a special task to accomplish and the Holy Spirit empowers us to carry out that task, a tremendously significant biblical truth becomes obvious: God does indeed have a plan for each of our lives. And He gives us the direction and power of His Holy Spirit to accomplish that plan.

If we do His will, we are living supernaturally, and our lives are greatly blessed, as are the lives of those around us. But if we fail to carry out God's plan for our lives, we are living carnal lives — frustrated and fruitless lives — without purpose and meaning.

Rewards in Heaven

At the judgment seat of Christ, we will be judged according to how well we have lived our lives according to God's plan:

"And no one can ever lay any other real foundation than that one we already have — Jesus Christ. But there are various kinds of materials that can be used to build on that foundation. Some use gold and silver and and jewels; and some build with sticks, and hay, or even straw.

"There is going to come a time of testing at Christ's judgment day to see what kind of material each builder has used. Everyone's work will be put through the fire so that all can see whether or not it keeps its value, and what was really accomplished" (1 Corinthians 3:11-13, TLB).

This will be a special judgment for believers only, and it pertains to our reward or loss in heaven as a result of our works. "But if the house he [the Christian] has built burns up, he will have a great loss. He himself will be saved, but like a man escaping through a wall of flames"

(1 Corinthians 3:15, TLB).

Serving God

The tragedy of many Christian lives is that believers are so involved in trying to discover or receive additional spiritual gifts that they are not developing and using their known gifts and abilities to do God's will.

For this reason, when I counsel in the area of Christian service, I do not suggest going to great lengths to discover spiritual gifts. Rather, I encourage full surrender to Jesus Christ and the importance of being filled with the Holy Spirit. Only then should one seek God's direction in life. Then, by faith and hard work, a person can set out with determination to accomplish that to which God has called him.

Paul wrote about this important principle in his letter to the Philippians: "Dearest friends, when I was there with you, you were always so careful to follow my instructions. And now that I am away you must be even more careful to do the good things that result from being saved, obeying God with deep reverence, shrinking back from all that might displease Him....

"For I can do everything God asks me to with the help of Christ who gives me the strength and power" (Philippians 2:12, 4:13, TLB). This, of course, can be done only if a Christian totally submits himself to the lordship of Jesus Christ.

Let me repeat what Paul wrote to the Christians in Rome: "And so, dear brothers, I plead with you to give your bodies to God. Let them be a living sacrifice, holy — the kind He can accept. When you think of what He has done for you, is this too much to ask?

"Don't copy the behavior and customs of this world, but be a new and different person with a fresh newness in all you do and think. Then you will learn from your own experience how His ways will really satisfy you.

"As God's messenger I give each of you God's warning:

Be honest in your estimate of yourselves, measuring your value by how much faith God has given you.

"Just as there are many parts to our bodies, so it is with Christ's body. We are all parts of it, and it takes every one of us to make it complete, for we each have different work to do. So we belong to each other, and each needs all the others.

"God has given each of us the ability to do certain things well" (Romans 12:1-6a, TLB).

Spiritual gifts can be a vibrant part of your supernatural life. But, as I have already cautioned, do not place such emphasis on gifts that your life becomes off-balance. The gifts of the Spirit are given for glorifying Christ *in love*, for equipping the saints *in love*, and for unifying the body of Christ *in love*.

CHAPTER TWENTY-EIGHT

Sharing The Supernatural Life

Sometime ago I was at a conference in St. Louis, anticipating an early adjournment so that I could catch a plane to Los Angeles and rejoin my waiting family.

When I arrived at the airport, I discovered that flight after flight had been cancelled because of poor weather conditions. Rushing from one airline ticket counter to another, I hoped to find one that was still flying its planes. Finally, to my disappointment, all the airlines cancelled their flights.

On one hand I was discouraged, but on the other I was encouraged by the promise of the Bible: "And we know that all that happens to us is working for our good if we love God and are fitting into His plans" (Romans 8:28, TLB).

Back at the hotel for the night, in the lobby I met a businessman who was hungry for God. As I shared Christ with him, I learned that he and his wife had been visiting a different church every Sunday for the past couple of years. They were looking for God — but could not find Him.

I explained to my new friend how to receive Christ. Together, then, we knelt and prayed, and he received Christ into his life as his personal Lord and Savior.

Eager to Receive Christ

With great joy and enthusiasm my new brother in Christ announced, "I want to take these things you have shared with me to my wife because she too is eager to receive Christ." Then he asked, "What do you do with your life?"

I told him that I travel the world, telling anyone who will listen about Christ. Then he made a statement I shall never forget: "You must bring a lot of happiness into this world."

Though I was disappointed at missing a flight home, I went to bed that night with a joyful heart, singing praises to God because I have the privilege of bringing a lot of happiness into this world. I awakened the next morning with that same melody in my heart — that statement running over and over in my mind, "You must bring a lot of happiness into this world." Now I am writing a book, especially for Christians: *How You Can Bring a Lot of Happiness Into This World.*

A Presidential Candidate

Recently I was witnessing to a man who professed to be a Christian. He was a very distinguished man — in fact, a presidential candidate. As our conversation progressed, I challenged him to make his life count for God.

He said, with a bit of impatience, "I don't wear my religion on my sleeve; it's personal and private, and I don't talk about it."

"Please forgive me," I said. "I don't want to offend you, but did it ever occur to you that in order for you to say that you are a Christian it cost the Lord Jesus Christ His life? He died for your sins.

"It cost all the disciples great persecution and most of them martyrdom. And through the centuries, millions of Christians have died as martyrs, getting this message through to you. Now, let me ask you, do you really think that your Christianity is personal and private and that you shouldn't talk about it?"

"No, sir! I'm wrong," he said. "Please help me to make Christ more a part of what I'm doing."

Longing to Know Christ Personally

Recently I was talking to a man who was attending one of our executive meetings. He had grown up in the church and was a trustee. Belonging to one of the leading families in the city, he was a man of great influence. When he heard my explanation of the gospel, he realized the difference between the *historical* Christian and the *personal* Christian. As a result of his new understanding, he received Christ into his life and became a "new creature."

The historical Christian is one who believes intellectually that Jesus Christ is the Son of God, that He died for our sins, that He was raised from the dead. Such a person is often very active in his church. He may be an elder or deacon, Sunday school teacher, even a minister or missionary.

He can believe all about Jesus — intellectually, but he doesn't know Him personally. For such a person there has never been a time, as an act of the will, when he has received Christ into his life as Savior and Lord by faith.

The apostle John wrote, "But to all who received Him, He gave the right to become children of God" (John 1:12, TLB).

The historical Christian has never experienced being born again as Jesus explained: "Unless one is born of water and the Spirit, he cannot enter the Kingdom of God. Men can only reproduce human life, but the Holy Spirit gives new life from heaven.... For God loved the world so much that He gave His only Son so that anyone who believes in Him shall not perish but have eternal life" (John 3:5, 6, 16, TLB).

The man to whom I referred fit the definition of a historical Christian, but he wanted to become a personal Christian. He wanted to know Christ in a personal way. And so, very simply, as he read the Four Spiritual Laws, a simple presentation of the gospel, he opened his heart to Christ and began immediately to rejoice in the assurance of his salvation.

Three days later, I had the opportunity to see my

friend in another situation. He was talking to a group of his peers — many of them leaders in the city — telling them about his new life in Christ.

This man is only one of millions of historical Christians in the world. Our surveys indicate that approximately 50% of the churchgoers in America — and up to 90% in some churches — are historical Christians who are unable to honestly say that they love and know the Lord Jesus Christ personally.

They have never received Christ as their personal Savior and Lord. They might know Him intellectually, but not personally. But when given a clear, simple presentation of the gospel — such as the one found in the Four Spiritual Laws booklet — most respond enthusiastically.

Fishing for Men

Nothing that you and I can do is more important in this world than reaching others with the gospel of Jesus Christ — helping them grow and become witnesses for our Savior and Lord.

Jesus explained the importance of such a fruitful witness: "By this is my Father glorified, that you bear much fruit, and so prove to be my disciples" (John 15:8, NAS). "Follow Me, and I will make you fishers of men" (Matthew 4:19, NAS).

As I already have stated, it is our responsibility to follow Christ. It is His responsibility to make us fishers of men. What a relief to know that the responsibility of bearing fruit is the Lord's.

God asks only that we make ourselves completely available to Him, that we trust Him and are obedient to Him. He wants us to live holy, righteous lives and to tell others about Christ at every opportunity, but their response is dependent upon the working of the Holy Spirit in their lives. *Success in witnessing is simply taking the initiative to share Christ in the power of the Holy Spirit and leaving the results to God.*

Work of the Spirit

Not once have I ever led anyone to Christ, and I never shall. However, I have had the privilege of praying with thousands of people who have received Christ as a result of my witness.

When a person receives Christ, it is the work of the Holy Spirit. That is why I cannot boast over much fruit or be discouraged over little fruit. The responsibility for fruit belongs to the Holy Spirit who works in and through the believer, producing fruit and changing the lives of those who respond favorable to our witness.

The power of our Lord Jesus is available to all who trust and obey Him. The apostle Paul writes, "I pray that you will begin to understand how incredibly great His power is to help those who believe Him. It is that same mighty power that raised Christ from the dead and seated Him in the place of honor at God's right hand in heaven, far, far above any other king or ruler or dictator or leader.

"Yes, His honor is far more glorious than that of anyone else either in this world or in the world to come. And God has put all things under His feet and made Him the supreme Head of the church — which is His Body, filled with Himself, the Author and Giver of everything everywhere" (Ephesians 1:19-23, TLB).

"I Am With You Always"

The Lord Jesus commissioned the disciples to go into all the world and preach the gospel, with the promise that He would always be with them. He said, "I have been given all authority in heaven and earth. Therefore go and make disciples in all the nations…and then teach these new disciples to obey all the commands I have given you" (Matthew 28:18, 20, TLB).

Jesus did not say to them, "Go into all the world…and good luck!" He said, "And be sure of this — that I am with you always, even to the end of the world" (Matthew 28:20, TLB). "I will never, never fail you nor forsake you" (Hebrews 13:5, TLB).

"You Shall Receive Power"

Now, carefully consider the last words the Lord spoke as He met with His disciples on the Mount of Olives only moments before He ascended into heaven. Jesus had previously commissioned His disciples to go into all the world and preach the gospel, and to make disciples of all nations. But He had told them not to leave Jerusalem until they were filled with the power of the Holy Spirit.

"You shall receive power," He said, "when the Holy Spirit has come upon you; and you shall be My witnesses both in Jerusalem, and in Judea and Samaria, and even to the remotest part of the earth" (Acts 1:8, NAS).

Power to Share

A very discouraged university student came to me for counsel after one of my messages. For several months, he had spent at least three hours each day reading his Bible, praying and sharing his faith with others. Yet, he had never introduced anyone to Christ. After a time of discussion, his problem became apparent — he was not controlled and empowered with the Holy Spirit, although he wanted to be.

After I shared with him from the Bible how to appropriate the filling of the Holy Spirit by faith, we prayed together, then by faith he appropriated the power of the Holy Spirit on the authority of God's Word.

That very day he had his first experience of introducing a person to Christ. The next day he successfully witnessed to another, and he has since introduced hundreds of people to the Lord. Obviously, his life was absolutely transformed by the simple act of claiming the fullness of the Holy Spirit by faith.

A very successful businessman and Christian layman came to Arrowhead Springs, our international headquarters, for training. He was the son of a minister, had been reared under the good influence of the church, had been a Sunday school teacher for years, a Sunday school superintendent, deacon, member of the board of trustees of one of America's leading theological seminaries, and president of all the laymen for his denomination for an entire state; yet, he had never to his knowledge introduced anyone to Christ.

Multiplied Ministry

During the training, he learned how to be filled with the Holy Spirit by faith and how to introduce others to Christ. Since that time, he has personally witnessed successfully to hundreds of people and has trained thousands of laymen and pastors through our Lay Institutes for Evangelism. Thousands of others have been introduced to Christ through those whom he has trained.

A pastor of a 1,500-member church attended one of our Pastors' Institutes for Evangelism at Arrowhead Springs where he appropriated the fullness of the Holy Spirit and learned how to introduce others to Christ as a part of our training.

During one afternoon of witnessing for Christ, 14 of the 15 people whom this pastor interviewed prayed with him and received Christ as Savior. Never had he had such an experience. He returned to his pulpit a new man. Soon, hundreds of his church members too had appropriated the fullness of the Holy Spirit by faith. Now they are sharing their enthusiasm for Christ, and through their witness many more are responding to the Savior.

Filled to Shared

The primary purpose for which we are filled with the

Holy Spirit is to make us witnesses for Christ through the life that we live and the words which we speak. I trust that as a result of reading this book you will by faith appropriate the fullness of the Holy Spirit and will witness for our Lord Jesus Christ as a way of life.

The greatest spiritual awakening since Pentecost, in my opinion, has already begun. Millions of Christians are discovering this great source of power which in the first century altered the course of history and turned a wicked Roman Empire upside down.

That same power, the power of the Holy Spirit, is being released through the lives of believing and obedient Christians in our generation to turn our world around and accelerate the fulfillment of the Great Commission in our generation.

As you share your faith in Christ in the power of the Holy Spirit, you too will "bring a lot of happiness into this world."

CHAPTER TWENTY-NINE

The Holy Spirit In A World Of Turmoil

More than a century ago, a missionary meeting was held in the First Baptist Church, Richmond, Virginia. When the offering for missions was taken, the people gave generously and sacrificially.

Later, when the ushers were counting the offering, they found in one basket a card on which was written the word, "Myself." It was singed, "John Lewis Shuck." The card was immediately carried to the pastor. With deep feeling he read it to the congregation.

John Lewis Shuck had heard the call of the Holy Spirit: "Whom shall I send, and who will go for us?" And he had responded, "Here am I; send me." He became the first Southern Baptist missionary to go to China. He had the spirit of revival in his heart and the goal of revival in his eyes.

A Call for Revival

The Holy Spirit has burdened my heart for revival, too-for our nation and for the world. There is no hope for civilization to escape another dark age unless God supernaturally intervenes, unless He touches us with His power.

The more I pray for this great need for the world — especially for the United States — the more I am gripped with the realization that revival will come only when we boldly move up to the front lines of spiritual battle in evangelism and discipleship.

I believe that God is going to touch us in supernatural ways, that our hearts will be deeply stirred and that anything that hinders the working of God's Spirit in our hearts will be removed. I believe that the divine fire of Heaven will come upon us, and be expressed through us.

Many of us have been praying for revival. We realize that our society is becoming paganized, that it has already reached the point of nausea in the eyes and heart of God. We have come to tolerate this decadent, godless nation of America because there is something about sin that, when thrust upon us from every sector, deadens our sensitivity.

The Tide of Secular Humanism

A rising tide of secular humanism is America is threatening this nation's very existence. And all to many of us have succumbed to its subtle encroachment.

Sergio Garcia, our Director of Affairs in Latin America, said, "American culture has been brainwashed by humanism. Humanism is the basis of communism, and there is no power in the Church today because we subscribe to a milk-toast Christianity.

"We must have a balance between a merciful, loving God and a God of judgment. All my life I have known the love of God, and I have preached the love of God. But I must tell my American brothers and sisters that the time has come for us to balance that message of the God of love with the message of the God of judgment.

"Our God is a holy God, a God of fire; He does not tolerate our sin. You and I are a part of a society that is disintegrating before our very eyes because we are not the 'salt of the earth' and are not the 'light of the world,' as our Lord commands us to be."

Our Nation's Christian Heritage

Little attention seems to be given in the secular world today to the many evidences of God's hand in the beginning of our nation. As Pastor Tim LaHaye writes in his timely new book, *The Battle for the Mind,* "In this world, there are two basic lines of reasoning that determine the morals, values, life-style and activities of mankind — the wisdom of man or the wisdom of God (see 1 Corinthians 1:17-25). Today they take the form of atheistic humanism or Christianity.

"Most people today," continues Dr. LaHaye, "do not realize what humanism really is and how it is destroying our culture, families, country — and one day, the entire world. Most of the evils in the world today can be traced to humanism, which has taken over our government, the UN, education, TV, and most of the other influential areas of life."

Dr. LaHaye, Pat Robertson, Jerry Falwell, Oral Roberts, Adrian Rogers, James Robinson and Billy Graham, to name a few, are concerned evangelical leaders who believe that there is a war being waged between the forces of Satan and the forces of God for the minds and souls of Americans. Many times in the current year alone, I have joined some of these and other great men of God to warn multitudes of people about the consequences if we as Christians do not fight against this onslaught of humanism.

Unless there is a mighty work of the Holy Spirit in the lives of Christians of United States, our great nation is doomed to go the way of ancient Rome and all other decadent nations in history.

God's Plan for America

Our current history books, written largely by humanists, usually fail to mention it, but even before America was named, God's plan was being worked out for this great nation to be used of Him to carry His message of love, forgiveness and salvation through Jesus Christ to the rest of the world.

I believe the Holy Spirit was guiding Christopher Columbus on his voyage to the new world when he discovered the North American continent. Not generally known is that the diaries of Columbus make clear that he interpreted his first name of Christopher to mean,

"Christ-bearer," and that he undertook his voyage in search of new lands in which to help establish the gospel of Jesus Christ.

All of the first colleges and universities founded in this country- including outstanding institutions such as Harvard, Princeton, Dartmouth, Yale and Columbia — were established largely for the purpose of acquainting young scholars with the knowledge of God and the Bible, upon which all other branches of wisdom and knowledge rest. During the colonial period, 70% of the graduates of Harvard entered the Christian ministry. The guiding hand of the Holy Spirit was obviously upon our country's institutions of higher learning.

Many of our founding fathers were humble servants of God in the establishment of our republic. Their deep awareness of God is explicit in such documents as the Declaration of Independence.

On July 20, 1775, the Continental Congress set aside the first national day of prayer and fasting, and General George Washington enforced it throughout the army.

He, himself, began and ended every day on his knees in Bible-reading and prayer. Ben Franklin testified at the Constitutional Convention to the truth that "God governs in the affairs of man."

It was a time of impasse — a crucial moment in the beginnings of our young nation. Ben Franklin boldly went on to declare: "If a sparrow cannot fall to the ground without His knowledge, neither can a nation rise without His benediction. I move that we adjourn for prayer."

History records that they followed his suggestion and immediately upon reconvening, the problem that had separated them was resolved.

This nation's greatness has been due, in my opinion, to its belief in God — its Christian heritage. It was not only because many of those who occupied the nation's high offices were obedient to God, but also the dedicated clergy of colonial America. None perceived the soul of the United States and its people more accurately than the distinguished French historian, Alexis de Tocqueville, who wrote in his classic study, *Democracy in America:*

"I sought for the greatness and genius of America in her commodious harbors and her ample rivers; and it was not there; in the fertile fields and the boundless prairies, and it was not there; in her rich mines and her vast world commerce, and it was not there.

"Not until I went into the churches of America, and heard her pulpits aflame with righteousness, did I understand the secret of her genius and power. America is great because she is good, and if America ever ceases to be good, America will cease to be great!"

Biblical Precedents

Whether or not they knew it, our forefathers and de Tocqueville were on firm biblical ground when they warned that, apart from God, America would flounder and break apart. Moses spoke in much the same spirit to the people of Israel just before he turned over the leadership to Joshua and left them, after having struggled for them and with them for more than 40 years of their wilderness experience.

In Deuteronomy 8, Moses recorded God's warnings to His people to keep Him first in their lives and to obey His commands or else He would send plagues on them:

"You must obey all the commandments I give you today. If you do, you will not only multiply and will go in and take over the land promised to your fathers by the Lord. . . .

"Obey the laws of the Lord your God. Walk in His ways and fear Him. . . . For when you have become full and prosperous and have built fine homes to live in, and when your flocks and herds have become very large, and your silver and gold have multiplied, that is the time to watch out that you don't become proud, and forget the Lord your God who brought you out of your slavery in the land of Egypt. . . .

"Always remember that it is the Lord your God who gives you power to become rich, and he does it to fulfill His promise to your ancestors. But if you forget about the Lord your God and worship other gods instead, and follow evil ways, you shall certainly perish, just as the Lord has caused other nations in the past to perish. That will be your fate, too, if you don't obey the Lord your God" (Deuteronomy 8:1, 6, 12-14, 18-20, TLB).

Further on in the book of Deuteronomy, Moses explained to the Israelites the many blessings of God that would be theirs if only they would continue to worship God:

"If you fully obey all of these commandments of the Lord your God, the laws I am declaring to you today, God will transform you into the greatest nation in the world. These are the blessings that will come upon you:

"Blessings in the city,

"Blessings in the field;

"Many children,

"Ample crops,

"Large flocks and herds;

"Blessings of fruit and bread;

"Blessings when you come in,

"Blessings when you go out.

"The Lord will defeat your enemies before you; they will march out together against you but scatter before you in seven directions! The Lord will bless you with good crops and healthy cattle, and prosper everything you do when you arrive in the land the Lord your God is giving you" (Deuteronomy 28:1-8, TLB).

Then Moses told his people what God would do if they turned their back on the Lord their God:

"If you won't listen to the Lord your God and won't obey these laws I am giving you today, then all of these curses shall come upon you:

"Curses in the city;

"Curses in the fields;

"Curses on your fruit and bread;

"The curse of barren wombs;

"Curses upon your crops;

"Curses upon the fertility of your cattle and flocks;

"Curses when you come in;

"Curses when you go out.

"For the Lord Himself will send His personal curse upon you. You will be confused and a failure in everything you do, until at last you are destroyed because of the sin of forsaking Him" (Deuteronomy 28:15-20, TLB)

The tragedy of the ancient Israelites is that they did not heed the warning of Moses. The fate of the children of Israel for their disobedience to God is lamented in Amos 4:

"'I sent you hunger,' says the Lord, 'but it did no good; you still would not return to me. I ruined your crops by holding back the rain three months before the harvest. I sent rain on one city, but not another. While rain fell on one field, another was dry and withered. People from two or three cities would make their weary journey for a drink of water to a city that had rain, but there wasn't ever enough. Yet you wouldn't return to me,' says the Lord.

"'I sent blight and mildew on your farms and your vineyards; the locusts ate your figs and olive trees. And still you wouldn't return to me,' says the Lord. 'I sent you plagues like those of Egypt long ago. I killed your lads in war and drove away your horses. The stench of death was terrible to smell. And yet you refused to come. I destroyed some of your cities, as I did Sodom and Gomorrah; those left are half-burned firebrands snatched away from fire. And still you won't return to me,' says the Lord.

"'Therefore I will bring upon you all these further evils I have spoken of. Prepare to meet your God in judgment, Israel. For you are dealing with the One who formed the mountains and made the winds, and knows your every thought; He turns the morning to darkness and crushes down the mountains underneath His feet: Jehovah, the Lord, the God of Hosts, is His name" (Amos 4:6-13, TLB).

Our holy, sovereign God demands no less in obedience from us, and He will chasten us no less for our disobedience.

The Fading Light

For about 175 years, the American republic acknowledged God as the source of its birth and strength. "In God We Trust" was stamped on our coins. "One Nation Under God" was our slogan. But then something started to go wrong. The fires of our Christian heritage began to die down, and the light of the gospel grew dim.

Ignoring God's warning to Israel, and — through Deuteronomy 8 — to those of us in America, we started to become fat and lazy, proud and rich. We became absorbed in the material things of the world and turned our backs on God. Even Christians began to let the world crowd us into its mold.

The Turning Point

I believe the major departure from our Christian heritage took place in 1963 when the highest court in the land — the Supreme Court of the United States — made a decision that was widely interpreted to mean that there is no place for God anymore in the schools. Prayer and Bible study were now considered illegal.

In my view, the evidence is exceedingly strong that that decision and its rippling effects were catastrophic in their impact on our society. After God had so greatly blessed this nation, the virtual rejection of the Lord from the public schools — which had been born in the cradle of the church — was especially affronting to God. He began immediately to judge and chasten us, both for the action itself and for what it symbolized about the spiritual direction of our country.

In my testimony before the House Judiciary Subcommittee on Courts, Civil Liberties, and Administration of Justice regarding the matter of school prayer, which was included in the Congressional Record of July 31, 1980, I tried to impress upon our political leaders the severity of the situation:

"It is the sad conclusion of many that our relationship with the God of our fathers is in greater peril at this moment than at any previous time in our history. For many, the depth of our rejection of God and the rich heritage of our nation's Judeo-Christian values was symbolized tragically in the 1963 decision of the U.S. Supreme Court in the case of *Abington Township v. Schempp*. This ruling had the effect of virtually banishing from the public schools all mention of the Divine Father whom we acknowledge on our coins and in so many other areas of public life.

"I am one who believes that our turning away from God in our prosperity — and especially our rejection of Him in this very basic way — has brought upon the United States the same chastening which the ancient nation of Israel so often experienced when the Israelites had turned aside from Him. I believe that the evidence is overwhelming that we in this country are under God's judgment, and that it is altogether likely that much worse troubles lie dead ahead of us if we do not leave the present course we are following."

God's Judgment

Consider some of the developments, or "plagues" if you will, which followed that decision. Within a short time, President Kennedy was assassinated. It would be easy to say, "Well, that would have happened anyway." The Vietnam War began to accelerate, and it was only a couple of years before the Gulf of Tonkin Resolution and the massive American buildup in Southeast Asia. "Well," one could say, "that would probably have happened anyway."

The drug culture began to escalate rapidly. Crime accelerated. American families began disintegrating at an ever faster rate as divorces began to increase dramatically. Racial conflict in cities turned bloody, and whole blocks were burned. Campuses became battlegrounds. Senator Robert Kennedy was assassinated, then Dr. Martin Luther King.

Sexual morality crumbled rapidly. The new doctrine, "If it feels good, do it," became extremely widespread. It was reflected, in part, in drastic declines in respect for chastity, and in soaring rates of teenage pregnancy and venereal disease. Economic problems, military problems, energy problems began to mount to the point that they are today at crisis levels. Abuse of trust has become commonplace.

The Supreme Court opened the floodgates to legalized abortion-on-demand, and, in the name of women's rights to control their bodies, the murder of the unborn became an accepted, legally respectable form of birth control. We have been horrified at the genocide in Cambodia, where several million people have either been allowed to starve or, in many cases, simply murdered.

A generation earlier the world was shocked and appalled at the systematic murder of some six million Jews by Hitler. And yet within less than a decade, some eight million pre-born infants — human lives in every sense except independent life support — have been slaughtered in our own country through abortion.

I shudder for America when I read what the Ten Commandments say about murder, what the Proverbs say about the shedding of innocent blood, and what Jesus had to say about children. I am afraid for our nation. I fear His indignation, His chastening and His judgment.

Pray for America

Humanism has become the unofficial religion of America. So, for this reason, I pray daily for revival in our country; for preservation of the privilege to preach the gospel and to see the fulfillment of the Great Commission. The United States represents the major source of manpower, money and technology to help reach the rest of the world for Christ.

Unless we repent, the one great burden of my heart — to see the whole world saturated with the gospel and every person with a chance to say "Yes" to Christ — will be forfeited for this generation, perhaps for a thousand years. We could well be plunged into another dark age, as some of our leading Christian intellectuals are now predicting.

The enemies of God are largely in control of the media, education and government, and they have permeated every other facet of society. Let there be no mistake about it. We cannot remain silent any longer, because if we are, we will march silently to our graves and the opportunity to preach the gospel to the world will be lost.

Sometime ago, as I considered the growing threat to our freedom, God reminded me of Psalms 2:1-5.

"What fools the nations are to rage against the Lord! How strange that men should try to outwit God! For a summit conference of the nations has been called to plot against the Lord and his Messiah, Christ the King.

"'Come, let us break his chains,' they say, 'and free ourselves from all this slavery to God.' But God in heaven merely laughs! He is amused by all their puny plans, and then in fierce fury he rebukes them and fills them with fear" (TLB).

No, you and I do not have anything to fear. Our God is the true God, the holy God. He is the God of justice, the God of love, the God of power. But we do not play games with Him. We do not compromise our moral standards. If we do, let me assure you, as David of old records in Psalms 32, "God chastens us when we are disobedient." And David knew what he was talking about. Having lied and committed adultery and murder, he began to feel God's chastening — until he repented.

If we go on living indifferent to the Scriptures and allow our moral standards to deteriorate, God will judge us and He will judge America. This nation which He has blessed so abundantly will forfeit the opportunity which He has given it to help fulfill the Great Commission and will quite likely lose our freedom as a result of our disobedience.

The Holy Spirit: The Key to Revival

The Holy Spirit is the key to revival. He is the key to revival because He is the key to supernatural living, and apart from living supernaturally — living in the fullness of the Holy Spirit — man can do nothing to save our country and help fulfill the Great Commission.

I love America for what it has been and for what it can be — with God's help. But I abhor the sins of our morally bankrupt nation today.

Difficult times are on the horizon for America — socially, economically, militarily, politically and in the areas of natural resources and energy. But, still, I remain optimistic because it is during times of trial and tribulation that man often turns to God for mercy. I believe that God will use the turmoil of the past two decades and the imminent future to bring us to our knees, literally, as a nation and as individuals.

The Holy Spirit is already convicting many Christians of their lethargy, and a spiritual Mt. St. Helens is about to erupt, spewing the good news of the love and forgiveness of Jesus Christ far and wide throughout our land and the world. We shall see a resurgence in evangelism and a zeal unparalleled in Church history as we endeavor — in the power of the Holy Spirit — to help fulfill the Great Commission.

The Holy Spirit will touch the hearts of Christians in every denomination and every independent local church in a way that can result only in a powerful, marching Body of Christ, united in God's love and for His kingdom as never before.

The spiritual balance within the Body of Christ will move toward a biblical base, and those who are living Spirit-filled, supernatural lives will assume greater leadership in the affairs of the Church and in secular society. Satanic opposition will intensify, but it will only strengthen the Church by placing her in greater reliance on the power and guidance of the Holy Spirit.

More Christians will exhibit the fruit of the Spirit and the working of spiritual gifts to a degree and in a measure never before witnessed. The Church is about to enter its finest hour on earth, and Jesus Christ will be glorified as never before.

The time of awakening has come, and the winds of revival are beginning to blow throughout the world. But world revival will come only when believers meet the biblical standards of revival and awakening.

"If my people, which are called by my name, will humble themselves, and pray, and seek my face, and turn from their wicked ways, then will I hear from heaven, and will forgive their sin, and will heal their land" (2 Chronicles 7:14, KJ).

So I urge you, join with me — and with millions of our brothers and sisters in Christ — as we look upon the majesty of God in a fresh, new way. Then answer the call of His Holy Spirit to live supernaturally, to respond to the Great Commission of the Lord Jesus Christ to help evangelize and disciple the nations of the world for the glory, honor and praise of our living God and Father.

Appendix A

Following are general definitions of the gifts of the Holy Spirit which are mentioned in the passages found in 1 Corinthians 12 and 14, Romans 12 and Ephesians 4:

WISDOM (1 Corinthians 12:8)

Wisdom is a natural ability that is generally developed over a long period of time by all people. The spiritual gift of wisdom, however, while usually acquired as the believer matures spiritually, can also be instantaneous in nature. That is to say that a Christian who has this gift can clearly discern the mind of Christ in applying specific knowledge to specific needs that arise within the body of Christ.

KNOWLEDGE (1 Corinthians 12:8)

Knowledge is another spiritual gift that has a counterpart in natural talent. Everyone is born with the natural ability to discover certain information and formulate ideas from that information. But the Christian who has the spiritual gift of knowledge has a supernatural ability to discover, accumulate, analyze and clarify information and ideas that are pertinent to the growth and well-being of the body of Christ.

FAITH (1 Corinthians 12:9)

All believers are given faith in some measure and for certain reasons. For example, every believer is given the ability to have faith in Christ for his salvation. Each Christian is also to live by faith. Beyond that, faith is a spiritual gift that the believer may develop and apply in virtually every area of life.

This gift is the special ability to discern with extraordinary confidence the will and purposes of God as they relate to the growth and well-being of the body of Christ. It is evident in the lives of those ministers and laymen who do believe, as contrasted with the lives of those who do not.

HEALING (1 Corinthians 12:8, 28)

The gift of healing does not suggest that the recipient of the gift is given supernatural powers over the human body and over disease. Rather, it means that the individual is given the privilege of being the vessel through which God's works of healing are directed.

Healing in a strict sense is a miracle of God. This gift is available in its application to all Christians through the ministry of the elders of the church. This is described in James 5:14, 15:

"Is anyone sick? He should call for the elders of the church and they should pray over him and pour a little oil upon him, calling on the Lord to heal him. And their prayer, if offered in faith, will heal him, for the Lord will make him well; and if his sickness was caused by some sin, the Lord will forgive him" (TLB).

Doctors and others in the medical profession may acquire certain skills and develop certain natural abilities in the areas of medicine, but the healing itself is a miraculous wonder of the life process which is uniquely controlled by God. Many Christian doctors have natural and acquired abilities which are complemented by the gift of healing.

MIRACLES (1 Corinthians 12:10, 28)

The gift of miracles is the supernatural ability given to certain believers through whom the Holy Spirit performs acts by means outside the ordinary laws of nature.

The Bible contains many illustrations of miracles, many of them performed by the Lord Himself. And, in Revelation 11, we read that at some future time believers will be given miraculous powers through the indwelling of the Holy Spirit. Nowhere in Scripture do we read that the granting of this very special gift has been temporarily held back by the Holy Spirit.

PROPHECY (1 Corinthians 12:10, 28)

The gift of prophecy is one of the most misunderstood of all the gifts. Many people consider it the ability to foretell the future. The word literally means to "preach" or to proclaim the Word of God to others. A prophet, biblically, called a nation to repentenance and to a return to God. Like Dr. Williams Evans, most believers who have this gift find that it takes much time, hard work and reliance on the power and control of the Holy Spirit to develop this gift.

Since so much of Scripture contains God's revelation of His future plans, the preaching of the Word from time to time includes dealing with things to come. Since the canon of Scripture is now "closed," or complete, such preaching on future things, if it is the result of being truly gifted, only confirms what the Bible says and does not add to the Scriptures.

DISCERNING OF SPIRITS (1 Corinthians 12:10)

The gift of discerning of spirits is the supernatural ability of certain believers to discern whether things said and done by others are true or false, are of God or of Satan, are of the Holy Spirit or of the flesh. The writer of the book of Hebrews tells us, "You will never be able to eat solid spiritual food and understand the deeper things of God's Word until you become better Christians and learn right from wrong by practicing doing right" (Hebrews 5:14, TLB).

This passage indicates to us that discernment of spirits is an ability which is learned over a period of time.

TONGUES (1 Corinthians 12:10, 28)

The gift of tongues is the supernatural ability to speak to others and/or to God in a language or utterance never learned by the speaker. Like all the other gifts of the Holy Spirit, the gift of tongues has been given to the Church in order to glorify Christ and to build up the body of Christ (1 Corinthians 14:26). Unhappily, however, tongues has often become a divisive issue among all too many Christians.

Many others have written extensively (and exhaustively) on the "issue" of tongues, and it is doubtful that much could be written here that has not already been stated. Let me stress only two biblical principles: First, the gift of tongues must always be exercised in accordance with the biblical guidelines as mentioned in 1 Corinthians 14. Second, those who have this gift must exercise it in love and humility, and those who do not have this gift must accept with love those who claim to have it.

We must aim for equality and not sameness among the members of the body of Christ (2 Corinthians 8:14). And in so doing, we must seek first to glorify Christ and then to build up one another toward unity in the Holy Spirit. I suggest that you read again and again the passage of Scripture found in 1 Peter 4:7-19.

INTERPRETATION OF TONGUES (1 Corinthians 14:13)

The gift of tongues may or may not be accompanied by the giving of another closely related gift, the interpretation of tongues. Whenever the gift of tongues is exercised in the presence of others, the person speaking in tongues is to "pray also for the gift of knowing what he

has said, so that he can tell people afterwards, plainly"
(1 Corinthians 14:13, TLB).

APOSTLESHIP (1 Corinthians 14:28, Ephesians 4:11)

Some Christians are given special abilities with which
to perform the functions of the office of the Church that
is termed *apostle*. Thus the gift of apostleship. It was
granted to the original 12 apostles, then others after
them, including Paul (Acts 1:26, Romans 1:1, Acts 14:14,
Romans 16:7, 1 Thessalonians 2:6).

Though we do not have people who could claim to
be apostles in the original sense — those who had been
eyewitnesses of the resurrected Christ (Acts 21:26) —
today we would have those who may function much
like an apostle. In a general sense, then, an apostle is
one who is gifted by the Holy Spirit with the special
ability to give leadership to a number of churches and
to show supernatural wisdom and authority in spiritual
matters that relate to those churches.

TEACHING (1 Corinthians 12:28; Romans 12:7; Ephesians 4:11)

The gift of teaching is the supernatural ability to explain information to members of the body of Christ in
such a way that they will be edified and able readily to
apply it in their lives. This gift develops with maturity.

Teaching is a very common natural talent. But not all
natural teaching is beneficial. Only the spiritual gift of
teaching can bring about righteous results in the lives
of others. This is true for two reasons:

First, the Christian's ability to teach is supernaturally
imparted by the Holy Spirit. Since God is holy, therefore,
any gift of His would be holy and could not be used in
an unholy fashion, if properly exercised in the power
and control of the Holy Spirit.

Second, for the Christian, the gift of teaching is the supernatural ability to teach *truths*. Since all truth is ultimately from God, it can have only a beneficial impact on the life of the student when properly applied.

HELPS, SERVICE AND MERCY (1 Corinthians 12:28; Romans 12:7, 8; Ephesians 4:12)

The spiritual gifts of helps, service and mercy are similar in many respects. All three are given for the building up of the body of Christ, but they differ slightly.

The gift of helps is characteristically more *task*-oriented. The gift of service is more people-oriented. The gift of mercy is extended usually to the infirm, the elderly or the injured, who are unable to totally care for themselves.

ADMINISTRATION (1 Corinthians 11:28)

The gift of administration (called "governments" in some translations of the Bible) is the special ability given by the Holy Spirit to some believers enabling them to understand the objectives of a particular group within the Body of Christ and to make and carry out plans for realizing those objectives.

We sometimes confuse this spiritual gift with the gift of leadership. While some leaders might also have the gift of administration, all do not. Conversely, not all who have the gift of administration have the gift of leadership.

LEADERSHIP (Romans 12:8)

The spiritual gift of leadership is the special ability given by the Holy Spirit to certain members of the Body of Christ for the purpose of setting goals and motivating and directing the activities of others in working together toward accomplishing those goals.

An individual who has the gift of leadership but not of administration would do well to have supportive staff who are gifted in administration. Otherwise, and we see this too often, a leader will emerge who will establish goals and highly motivate people to work together to reach those goals only to fail because of poor planning, organization, direction and controls.

Likewise, a well-organized local church which lacks a leader may flounder from misdirection or stagnancy and its people may become frustrated and unfulfilled because of the slow rate or lack of progress in the life and growth of the church.

EXHORTATION (1 Corinthians 12:10)

The gift of exhortation is the special ability given by the Holy Spirit to certain members of the Body of Christ to minister to groups or to individuals, on a short-term basis, words of comfort, consolation, encouragement and counsel. The result of such counseling to other members of the body of Christ is that those exhorted will feel helped and healed.

Another term for exhortation would be to "build up" one another in Christ. Hebrews 3:13 tells us to do just that: "Exhort one another daily." Each of us is told to exercise this special ability, and therefore each of us, as Christians, is assured that the Holy Spirit will empower us with this gift: "For I can do everything God asks me to with the help of Christ who gives me the strength and power" (Philippians 4:13, TLB).

GIVING (Romans 12:8)

In my many years with the ministry of Campus Crusade for Christ, I have seen the gift of giving demonstrated over and over again. This gift is the supernatural ability to acquire money for the purpose of giving it to others for the sole purpose of carrying out the work of God.

Those who possess this gift are among the happiest and most cheerful people I know. This is proof of the Lord's promise, "It is more blessed to give than to receive" (Acts 20:35, TLB). We cannot outgive God. "Give, and it will be given to you" (Luke 6:38, NAS).

EVANGELISM (Ephesians 4:11)

Ephesians 4:11 refers to evangelism as an office; however, I believe it is also a special ability given by the Holy Spirit to certain believers, though granted in different and varying amounts. While some are given this special ability, the Bible teaches that the Church is commissioned to preach the gospel throughout the world (Matthew 28:19, 20), and that the Lord promised that the Holy Spirit would indwell all believers for the specific purpose of witnessing for Him (Acts 1:8).

Out of love for the Lord and in obedience to His command, all believers are to be witnesses for Him as a way of life. The supernaturalness of this gift lies in our motivation that is prompted by the Holy Spirit to want to share Christ, and in the power of the Holy Spirit to open minds to the gospel when it is shared. All Christians should share Christ with others. Those who are more gifted in evangelism should devote even more time to seeking to reach others for Christ.

PASTORING (Ephesians 4:11)

The office of pastor, as listed in Ephesians 4, indicates that certain members of the body of Christ are given special abilities by the Holy Spirit to pastor or "shepherd" the members of that unit of the Church. This gift gives one the ability to care for the interests of those believers whom God has committed to that person's care.

The gift of pastoring, however, is not limited to those who hold the church office of pastor. A lay person who has a strong desire to disciple or shepherd a group of people in his home may well have the gift of pastoring. All too often the entire responsibility of pastoring in a local church is limited to the office of pastor. Among the most dynamic local churches I have seen are those in which the gift of pastoring is recognized among the laity and its practice encouraged.

TOTAL AVAILABILITY TO GOD

As we have seen in this appendix, many of the spiritual gifts are similar in nature, and many times individuals may have two or more gifts that greatly complement one another. Again, I want to say that knowing what our spiritual gifts are is much less important than being available to God at all times and in every way to build up the body of Christ.

Remember too that spiritual gifts are not a mark of spirituality. That was obvious in the Corinthian church, one of the most carnal churches of all, and yet one in which there was a wrongly motivated overemphasis on spiritual gifts.

Finally, we can know that we are living Spirit-filled lives, not by the manifestation of spiritual gifts but when the fruit of the Spirit, which is primarily love, becomes increasingly evident in our lives.

Have You Heard of The
Four Spiritual Laws?

Just as there are physical laws that govern the physical universe, so are there spiritual laws which govern your relationship with God.

LAW ONE

GOD **LOVES** YOU, AND OFFERS A WONDERFUL **PLAN** FOR YOUR LIFE.
(References should be read in context from the Bible wherever possible.)

God's Love

"For God so loved the world, that He gave His only begotten Son, that whoever believes in Him should not perish, but have eternal life" (John 3:16).

God's Plan

(Christ speaking) "I came that they might have life, and might have it abundantly" (that it might be full and meaningful) (John 10:10).

Why is it that most people are not experiencing the abundant life?

Because . . .

LAW TWO

MAN IS **SINFUL** AND **SEPARATED** FROM GOD. THEREFORE, HE CANNOT KNOW AND EXPERIENCE GOD'S LOVE AND PLAN FOR HIS LIFE.

Man Is Sinful

"For all have sinned and fall short of the glory of God" (Romans 3:23).

Man was created to have fellowship with God; but, because of his stubborn self-will, he chose to go his own independent way and fellowship with God was broken. This self-will, characterized by an attitude of active rebellion or passive indifference, is evidence of what the Bible calls sin.

Man IS Separated

"For the wages of sin is death" (spiritual separation from God) (Romans 6:23).

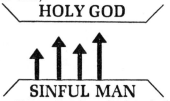

This diagram illustrates that God is holy and man is sinful. A great gulf separates the two. The arrows illustrate that man is continually trying to reach God and the abundant life through his own efforts, such as a good life, philosophy or religion.

The third law explains the only way to bridge this gulf . . .

LAW THREE

JESUS CHRIST IS GOD'S **ONLY** PROVISION FOR MAN'S SIN. THROUGH HIM YOU CAN KNOW AND EXPERIENCE GOD'S LOVE AND PLAN FOR YOUR LIFE.

He Died in Our Place

"But God demonstrates His own love toward us, in that while we were yet sinners, Christ died for us" (Romans 5:8).

He Rose from the Dead

"Christ died for our sins . . . He was buried . . . He was raised on the third day, according to the Scriptures . . . He appeared to Peter, then to the twelve. After that He appeared to more than five hundred . . ." (I Corinthians 15:3-6).

He Is the Only Way to God

"Jesus said to him, 'I am the way, and the truth, and the life; no one comes to the Father, but through Me' "(John 14:6)

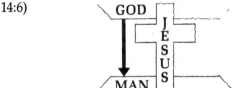

This diagram illustrates that God has bridged the gulf which separates us from God by sending His Son, Jesus Christ, to die on the cross in our place to pay the penalty for our sins.

It is not enough just to know these three laws . . .

LAW FOUR

WE MUST INDIVIDUALLY **RECEIVE** JESUS CHRIST AS SAVIOR AND LORD; THEN WE CAN KNOW AND EXPERIENCE GOD'S LOVE AND PLAN FOR OUR LIVES.

We Must Receive Christ

"But as many as received Him, to them He gave the right to become children of God, even to those who believe in his name" (John 1:12).

We Receive Christ Through Faith

"For by grace you have been saved through faith; and that not of yourselves, it is the gift of God; not as a result of works, that no one should boast" (Ephesians 2:8,9).

When We Receive Christ, We Experience A New Birth

(Read John 3:1-8).

We Receive Christ by Personal Invitation

(Christ is speaking) "Behold, I stand at the door and knock; if any one hears My voice and opens the door, I will come in to him" (Revelation 3:20).

Receiving Christ involves turning from self to God (repentance) and trusting Christ to come into our lives to forgive our sins and to make us the kind of person He wants us to be. Just to agree intellectually that Jesus Christ is the Son of God and that He died on the cross for our sins is not enough. Nor is it enough to have an emotional experience. We receive Jesus Christ by faith, as an act of the will.

These two circles represent two kinds of lives:

SELF-DIRECTED LIFE

S—Self on the throne

†—Christ is outside the life

•—Interests are directed by self, often resulting in discord and frustration

CHRIST-DIRECTED LIFE

†—Christ is in the life

S—Self is yielding to Christ

•—Interests are directed by Christ, resulting in harmony with God's plan

Which circle best represents your life?

Which circle would you like to have represent your life?

The following explains how you can receive Christ:

YOU CAN RECEIVE CHRIST RIGHT NOW BY FAITH THROUGH PRAYER

(Prayer is talking with God)

God knows your heart and is not so concerned with your words as He is with the attitude of your heart. The following is a suggested prayer:

"Lord Jesus, I need You. Thank You for dying on the cross for my sins. I open the door of my life and receive You as my Savior and Lord. Thank You for forgiving my sins and giving me eternal life. Make me the kind of person You want me to be."

Does this prayer express the desire of your heart?

If it does, prayer this prayer right now, and Christ will come into your life, as He promised.

Have You Made
the Wonderful Discovery
of the Spirit-Filled Life?

EVERY DAY CAN BE AN EXCITING ADVENTURE FOR THE CHRISTIAN who knows the reality of being filled with the Holy Spirit and who lives constantly, moment by moment, under His gracious direction.

The Bible tells us that there are three kinds of people:
1. NATURAL MAN
   (One who has not received Christ)
"But a natural man does not accept the things of the Spirit of God; for they are foolishness to him, and he cannot understand them, because they are spiritually appraised" (I Corinthians 2:14).

SELF-DIRECTED LIFE
S—Ego or finite self is on the throne
†—Christ is outside the life
•—Interests are directed by self, often resulting in discord and frustration

2. SPIRITUAL MAN
   (One who is directed and empowered by the Holy Spirit)
"But he who is spiritual appraises all things . . ." (I Corinthians 2:15).

CHRIST-DIRECTED LIFE
†—Christ is in the life and on the throne
S—Self is yielding to Christ
•—Interests are directed by Christ, resulting in harmony with God's plan

2. CARNAL MAN
   (One who has received Christ, but who lives in defeat
   because he trust in his own efforts to live the Christian
   life)
"And I, brethren, could not speak to you as to spiritual
men, but as to carnal men, as to babes in Christ. I gave
you milk to drink, not solid food; for you were not yet
able to receive it. Indeed, even now you are not yet able,
for you are still carnal. For since there is jealousy and
strife among you, are you not fleshly, and are you now
walking like ere men?" (I Corinthians 3:1-3).

SELF-DIRECTED LIFE
S—Self is on the throne
†—Christ dethroned and not allowed to direct
   the life
•—Interests are directed by self, often
   resulting in discord and frustration

1. GOD HAS PROVIDED FOR US AN ABUNDANT
   AND FRUITFUL CHRISTIAN LIFE.
Jesus said, "I came that you might have life, and might
have it abundantly" (John 10:10).
"I am the vine, you are the branches; he who abides in
Me, and I in him, he bears much fruit; for apart from
Me you can do nothing" (John 15:5).
"But the fruit of the Spirit is love, joy, peace, patience,
kindness, goodness, faithfulness, gentleness, self-con-
trol; against such things there is no law" (Galatians
5:22,23).
"But you shall receive power when the Holy Spirit has
come upon you; and you shall be My witness both in
Jerusalem, and in all Judea and Samaria, and even to
the remotest part of the earth" (Acts 1:8).

THE SPIRITUAL MAN — Some personal traits which result from trusting God:
Christ-centered
Empowered by the Holy Spirit
Introduces others to Christ
Effective prayer life
Understands God's Word
Trust God
Obeys God
Love
Joy
Peace
Patience
Kindness
Faithfulness
Goodness

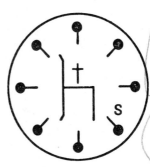

The degree to which these traits are manifested in the life depends upon the extent to which the Christian trusts the Lord with every detail of his life, and upon his maturity in Christ. One who is only beginning to understand the ministry of the Holy Spirit should not be discouraged if he is not as fruitful as more mature Christians who have known and experienced this truth for a longer period.

Why is it that most Christians are not experiencing the abundant life?

2. CARNAL CHRISTIANS CANNOT EXPERIENCE THE ABUNDANT AND FRUITFUL CHRISTIAN LIFE.
The carnal man trusts in his own efforts to live the Christian life:
   A. He is either uninformed about, or has forgotten,

God's love, forgiveness, and power (Romans 5:8-
10; Hebrews 10:1- 25; I John 1; 2:1-3; II Peter 1:9;
Acts 1:8).
B. He has an up-and-down spiritual experience.
C. He cannot understand himself — he wants to do
what is right, but cannot.
D. He fails to draw upon the power of the Holy Spirit
to live the Christian life.

(I Corinthians 3:1-3; Romans 7:15-24; 8:7; Galatians
5:16-18)

THE CARNAL MAN — Some or all of the following traits
may characterize the Christian who does not fully trust
God:

Ignorance of his spiritual
  heritage
Unbelief
Disobedience
Loss of love for God and
  for others
Poor prayer life
No desire for Bible study
Legalistic attitude
Impure thoughts
Jealousy
Guilt
Worry
Discouragement
Critical spirit
Frustration
Aimlessness

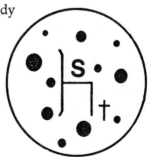

(The individual who professes to be a Christian but who
continues to practice sin should realize that he may not
be a Christian at all, according to I John 2:3, 3:6, 9: Ephesians 5:5.)

*The third truth gives us the only solution
to this problem . . .*

3. JESUS PROMISED THE ABUNDANT AND FRUIT-
   FUL LIFE AS THE RESULT OF BEING FILLED (DI-
   RECTED AND EMPOWERED) BY THE HOLY SPIRIT.
The Spirit-filled life is the Christ-directed life by which
Christ lives His life in and through us in the power of
the Holy Spirit (John 15).
   A. One becomes a Christian through the ministry of
      the Holy Spirit, according to John 3:1-8. From the
      moment of spiritual birth, the Christian is indwelt
      by the Holy Spirit at all times (John 1:12; Colossians
      2:9,10; John 14:16,17). **Though all Christians are
      indwelt by the Holy Spirit, not all Christians are
      filled (directed and empowered) by the Holy
      Spirit.**
   B. The Holy Spirit is the source of the overflowing
      life) John 7:37-39).
   C. The Holy Spirit came to glorify Christ (John 16:1-
      15). When one is filled with the Holy Spirit, he is
      a true disciple of Christ.
   D. In His last command before His ascension, Christ
      promised the power of the Holy Spirit to enable
      us to be witnesses for Him (Acts 1:1-9).
How, then can one be filled with the Holy Spirit?

4. WE ARE FILLED (DIRECTED AND EMPOWERED) BY THE HOLY SPIRIT BY FAITH; THEN WE CAN EXPERIENCE THE ABUNDANT AND FRUITFUL LIFE WHICH CHRIST PROMISED TO EACH CHRISTIAN.

You can appropriate the filling of the Holy Spirit **right now** if you:

A. Sincerely desire to be directed and empowered by the Holy Spirit (Matthew 5:6; John 7:37-39).

B. Confess your sins.
By **faith** thank God that He **has** forgiven all of your sins — past, present, and future — because Christ died for you (Colossians 2:13-15; I John 1; 2:1-3; Hebrews 10:1-17).

C. Present every area of your life to God (Romans 12:1,2).

D. By **faith** claim the fullness of the Holy Spirit, according to:
1. HIS COMMAND — Be filled with the Spirit.
"And do not get drunk with wine, for that is dissipation, but be filled with the Spirit" (Ephesians 5:18).
2. HIS PROMISE — He will always answer when we pray according to His will. "And this is the confidence which we have before Him, that, if we ask anything according to His will, He hears us. And if we know that He hears us in whatever we ask, we know that we have the requests which we have asked from Him" (I John 5:14,15).

Faith can be expressed through prayer . . .

HOW TO PRAY IN FAITH TO BE FILLED WITH THE HOLY SPIRIT

We are filled with the Holy Spirit by **faith** alone. However, true prayer is one way of expressing your faith. The following is a suggested prayer:

"Dear Father, I need You. I acknowledge that I have been directing my own life and that, as a result, I have sinned against You. I thank You that You have forgiven my sins through Christ's death on the cross for me. I now invite Christ to again take His place on the throne of my life. Fill me with the Holy Spirit as You **commanded** me to be filled, as as You **promised** in Your Word that You would do if I asked in faith. I pray this in the name of Jesus. As an expression of my faith, I now thank You for directing my life and for filling me with the Holy Spirit."

Does this prayer express the desire of your heart? If so, bow in prayer and trust God to fill you with the Holy Spirit **right now**.

HOW TO KNOW THAT YOU ARE FILLED (DIRECTED AND EMPOWERED) BY THE HOLY SPIRIT

Did you ask God to fill you with the Holy Spirit? Do you know that you are now filled with the Holy Spirit? On what authority? (On the trustworthiness of God Himself and His Word: Hebrews 11:6, Romans 14:22,23.)

Do not depend upon feelings. The promise of God's Word, not our feelings, is our authority. The Christian lives by faith (trust) in the trustworthiness of God Himself and His Word. This train diagram illustrates the relationship between **fact** (God and His Word), **faith** (our trust in God and His Word), and **feeling** (the result of our faith and obedience) (John 14:21).

The train wil run with or without the caboose. However, it would be futile to attempt to pull the train by the caboose. In the same way, we, as Christians, do not depend upon feelings or emotions, but we place our faith (trust) in the trustworthiness of God and the promises of His Word.

HOW TO WALK IN THE SPIRIT

Faith (trust in God and in His promises) is the only means by which a Christian can live the Spitit-directed life. As you continue to trust Christ moment by moment:

A. Your life will demonstrate more and more of the fruit of the Spirit (Galatians 5:22,23) and will be more and more conformed to the image of Christ (Romans 12:22; II Corinthians 3:18).

B. Your prayer life and study of God's Word will become more meaningful.

C. You will experience His power in witnessing (Acts 1:8).

D. You will be prepared for spiritual conflict against the world (I John 2:15-17); against the flesh (Galatians 5:16,17); and against Satan (I Peter 5:7-9; Ephesians 6:10-13).

E. You will experience His power to resist temptation and sin (I Corinthians 10:13; Philippians 4:13; Ephesians 1:19-23; 6:10;II Timothy 1:7; Romans 6:1-16).

SPIRITUAL BREATHING

By faith you can continue to experience God's love and forgiveness.

If you become aware of an area of your life (an attitude or an action) that is displeasing to the Lord, even though you are walking with Him and sincerely desiring to serve Him, simply thank God that He has forgiven your sins — past, present and future — on the basis of Christ's death on the cross. Claim His love and forgiveness by faith and continue to have fellowship with Him.

If you retake the throne of your life through sin — a definite act of disobedience — breathe spiritually.

Spiritual breathing (exhaling the impure and inhaling the pure) is an exercise in faith and enables you to continue to experience God's love and forgiveness.

1. **Exhale** — confess your sin — agree with God concerning your sin and thank Him for His forgiveness of it, according to I John 1:9 and Hebrews 10:1-25. Confession involves repentance — a change in attitude and action.

2. **Inhale** — surrender the control of your life to Christ, and appropriate (receive) the fullness of the Holy Spirit by faith. Trust that He now directs and empowers you, according to the **command** of Ephesians 5:18 and the **promise** of I John 5:14, 15.

Resources to Help You Grow and Share the Good News

Qty.   Total

Transferable Concepts to help you experience and share the abundant Christian life. Bill Bright.

____ *How You Can Be Sure You Are a Christian* $1.99 ____

____ *How You Can Experience God's Love and Forgiveness* $1.99 ____

____ *How You Can Be Filled With the Holy Spirit* $1.99 ____

____ *How You Can Walk in the Spirit* $1.99 ____

____ *How You Can Be a Fruitful Witness* $1.99 ____

____ *How You Can Introduce Others to Christ* $1.99 ____

____ *How You Can Help Fulfill the Great Commission* $1.99 ____

____ *How You Can Love By Faith* $1.99 ____

____ *How You Can Pray With Confidence* $1.99 ____

____ *How You Can Experience the Adventure of Giving* $1.99 ____

____ **A Man Without Equal.** Bill Bright. A fresh ____ look at the unique birth, life, teachings, death, and resurrection of Jesus and how He continues to change the way we live and think today. $4.99

____ **Witnessing Without Fear.** Bill Bright, with a ____ foreword by Billy Graham. A step-by-step guide to sharing your faith with confidence. Ideal for both individual and group study; a Gold Medallion Award winner. $10.99

____ **Have You Heard of the Four Spiritual** ____ **Laws?** Bill Bright. One of the most effective evangelistic tools ever developed, the *Four*

_____ *Spiritual Laws* provides an easy-to-use way of _____
sharing your faith with others. More than 1.5
billion copies have been distributed around
the world in all major languages. Package of
50/$9.99

_____ **Would You Like to Know God Personally?** _____
Bill Bright. A conversational, reader-friendly
adaptation of the *Four Spiritual Laws*, presented as four principles for establishing a personal relationship with God through faith in
Jesus Christ. Package of 50/$9.99

_____ **Have You Made the Wonderful Discovery** _____
of the Spirit-filled Life? Bill Bright. Discover
the reality of the Spirit-filled life and how to
live in moment-by-moment dependence on
Him. Package of 25/$6.99

_____ **Ten Basic Steps.** Bill Bright. A comprehen- _____
sive curriculum for the new Christian or anyone who wants to master the basics of Christian growth. These studies have been used
by hundreds of thousands in many languages worldwide.

_____	*Introduction: Uniqueness of Jesus*	$5.99	_____
_____	*Step 1: The Christian Adventure*	$5.99	_____
_____	*Step 2: The Christian and the Abundant Life*	$5.99	_____
_____	*Step 3: The Christian and the Holy Spirit*	$5.99	_____
_____	*Step 4: The Christian and Prayer*	$5.99	_____
_____	*Step 5: The Christian and the Bible*	$5.99	_____
_____	*Step 6: The Christian and Obedience*	$5.99	_____
_____	*Step 7: The Christian and Witnessing*	$5.99	_____
_____	*Step 8: The Christian and Giving*	$5.99	_____
_____	*Step 9: Exploring the Old Testament*	$5.99	_____
_____	*Step 10: Exploring the New Testament*	$5.99	_____

Qty.		Total
____	*Leader's Guide*	$14.99 ____
____	*A Handbook for Christian Maturity*	$16.99 ____

____ **A Man Without Equal (video).** Featuring ____ Bill Bright, this intriguing 30-minute video explores the uniqueness of Jesus through dramatic recreations and breathtaking portraits from the great Masters. An effective evangelism tool. $14.99

____ **The Holy Spirit: Key to Supernatural** ____ **Living.** Bill Bright. This book helps you enter into the Spirit-filled life and shares how you can experience a life of supernatural power and victory. $7.99

These products are available through your local Christian bookstore. If not, you may order through NewLife Publications. Please allow 2 to 4 weeks for delivery.

✂ --

ORDER FORM

❑ Enclosed is my check payable to Campus Crusade for Christ

❑ Bill my Mastercard, VISA, or Discover Card (circle one)

Card Number _____

Exp. Date ____ / ____ Signature _____

Name _____

Address _____

City _____ State _____

Zip_____ Phone _____

Clip and mail to:

NewLife Publications
P.O. Box 593684
Orlando, FL 32859-3684

Response Form

☐ I have recently received Jesus Christ as my Savior and Lord as a result of reading this booklet.

☐ I am a new Christian and want to know Christ better and experience the abundant Christian life.

☐ Please send me **free** information on staff and ministry opportunities with Campus Crusade for Christ.

☐ Please send me **free** information about other books, booklets, audio cassettes, and videos by Bill Bright.

NAME _____

ADDRESS _____

CITY _____

STATE _____ ZIP _____

PHONE _____

Please check the appropriate box(es) and mail this form in an envelope to:

Dr. Bill Bright
Campus Crusade for Christ
P.O. Box 593684
Orlando, Fl 32859-3684

You may also fax your response to (407) 826-2149 or send E-mail to:

CompuServe: 74114,1206
Internet: newlife@magicnet.net